Embedded Software Development with C

T0134807

Kai Qian • David den Haring • Li Cao

Embedded Software
Development with C

Kai Qian
Dept. of Computer Science
Southern Polytechnic University
Marietta GA 30060
USA
kqian@spsu.edu

David den Haring
Atronix Engineering Inc.
3100 Medlock Bridge Road
Suite 110
Norcross GA 30071
USA
ddharing@atronixengineering.com

Li Cao
University of Texas at Austin
2500 San Jacinto Blvd.
Austin TX 78705
USA
lcao@x85.com

ISBN 978-1-4899-8499-9   ISBN 978-1-4419-0606-9 (eBook)
DOI 10.1007/978-1-4419-0606-9
Springer Dordrecht Heidelberg London New York

Printed on acid-free paper

Springer is part of Springer Science+Business Media (www.springer.com)

Preface

Welcome to the world of embedded systems software development with the C language. This book is an introductory text intended primarily for undergraduate students in computer science, electrical engineering, software engineering and other related engineering majors. If you are not a student, however, please don't let that stop you from reading and using this book to help satisfy your curiosity about embedded systems or to help move your career forward.

Overview

This is a practical book. It won't waste your time. Here are three reasons why:

1. **The C programming language.** C has a long history and is the defacto high-level language in the embedded systems world. It is also used widely for operating system and application development for all important platforms like Windows, UNIX, Macintosh and Linux. Learning C is definitely not a waste of time – it's used everywhere.
   This book assumes that you have a basic knowledge of C, but not much more than that. If you need a quick review, check out Appendix A and B.
2. **The 8051 microcontroller.** Like C, the 8051 microcontroller (originally developed by Intel) has a long history and remains a popular and relevant platform for designing embedded systems.
3. **Bundled hardware and software.** Learn best by doing! This book has complete, self-contained labs. The book can be bundled with the Silicon Labs 8051 development kit (C8051F005DK), all lab materials (e.g. breadboard, LEDs, resistors, etc) and the Keil C software. This optional bundling is convenient for both the university and the individual.

Whether you are a student, educator or working professional, this book will give you a solid foundation in the hardware and software aspects of embedded systems development.

Roadmap

This book basically consists of 4 parts.

Part I: Getting Started with the Microcontroller and Embedded Systems Development

- Chapter 1 provides an overview of microcontrollers, embedded systems and their application.
- Appendix A gives a review of C programming. The reader can skip it if you have experience with C.
- Appendix B and C help the reader get started with the Keil and Silicon Labs development tools:

After the completion of Part 1, the reader will have a better understanding of microcontrollers and embedded systems and will be able to develop simple embedded application using Keil and C8051F005DK with 8051 MCU.

Part II: Embedded System Fundamentals

- Chapter 2 gets serious (briefly) and discusses requirements analysis and software design.
- Chapter 3 takes the reader on a tour of hardware fundamentals that are common to all embedded systems.
- Chapter 4 shifts attention to the C language and how to use it properly in an embedded environment where CPU and memory resources are limited.
- Chapter 5 provides an introduction to the RTOS (Real Time Operating System) and presents a simple RTOS for the 8051 microcontroller.
- Chapter 6 introduces the reader to serial communications, UART, and serial communication programming in the 8051. Software and hardware handshaking are also discussed.

Part III: Popular Microcontrollers and Ethernet Application Development

- Chapter 7 pulls away from all the low level detail and puts the 8051 microcontroller in perspective with other popular microcontrollers like the ARM, PIC and Rabbit.
- Chapter 8 discusses Ethernet applications and the future of the microcontroller. This is not a survey chapter. It introduces TCP/IP and features one case study and a complete example. All source code is provided. To work the example in this chapter, the Silicon Labs ETHERNETDK kit is required. The chapter concludes with a look at the possible future of the microcontroller.

Part IV: Hands-on Project Labs

- Chapter 9 is the lab chapter. There are eight labs with step-by-step instructions, circuit diagrams, finished lab photos and complete source code.
- Appendix D is an introductory lab that explains in more detail than chapter 9 how to breadboard circuits. If you find the first few labs in Chapter 9 difficult, check out Appendix D for a softer introduction.
- Appendix E is only available at http://embeddedbook.x85.com. It features an advanced project that demonstrates PC to 8051 communications over a Bluetooth wireless network.

The authors firmly believe that people learn by studying the example of others and then learn by doing. With that said, source code is included with each lab for study and modification. That's the *"learn by example"* part.

The student must wire the circuits and use the IDE tools to download and debug the software. There are also lab questions and optional exercises which will require students to modify the code, write new functions and add additional hardware components. That's the *"learn by doing"* part. This two-step approach will allow instructors to provide students with labs of varying length and difficulty.

The authors designed, built and tested all of the labs. The labs are available for download at http://embeddedbook.x85.com/. Additionally, full source code is included in the text. Instructors can get access to testbank material based on the topics brought up in this text by sending E-mail to kqian@spsu.edu.

We enjoyed writing this book and hope that you learn and benefit from it in your academic and professional career.

Acknowledgements

Thanks to all those who reviewed this book for their constructive comments, suggestions, and encouragements. Thanks to Iqbal Ahmed for his help in development of the uWeb Embedded Web Server. We appreciate the hard work and support of the editorial and production teams at the Springer publishing.

June, 2009   Kai Qian
                                                                            David den Haring
                                                                                      Li Cao

Contents

Chapter 1
Introduction to Embedded Systems

Objectives

- Understand the purpose and categories of embedded systems
- Understand the embedded system hardware and software
- Use Keil μVision3 C51 Development Kit
- Use C8051F005DK microcontroller development kit

1.1 Overview

We can easily find embedded systems everywhere in our daily lives. The numbers of embedded systems are rapidly growing especially in wireless and web applications. The embedded systems market is one of the fastest growing areas in the world. By name, an embedded system is a special-purpose computing device designed to perform dedicated functions. Some of the embedded systems with real-time constraints are called real-time embedded systems. An embedded system consists of its hardware and software. The hardware includes a microprocessor or microcontroller with additional attached external memory, I/O, and other components such as sensors, keypad, LEDs, LCDs, and any kind of actuators. The embedded software is the driving force of an embedded system. Most real-time embedded systems software has specific application programs supported by a Real Time Operating System (RTOS). The embedded software is usually called firmware because this type software is loaded to ROM, EPROM, or Flash memory, and once it is loaded it will never be changed unless it needs to be reloaded or replaced. This book introduces the fundamentals of embedded system design and development. The focus is emphasized on the software aspect of embedded systems design and development. You will enjoy the hands-on experience of building embedded systems on your own with this book.

For a general-purpose computer, you can install any software to do all kinds of jobs such as word processing, book keeping, database management, and others depending on your purposes. The embedded systems are only used to repeatedly carry out particular designated functions. Embedded systems have been used for

K. Qian et al., *Embedded Software Development with C*,
DOI 10.1007/978-1-4419-0606-9_1, © Springer Science+Business Media, LLC 2009

almost a half century since the microprocessor was developed. The first Intel micro-processor chip was designed for calculators and other simple systems in 1960's. Since then, as the cost of microprocessors and microcontrollers fell and function power is enriched, it became feasible to replace many expensive products and systems with microprocessor and microcontroller powered embedded systems.

The embedded system makes the world smarter and more advanced.

1.2 Categories of Embedded Systems

Embedded systems can be classified into the following categories based on the functional and performance requirements:

- Stand-alone embedded systems

A stand-alone embedded system works by itself. It is a self-contained device. It takes either digital or analog inputs from its input ports, calibrates, converts, and processes the data, and outputs the resulting data to its attached output device, which either displays data, or controls and drives the attached devices. Entertainment devices such as video game console and MP3 players, digital cameras, and microwaves are typical systems that fall into this category.

- Real-time embedded systems

A system is said to be real-time if the response time is critical. In other words, some particular work must be done in a specified time period. In addition to functional correctness, the time constraint must also be satisfied.

There are two types of real-time embedded systems: hard real-time and soft real-time embedded systems.

– Hard real-time systems.

For a hard or immediate real-time system, the completion of an operation after its deadline may lead to a critical failure and result in loss of life or property damage. The response time deadline for such systems is very critical (in milliseconds or even shorter). For example, missing a deadline in a missile control embedded system or carbon-oxygen monitoring embedded system will lead to catastrophe or disaster. These systems usually interact directly with physical hardware instead of through a human being. You can even find hard real-time embedded system in your daily life. For example, a car airbag control system is a hard real-time system, because a delayed reaction may cost a driver his life, and a delay response in pacemakers will also lead a severe result. It is imperative for such a system to react to an event within a strict deadline, and missing a deadline will constitute failure of the system. The hardware and software of hard real-time systems must allow a worst case execution (WCET) analysis that guarantees the execution be completed within a strict deadline. The chip selection and RTOS selection become important factors for hard real-time system design.

– Soft real-time system

In some other embedded system, there is a response deadline, but lateness can be tolerated in some degrees. The violation of time constraints will result in degraded quality, but the system can continue to operate. Microwaves and washing machines fall into this sub-category. Although there is a response time deadline for any operation, the allowed latency delay can be seconds rather than milliseconds. In soft real-time systems, the design focus is to offer a guaranteed bandwidth to each real-time task and to distribute the resources to the tasks.

Actually, many real-time systems have both hard and soft events mixed. The hardware resource (CPU time) and software resources (high priority interrupts) should be allocated to these processes handling hard real-time events.

- Networked embedded systems

The networked embedded systems connect to a network with network interfaces to access resources. The connected network can be Local Area Network (LAN), Wide Area Network (WAN), or the Internet. The connection can be wired or wireless. You can simply group the networked embedded systems into wired and wireless sub-categories, but in many systems these two type systems are merged together.

A home security system is an example of a LAN networked embedded system where all sensors (e.g. motion detectors, press sensors, light sensors, or smoke sensors) are wired and running on the TCP/IP protocol. A home security system can be integrated into a web based security system with an additional web camera running on HTTP protocol.

Pervasive computing is the new trend of networked embedded systems with application towards increasingly ubiquitous environment using all very tiny or even invisible embedded devices. They can be mobile or embedded in almost any type of object where information and computational resources are organized as a ubiquitous service grid.

The networked embedded system is the fastest growing area in embedded systems applications. The embedded web server is such a system where all embedded devices are connected to a web server and can be accessed and controlled by any web browser.

Although all embedded systems are classified into these three major categories, the division is not absolute. A sub-system of a networked embedded system can be real-time or not real-time. A real-time system can be stand-alone or networked. The most important issues are the difference in the characteristics and the features among these different type systems so you can take that into account in the embedded systems design and implementation.

The embedded system can also be classified into scale categories. For example, a small scaled embedded system supported by a single 8–16 bit microprocessor or microcontroller with on-chip RAM and ROM is designed to perform simple tasks; medium scaled embedded system supported by a 16–32 bit microprocessor or microcontroller with external RAM and ROM can perform more complex operations; large scaled networked embedded system supported by 32-bit or 64-bit multiple chips can conduct distributed jobs.

1.3 Application Areas of Embedded Systems

Embedded systems range in complexity from single unit portable devices such as a Personnel Data Assistant (PDA) to large complex traffic control systems and manufacturing factory controller systems. The embedded systems have a huge variety of application domains which varies from very low cost and very large market to very high cost and few markets, from daily life consumer electronics to industry automation equipments, from entertainment devices to academic equipments, and from medical instruments to aerospace and weapon control systems. Embedded systems span all aspects of our modern life.

Here is a short list summarizing some embedded systems applications.

Some reports estimate that on average a middle-class household in U.S. has 50 microcontrollers embedded in the devices used at home.

1.4 Characteristics of Embedded systems

Design and development of embedded systems face a lot of challenges.

All embedded systems are dedicated to performing specific jobs. The lifetime of the embedded system should be long, e.g., more than 5 years. For high-volume

Table 1.1 Embedded System Applications

Home Appliances	Dishwasher, washing machine, microwave, Top-set box, security system, HVAC system, DVD, answering machine, garden sprinkler system
Office Automation	Fax, copy machine, smart phone system, modern, scanner, printer
Security	Face recognition, finger recognition, eye recognition, building security system, airport security system, alarm system
Academia	Smart board, smart room, OCR, calculator, smart cord
Instrumentation	Signal generator, signal processor, power supplier
Telecommunication	Router, hub, cellular phone, IP phone, web camera
Automotive	Fuel injection controller, anti-locking brake system, air-bag system, GPS, cruise control
Entertainment	MP3, video game, Mind Storm, smart toy
Aerospace	Navigation system, automatic landing system, flight attitude controller, space explorer, space robotics
Industrial automation	Assembly line, data collection system, monitoring systems on pressure, voltage, current, temperature, hazard detecting system, industrial robot
Personal	PDA, iPhone, palmtop, data organizer
Medical equipment	CT scanner, MRI, Glucose monitor, blood pressure monitor, medical diagnostic device
Business automation	ATM, smart vendor machine, cash register
Misc.	Elevator, tread mill, smart card, security door

embedded systems, the System on Chip (SoC), Application-Specific Integrated Circuit (ASIC), and Field-Programmable Gate Array (FPGA) can be solutions.

Reliability is a very important characteristic for embedded systems.

Many systems work in mission-critical and life-threatening environments, where system reliability is crucial. Embedded systems are often embedded in machines that are expected to run continuously for years without faults, and tolerate the errors by themselves if an error occurs. Therefore, the software is usually developed and tested more thoroughly than that for personal computers. Most embedded systems cannot be shut down for maintenance, or it is very difficult to repair, such as aerospace systems. Some systems will lose large amounts of money when they are shut down: Telephone switches, factory controls, bridge and elevator controls, funds transfer and market making, automated sales and service.

Most embedded systems work 24/7/365 and cannot stop for safety or financial reasons. They can't reboot at all and no human intervention is provided in many cases. No change or update is allowed for embedded software after release to the market. Durability is a very important issue for any embedded system.

Many other constraints for embedded system are listed below.

- Resource constraints: Embedded systems are constrained for their size, power capacity (may be battery operated), limited memory capacity(especially RAM size), CPU speed and function capacity
- Time constraints: Real-time system has response time deadline to meet.
- Environment constraint: Extreme operating conditions such as high or low temperature, high pressure, high humidity, under water, under collision, etc.
- Cost Constraint: Cost reduction of products has huge impact on the market competition because of the large volume of products for high volume systems such as MP3 players or PDAs. Minimizing cost is usually the primary design consideration. The selected hardware should be just "good enough" to cover the necessary functions.
- Time to market constraint: Design and development cycle is very limited in order to beat the competition to the market.

The other challenges of embedded systems design and development are:

- Wide variety of chips for selection
- Many RTOS selections available, even the selection of using RTOS or not
- Language selections of high level or assembly
- Many I/O accessory components selections
- Programming on direct port operations
- Programming with multi-tasking and multi-threading execution
- Must use cross compiler and development tools
- Need emulator to provide simulation of all aspects of the hardware and allow debugging on a normal PC.
- Need special emulation tools to debug
- Testing on multitasking and scheduling execution
- Testing on the real world environment because embedded software is embedded into devices.

1.5 Hardware Overview

1.5.1 Overall Architecture

Every embedded system consists of customer-built hardware components supported by a Central Processing Unit (CPU), which is the heart of a microprocessor (μP) or microcontroller (μC). A microprocessor is a stand-alone CPU chip, and memory and I/O ports can be custom designed and expanded. There is no on-chip memory or ports on the microprocessor. A microprocessor chip is a single integrated circuit intended to operate for general purpose and can be embedded into embedded electronics hardware. A microcontroller is an integrated chip which comes with built-in memory, I/O ports, timers, and other components. Most embedded systems are built on microcontrollers, which run faster than a custom-built system with a microprocessor, because all components are integrated within a single chip. There is a wide variety of microprocessors and microcontrollers available. Figure 1.1 shows a typical layout of a microcontroller.

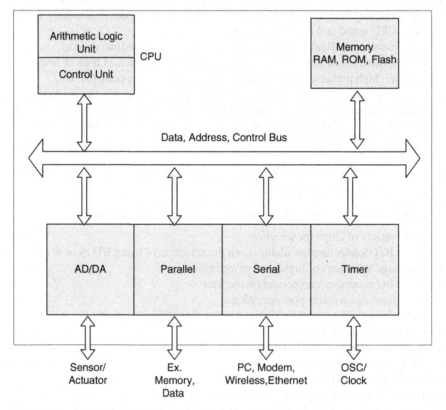

Fig. 1.1 Microcontroller and its connected I/O devices

First, let's review the basic concepts of the microprocessor or CPU, i.e. how it works. You have heard of 8-bit, 16-bit, 32-bit, or 64 bit CPU chips or computers. What do they mean? What is the CPU frequency? What does the MIPS tell? You will get all the answers here.

A CPU is composed of an Arithmetic Logic Unit (ALU), a Control Unit (CU), and many internal registers that are connected by buses.

The ALU performs all the mathematical operations (Add, Sub, Mul, Div), logical operations (AND, OR), and shifting operations within CPU.

The timing and sequencing of all CPU operations are controlled by the CU, which is actually built of many selection circuits including latches and decoders. The CU is responsible for directing the flow of instruction and data within the CPU and continuously running program instructions step by step.

There are many internal registers such as:

The accumulator (Acc) is a special data register that stores the result of ALU operations. It can also be used as an operand.

The Program Counter (PC) stores the memory location of the next instruction to be executed. The Instruction Register (IR) stores the current machine instruction to be decoded and executed.

The Data Buffer Registers store the data received from the memory or the data to be sent to memory. The Data Buffer Registers are connected to the data bus.

The Address Register stores the memory location of the data to be accessed (get or set). The Address Register is connected to the address bus.

In an embedded system, the CPU may never stop and run forever.

The CPU works in a cycle of fetching an instruction, decoding it, and executing it, known as the *fetch-decode-execute cycle*. The cycle begins when an instruction is fetched from a memory location pointed to by the PC to the IR via the data bus.

Each instruction is composed of two parts: the op-code and the operand. The decoding is performed in the IR. The op-code of the instruction is extracted to recognize the type of operation, and the operand is extracted to identify the location of data operands. The operand may be a CPU register or memory data.

The execution of the instruction may involve reading data from memory, storing data to memory, or activating the ALU to perform a mathematical or logical operation.

Each time an instruction is completed, the program counter is already updated to the next instruction location so that a new cycle begins again with the next instruction.

For embedded system design, many factors impact the CPU selection, e.g., the maximum size (number of bits) in a single operand for ALU (8, 16, 32, 64 bits), and CPU clock frequency for timing tick control, i.e. the number of ticks (clock cycles) per second in measures of MHz. Each instruction takes a few time ticks to complete.

MIPS (Million Instructions per Second), i.e. the number of machine instructions completed per second, is another index to tell the CPU speed. One machine cycle of the 8051 has 12 ticks. If the clock is 12 MHz, then its MIPS is 1 MIPS. A simple instruction only needs a single machine cycle, but some other instructions may need multiple cycles.

Here is a list of microprocessors and their MIPS/MHz.

Table 1.2 Microprocessors

Microprocessor	CPU MIPS at MHz	Year released
Intel 8080	640 kIPS / 2 MHz	1974
Motorola 68000	1 MIPS / 8 MHz	1979
Intel 286	2.66 MIPS / 12 MHz	1982
Motorola 68020	4 MIPS / 20 MHz	1984
ARM2	4 MIPS / 8 MHz	1986
Motorola 68030	11 MIPS / 33 MHz	1987
Intel 386DX	8.5 MIPS / 25 MHz	1988
Motorola 68040	44 MIPS / 40 MHz	1990
Intel 486DX	54 MIPS / 66 MHz	1992
PowerPC 600s (G2)	35 MIPS / 33 MHz	1994
Motorola 68060	88 MIPS / 66 MHz	1994
Intel Pentium Pro	541 MIPS / 200 MHz	1996
ARM 7500FE	35.9 MIPS / 40 MHz	1996
PowerPC G3	525 MIPS / 233 MHz	1997
Zilog eZ80	80 MIPS / 50 MHz	1999
Intel Pentium III	1,354 MIPS / 500 MHz	1999
AMD Athlon	3,561 MIPS / 1.2 MHZ	2000
AMD Athlon XP 2400+	5,935 MIPS / 2.0 GHz	2002
Pentium 4 Extreme	9,726 MIPS / 3.2 GHz	2003
AMD Athlon 64 3800+ X2 (Dual Core)	14,564 MIPS / 2.0 GHz	2005
Intel Core 2 X6800	27,079 MIPS / 2.93 GHz	2006
Intel Core 2 Extreme QX9770	59,455 MIPS / 3.2 GHz	2008

In addition to the CPU, a microcontroller typically includes small amounts of RAM, PROM, timers, and I/O ports. All of them are collected by the buses. Two popular microcontrollers used for embedded systems, the Intel 8051 and Motorola 68HC11, are shown in the following block diagrams.

The Intel 8051 microcontroller has an 8-bit microprocessor running at 1MIPS/ 12MHz with small on-chip RAM of 128 bytes for data and 4K on-chip ROM for code. It is integrated with 4 bi-directional I/O ports, two counter/timers, and Universal Asynchronous Receiver Transmitter (UART) for RS232 serial communication. It can support up to 64K external RAM and ROM. We chose the 8051 microcontroller to discuss in this book due to its popularity, low cost, and especially the availability of many affordable IDE development kits such as the Keil μVision development kit and the C8051F005DK development kits (target board included) with support for C programming language for the lab experiments in the book.

The 16-bit Intel 80×86 microcontrollers come with more RAM, timers, and DMAs.

The Motorola (Freescale) 68HC16 is a 16-bit microcontroller compatible upgrade of the 68HC11 with up to 768 bytes on-chip RAM and 64K extended RAM.

Both the 8051 family and 6800 family of microcontrollers are widely used for small and medium scale embedded systems, e.g. you can use 8051 or 68HC11 microcontrollers to design an embedded system to control a motor running at 10 rotates/second. You may use 80×86 microcontrollers for a voice signal processing system, because it needs to handle the voice data at 100 kbps.

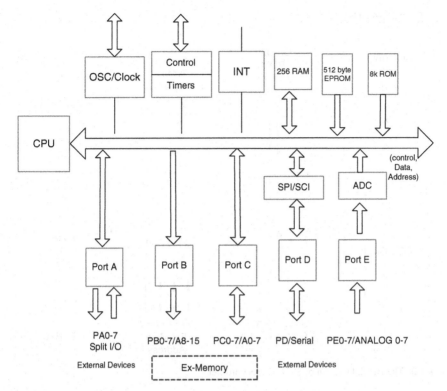

Fig. 1.2 Block Diagram of 68HC11 Microcontroller

The Microchip's PIC16 × 84 (68 bytes on-chip RAM, 14 bit instruction) micro-controllers are Programmable Intelligent Computer (PIC) family members, which are also commonly used for embedded systems. The PICs are popular to developers due to their low cost, wide availability, large user base, and extensive collection of application notes, rich and affordable development tools, and re-programming with flash memory capability. They are good fits to smart cars and other systems with lower power consumption especially for battery supplied systems.

The Atmel (Advanced RISC Machine) ARMx family microcontrollers with 32-bit CPU, MIA PowerPC, and the Intel i960 are widely used advanced micro-controllers for large scale embedded systems.

1.5.2 Memory

Embedded system memory can be on-chip or off-chip. For same type memory, on-chip memory access is much fast than off-chip memory, but the size of on-chip memory is much smaller than the size of off-chip memory. Usually, it takes at least two I/O ports as external address lines plus a few control lines such as R/W and

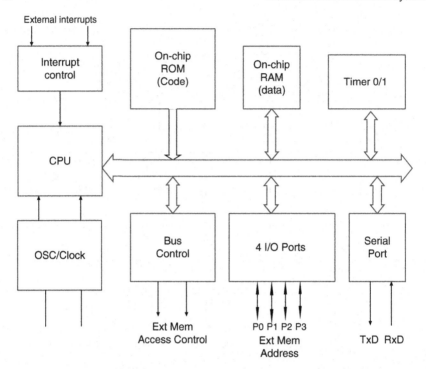

Fig. 1.3 The Block Diagram of 8051 Microcontroller

ALE control lines to enable the extended memory. For example, 16 bits of I/O port P0 and P2 are used to address 64k external memory in 8051. ($2^{16} = 2^6 \times 2^{10} = 64k$ byte memory space)

1.5.2.1 RAM

The 8051 memory is divided into Data Memory and Code Memory. Most of data is stored in Random Access Memory (RAM) and code is stored in Read Only Memory (ROM). This is due to the RAM constraint of the embedded system and the memory organization.

The RAM is readable and writable, faster access and more expensive volatile storage, which can be used to store either data or code. Once the power is turned off, all information stored in the RAM will be lost.

The RAM size of a microprocessor and microcontroller is rather small (<256 bytes in most cases). In order to access any byte in a 256 bytes memory space, there needs to be 8 address lines (internal address bus) because $2^8 = 256$.

One ASCII character takes one byte of memory space. For example, character 'A' has its ASCII code 65_{10}, i.e. in binary 01000001_2 (8 bits = 1 byte); an integer number 1024_{10} takes 11 bits (10000000000_2) which needs 2 bytes to store it. The simplest machine instructions can take one byte, but some other memory access machine instructions take multiple bytes.

The small amount of automatic variable data (local variables of functions and interrupt service routine functions, stacks) are stored on the on-chip RAM for fast and frequent access and update, while the large amount temporary data (array, table) can be stored in off-chip RAM.

The RAM chip can be SRAM (static) or DRAM (dynamic) depending on the manufacturer. SRAM is faster than DRAM, but is more expensive.

1.5.2.2   ROM

The ROM, EPROM, and Flash memory are all read-only type memories often used to store code in an embedded system. The embedded system code does not change after the code is loaded into memory. The ROM is programmed at the factory and can not be changed over time. The newer microcontrollers come with EPROM or Flash instead of ROM. Most microcontroller development kits come with EPROM as well.

EPROM and Flash memory are easier to rewrite than ROM. EPROM is an Erasable Programmable ROM in which the contents can be field programmed by a special burner and can be erased by a UV light bulb. The size of EPROM ranges up to 32kb in most embedded systems.

Flash memory is an Electrically EPROM which can be programmed from software so that the developers don't need to physically remove the EPROM from the circuit to re-program it. It is much quicker and easier to re-write Flash than other types of EPROM.

All ROM type memories are non-volatile. This is one of the reasons the embedded code firmware is stored in ROM type memory.

When the power is on, the first instruction in ROM is loaded into the PC and then the CPU fetches the instruction from the location in the ROM pointed to by the PC and stores it in the IR to start the continuous CPU fetch and execution cycle. The PC is advanced to the address of the next instruction depending on the length of the current instruction or the destination of the Jump instruction.

The 68HC11 comes with 256 bytes RAM, 512 bytes EPROM, and 8k bytes ROM. Here 1k is 1024 bytes (2^{10}) and 8k $= 2^{13}$ bytes. There needs to be 13 address lines available to cover 8k bytes space.

The 8051 comes with 128 bytes RAM and 4k ROM. The EPROM or Flash memory can be attached as extended memory.

1.5.3   Bus

From the previous block diagrams, you can see all the CPU, memory, and I/O ports are connected by the buses. There are three type buses: data bus, address bus, and control bus.

The bus is a pathway to collect all the microcontroller components. An 8-bit or 16-bit microcontroller has an 8-bit or 16-bit data bus to deliver data from one component to another component within the microcontroller. The address bus is used to specify the memory location for the CPU to load instructions to be executed or to access data in the memory or ports. The control bus is used for the CPU to control the operation in sequence with the timing tick paces and specify the read/write memory access operation. Just as you have seen before, in order to run an instruction in the ROM, the CPU needs to load the instruction from the ROM to IR based on the PC, extract the op-code and operands, load the operands from memory, perform the instruction operation in the ALU, store the results in the destination, and start a new fetch-execution cycle. All of these are controlled by the control signals on the control bus issued by the CU.

The external bus is used for microcontroller to connect to the external devices.

1.5.4 I/O Ports

The I/O ports are used to connect input and output devices. The common input devices for an embedded system include keypads, switches, buttons, knobs, and all kinds of sensors (light, temperature, pressure, etc).

The output devices include Light Emitting Diodes (LED), Liquid Crystal Displays (LCD), printers, alarms, actuators, etc.

Some devices support both input and output, such as communication interfaces including Network Interface Cards (NIC), modems, and mobile phones.

1.5.4.1 Parallel Port

A microcontroller is integrated with several parallel I/O ports, which are used to interface the microcontroller to outside devices such as switches, LCDs, keypads, and actuators. The parallel ports get or send 8 bits of data at a time to and from connected outside devices.

Many microcontrollers have 4-8 ports, e.g. both the 8051 and 68HC11 have 8-bit I/O ports.

In 68HC11some of the ports are input only to connect input devices such as keypads and sensors, some other ports are used for output only (Port D of 68HC11) to connect output devices such as LCDs and any actuators, and some I/O ports are partial input/output. The bi-directional ports are the most common I/O ports in any microcontroller. The 8051 I/O ports are all bi-directional.

The multiplexers and de-multiplexers facilitate multiple channel communications via a single common port.

Figure 1.4 shows an 8051 chip connected to a LCD for data display.

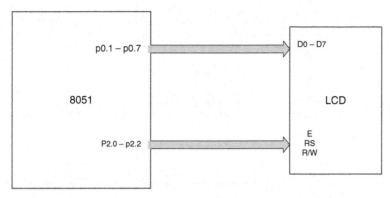

Fig. 1.4 LCD connected to the chip

1.5.4.2 Serial Ports

Some I/O ports such as the port D of the 68HC11 and port 3 of the 8051 can be used to connect an external serial device. Instead of 8 parallel lines in parallel I/O communication, the serial communication exchanges data one bit at a time with a single data line plus reference lines if needed. The typical application of serial ports is to connect a PC with a serial cable to take advantage of the PC for cross-platform embedded software debugging, testing, and deployment. Serial ports also allow data to flow between microcontrollers or between the microcontroller and any serial devices.

In order to make it work, there must be a protocol (rule) to govern the handshaking between two parties so that the receiver can recognize the beginning of the new coming byte and the end of the byte.

Assume the base logic is high "1" in discussion. Once the transfer starts, the line is lowered to "0" for a period of time to signal the receiver that the start bit is coming soon. Then the receiver activates its accepting circuit. Both sender and receiver follow the same clock pace, so that the receiver can sample the right data. The logic "1" is resumed after the 8 bits are delivered to mark the end of transmission of one byte data.

Figure 1.5 below describes the basic concept of serial communication. The RS232 is a serial communication standard which specifies the handshaking rules between two sites, e.g. the communication of a 9-pin COM port connecting to a PC COM port via serial cable complies with the RS232 protocol. The data is transferred at a specified baud rate (bps – number of bits per second). The baud rate at both sites must be the same so that the signals can be synchronized. It is called asynchronous communication because there is no clock control line between the transmitter and receiver to synchronize the pace.

The asynchronous serial communication is support by a built-in UART circuit.

It is possible to get and send data at the same time in a full-duplex mode or at separate times in the half-duplex mode. In transmission, the UART streams out 8 bits in sequence via the TxD pin at the specified baud rate. After 1 byte data is

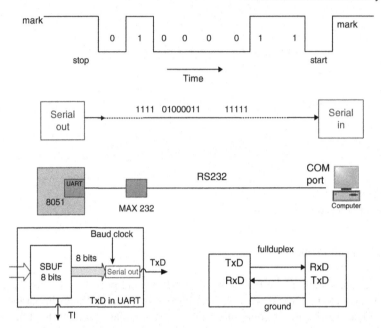

Fig. 1.5 Serial Communications

out, the UART sets the TI flag to 1 to signal the completion of the transmission and makes the buffer ready for the next data byte. The 68HC11 or 8051 provides TxD and RxD pins for the microcontroller to send and get data to and from a connected serial device. The lower left block diagram depicts the role of UART in transition. The receiver works in the opposition direction via the RxD pin and the completion of receiving one byte is notified by the RI flag.

1.5.5 Clock Oscillator, Timer and Watchdog

You know that time is a very important factor to consider in embedded system design. All microcontrollers need an oscillator clock unit which generates the clock tick at a predetermined rate. The clock is used to control the clocking requirement of the CPU for executing instructions and the configuration of timers. For example, a classic 8051 clock cycle is $(1/12)10^{-6}$ second ($1/12\,\mu s$) because the clock frequency is 12MHz. A simple 8051 instruction takes 12 cycles ($1\,\mu s$) to complete. Of course, some multi-cycle instructions take more clock cycles.

A timer is a real-time clock for real-time programming. Every timer comes with a counter which can be configured by programs to count the incoming pulses. When the counter overflows (resets to zero) it will fire a timeout interrupt that triggers predefined actions. Many time delays can be generated by timers. For example, a timer counter configured to 24,000 will trigger the timeout signal in $24,000 \times 1/12\,\mu s = 2\,ms$.

Each microprocessor provides multiple timers. The 8051 has two timers: Timer 0 and Timer 1. The 8052 has a third timer – Timer 2.

In addition to time delay generation, the timer is also widely used in the real-time embedded system to schedule multiple tasks in multitasking programming.

The watchdog timer is a special timing device that resets the system after a preset time delay in case of system anomaly. The watchdog starts up automatically after the system power up.

You need to reboot your PC time to time due to various faults caused by hardware or software. An embedded system cannot be rebooted manually, because it has been embedded to its system. That is why many microcontrollers come with an on-chip watchdog timer which can be configured just like the counter in the regular timer. After a system gets stuck (power supply voltage out of range or regular timer does not issue timeout after reaching zero count) the watchdog eventually will restart the system to bring the system back to a normal operational condition.

1.5.6 *Analog to Digital Converter (ADC) and DAC*

Many microcontroller kits integrate ADC and DAC units into the chip. Many embedded system application need to deal with non-digital external signals such as electronic voltage, music or voice, temperature, pressures, and many other signals in the analog form. The digital computer does not understand these data unless they are converted to digital formats.

The ADC is responsible for converting analog values to binary digits. The DAC is responsible for outputting analog signals for automation controls such as DC motor or HVDC furnace control.

Figure 1.6 shows an 8051 microcontroller connected to an ADC chip to convert the analog signals from sensor to digital signals to be processed by the microcontroller.

1.6 Embedded Software Design and Development

The embedded system software is an application-specific software that is dedicated to perform predesigned specific tasks repeatedly that users don't need to intervene the operation except the simple reset operation, i.e., once the embedded software is loaded into the system, the software is expected to run for a very long time by itself without any changes to the software. The software developers must guarantee the reliability, safety, and correctness of the embedded software.

The other challenges for software design include constraints on the software size, time-to-prototype, time-to-market, etc. An engineering discipline is needed for the embedded software design and development.

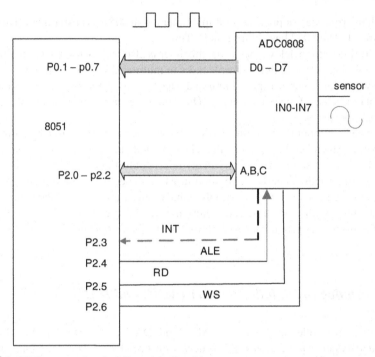

Fig. 1.6 ADC connected to the Microcontroller chip

1.6.1 Software Engineering Life cycle

The Software Development Life Cycle (SDLC) in software engineering is recommended for a complex embedded system software development project.

The entire development covers the specification and modeling, design, coding, testing, and integration as follows.

Various methodologies can be applied to each phase of the SDLC that will be discussed in the next chapter. The SDLC of an embedded system project can also be divided into two stages based on the system prototype paralleled with the hardware development.

On the first stage, embedded system software designers and developers need to set up the model, map the model to code, and implement and test the code in a cross-platform development environment with the simulation development tools.

On the second stage, the developers must load the host image (the executable code produced in the host machine) into the target machine (the embedded system itself) to run this target image on the target machine for the integration testing.

Almost all the embedded software is generated by a cross-compiler. The compiler runs on one kind processor(e.g., 80×86 PC) and generates target code for another processor(e.g., 8051) so that the resulting executable target code is run on a target machine as shown in Figure 1.7.

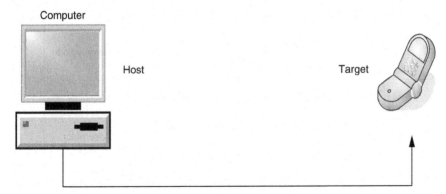

Fig. 1.7 Hosts and Target in Embedded Software Development

The flow chart in Figure 1.8 below shows the embedded C software compilation and link process in the 8051 family microcontroller. Although more and more embedded software is developed in C, sometimes critical jobs are still better when coded in assembly language for performance purposes. The C51 can mix C code and assembly code by #PRAGMA directives (will be discussed in chapter 4) so that the C can embed inline assembly code or assembly routines when it is necessary. The SRC option of C51 compiler can produce the assembly source code from C source code. The C51 compiler compiles the C source code into object code, while the A51 assembler assembles the assembly source code into objective code. The object code is not executable which has reference to library, external variable and external functions, and public symbol tables which help the linker to link all objective files and library file together to produce the absolute target code to run on the target. The bl51 is a linker/locator which links all objective files into a single relocatable machine code, and then generates executable binary code with located fixed address so that the program code can be loaded into ROM and data can be loaded into RAM in the located memory locations in the target machine.

1.6.2 Choose RTOS and Programming Language

Most embedded software is multitasking-based software, which supports multiple tasks running concurrently on the same CPU. One CPU can only run one instruction at a time, but multiple tasks are running simultaneously in a macro view, e.g. a temperature control embedded system has a thermal sensor and control panel with keypad and LCD.

The embedded system maintains the room temperature with a range of 70F $\sim$ 80F. If the temperature goes above 80, then a red LED is turned on; if it falls below 70F, then a green LED is on. Both LEDs are off if the temperature is between the upper and lower bounds. The current temperature is always displayed on the LCD. Users can reset the upper and lower bounds by the keypad at any time.

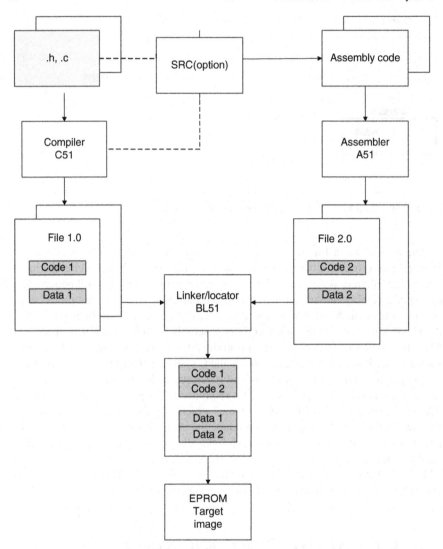

Fig. 1.8 C and Assembly Language and Objective Target Code

The software must run at least two tasks concurrently.

```
Task1                              Task2
   while(1)                           while(1)
   {                                  {

       sample ADC with sensor;            switch (key)
                                          {
       rest temp;                           Up: set up_T;
                                                break;
```

```
        if (temp>up_T) turn on Red;
        else if(temp<low_T) turn on Green;          Low: set low_T
        else turn off both                               break;
                                                    }

        wait (100ms);
                                                    }
    }
```

Task1 mainly monitors the current temperature and takes action when the temperature goes beyond the limits. It samples the sensor every 100 ms.

Task2 is ready to take user inputs from the keypad to reset the temperature upper and lower limits.

This simple embedded software deals with real-time and multiple tasks. You can design this software for multi-tasking by using a Real-Time Operating System (RTOS) or using the interrupt mechanisms supported by all microcontrollers.

There are many commercial or open source RTOS available for you to choose from based on the microcontroller system. RTX51 is a RTOS which comes with the Keil development kit.

1.7 Practice Labs

1.7.1 Getting Started with the Keil μVision3 C51 Development Kit

The standalone Keil Software development tool is widely used in embedded C software development for the 8051, 151, 251, and 166 microcontroller families. This tool suite includes C compilers, cross-compilers, assemblers, real-time executives, debuggers, simulators, and integrated environments. The Keil Software delivers its software in two types of kits: evaluation kits and production kits.

The free evaluation kit lets you generate applications up to 2 Kbytes in size and only includes a limited version of RTOS – RTXTiny. This kit can be used to generate small target applications. The Keil evaluation μVision3 development tools for 8051 Microcontrollers are available to download at https://www.keil.com/c51/demo/eval/c51.htm and the Getting Started tutorials of Keil μVision3 development are available at http://www.keil.com/uvision/ide_ov_starting.asp

The Production Kit (full version) provides the unlimited versions of their 8051 tools along with complete manuals. The production kits come with a full version of RTOS and some technical support and product updates.

Keil's compiler for the 8051 is called c51, which offers almost all the functions and syntax of 8051 C. In addition to command line compilation, Keil provides an IDE interface to cross-compile 8051 C source code. The code can run in a PC emulator or the 8051.

The demonstration here shows you how to write your first 8051 C language program using the popular Keil tool.

STEP 1: Creating Projects

You can download and install the current evaluation version of the Keil μVision3 for free including a project manager which makes it easy to design applications for the 8051 family targets.

First, go to Program -> Keil μVision3 to start Keil μVision3. You will see the opening page:

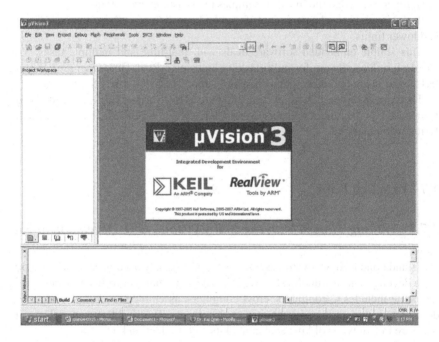

Select New Project from the Project menu to create a new project.

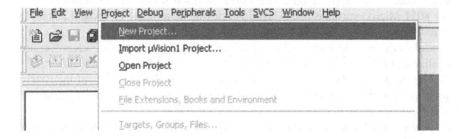

Create a new project named *myFirst* and save it in a directory called *myFirst* on the C drive. You can also save the project file anywhere you want.

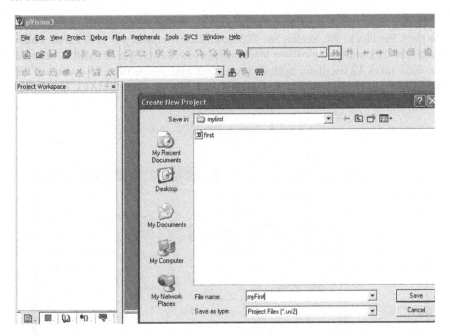

The new created project contains a default target, Target1, and file group name. You can see these file names in the Project Window on the lower left side of the window.

In the Project menu, select Option for Target to choose the particular 8051 chip you want to simulate. You can select generic 8051 driver.

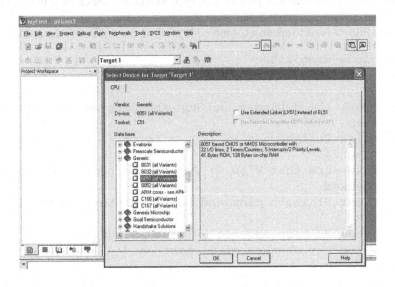

Next, go to Project -> Option for Target 1 to set the crystal oscillator frequency for the CPU clock. We assume the 8051 oscillator frequency is 12.0 MHz, which makes the CPU run at one million Machine Instructions per Second (MIPS), because the 8051 takes 12 oscillator cycles to run a machine instruction. Also you can set the memory model to SMALL, COMPACT, or LARGE, where SMALL is default.

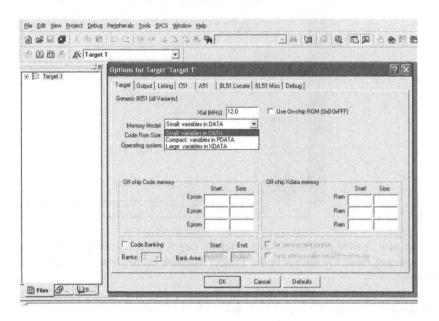

After you create your new project, you need to add the source code file into the project.

Go to File -> New to create a C source file *first.c* in the *myFirst* folder as follows.

```
#include <reg52.h>

/*
1. Start the debugger and Run the program step by
   step.
2. Click Peripherals -> I/O -> Ports -> Port 1 to
   view P1.
3. Make sure that View -> Periodic Window Update is
   checked.
4. Clear P1 (both pins and port register) in the P0
   box
5. Clear P0 port and set P0 pins as 00001010
6. Watch the changes of P1 port
*/
```

```
void main (void)
{
P0 = 0XFF; /*set P0 port as an input port in all 1s*/

while (1)
  {
  P1 = P0 ^ 0X0F; /*write (00001010 XOR 00001111) to
                        P1 */
  }
}
```

Right click the source group of the default target as follows.

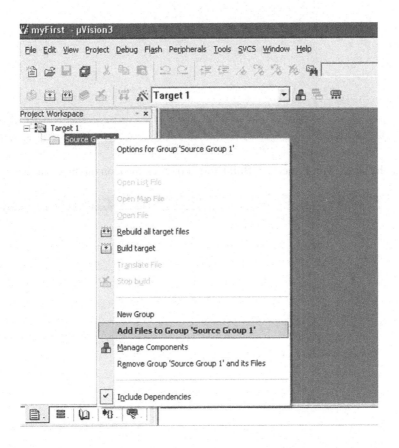

Click the *first.c* to display the code in the edit window.

Build the target with Project -> Build Target or click the icon on the menu bar.

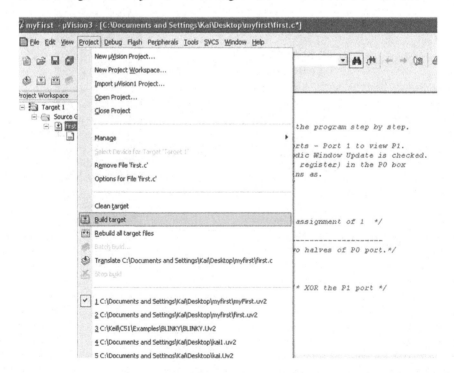

The output window indicates that the build process is well done.

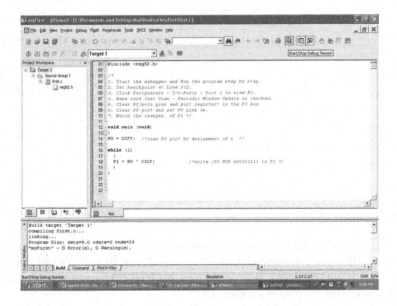

STEP 2: Run the Target

In order to simulate the input to the port pines and monitor the port changes, you go to Peripheral -> I/O Port, select port 0 and port 1 to bring these two port windows on the screen.

Go to View -> Periodic Window Update to activate the port window.

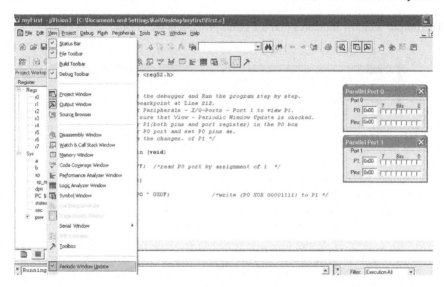

You can set a breakpoint at line 18 right before the P1 assignment statement is executed so that you can manipulate the P0 port and clear P1 port. The P1 pins can not be manipulated because it is an output port, but P0 is configured as an input port so that you can set the pins of P0 manually.

The bits above the pins in the port window are the port registers which you can initialize.

After you run the target by clicking the "RUN" icon or choosing Project -> Run, you will see the change in the P1 port. You can explain yourself why the result is "00000101".

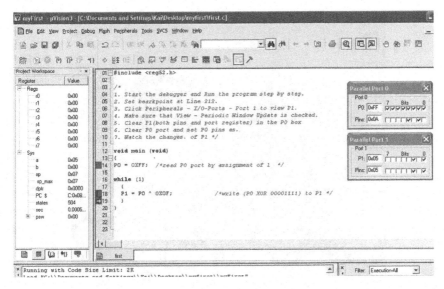

1.7.2 Lab with 8051 Microcontroller Development Kit

In this section you will have a hands-on lab exercise with an 8051 based microcontroller board. All the embedded system labs in this book are designed with the Keil 8051 software and the C8051F005DK development kit by the Silicon Laboratories, Inc. If you don't have this kit with you at this time, you can use the Keil software to simulate and practice this lab. The C8051F005DK kit is a 25 MIPS 8051 microcontroller with 32K in-system programmable FLASH, 256 bytes RAM, 2K-bytes XRAM, SPI, UART; 12-bit 8-channel A/D and 12-bit 2-channel D/A. Its Integrated Development Environment (IDE) is a complete, standalone software program that provides designers with the Keil software 8051 development tools (assembler-A51, C compiler-C51, linker-BL5, debugger, project interface, configuration wizard) that make the embedded software design and testing much easier. The picture below shows the target board and USB debug adapter which connect a JTAG connector on the board to the PC USB port for embedded software debugging, testing, and deployment. The Joint Test Action Group (JTAG) is the usual name for the IEEE 1149.1 Standard Test Access Port and Boundary-Scan Architecture for test access ports used for testing printed circuit boards. The C8051F005DK development kit is available for purchase at https://www.silabs.com/products/mcu/Pages/C8051F005DK.aspx

The target board has a C8051F005 microcontroller chip and 64-pin I/O connector for all I/O signals. In addition, it provides a power connector (AC adapter is included in the kit) and power indicator, a system reset button, a user switch, a user LED, ADC/DAC connector, a JTAG interface connector, and a proto board.

The C8051F005DK kit comes with a CD of development kit tools, which includes all the required software you need to install and a document CD. In case the CD does not work for your platform for any reason, you can download the software online. The current IDE kit software and the required Keil software for the kit are available online to download at https://www.silabs.com/products/mcu/Pages/SoftwareDownloads.aspx

You need to install the following three software components.

1. **Development Kit IDE**
   https://www.silabs.com/Support%20Documents/Software/mcu_ide.zip
2. **Configuration Wizard**
   https://www.silabs.com/Support%20Documents/Software/Software/ConfigAnd Config2Install.zip
3. **The Keil Compiler Tools Evaluation**
   https://www.silabs.com/Support%20Documents/Software/KeilV8Tools_ Installer.zip

The supporting materials for Silicon Labs development kit can be found at: https://www.silabs.com/support/pages/support.aspx?ProductFamily=Precision+ Mixed-Signal+MCUs

After you download the above software, you can set up the target board and debug adapter following the instructions on the quick start chart which comes with the kit. The following steps show the software installation.

Select the kit you have as follow.

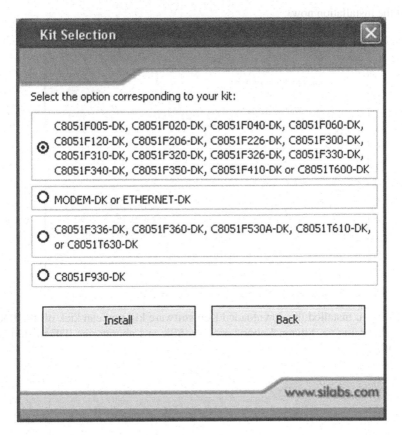

Select the components you want to install.

Start the installation now.

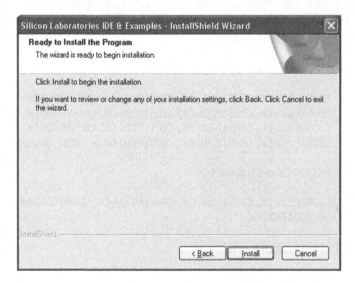

After you installed the downloaded Keil software kit, you can kick off the IDE: go to Programs -> Silicon Laboratories -> Silicon Laboratories IDE to start up the IDE.

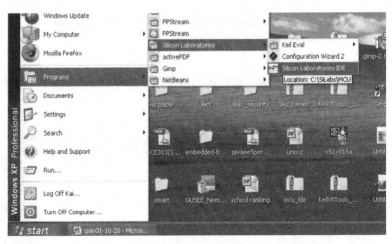

First, set the USB Debug Adapter and JTAG in the connection option.

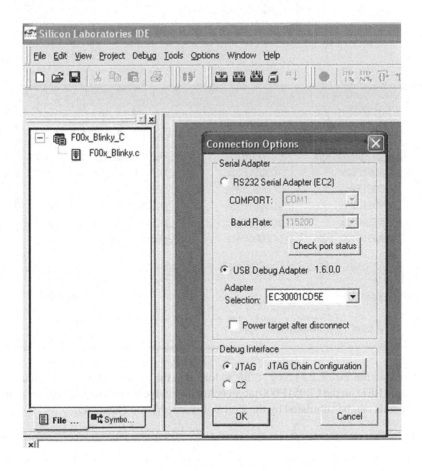

Let's practice an example project called `blinky`, which is available in the `silabs\mcu\examples\blinky` directory.

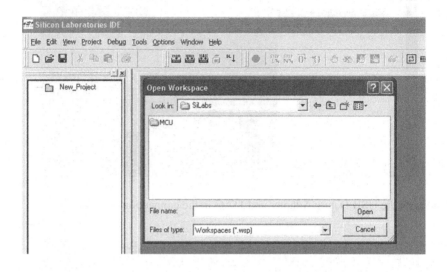

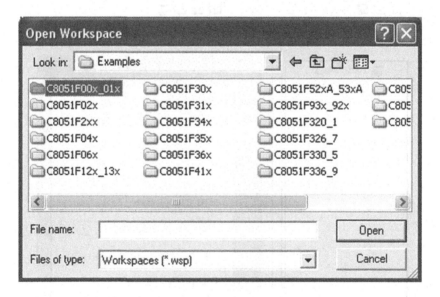

Click on the `f00x_blinky.C` file to load it to the project. This program flashes the green LED on the C8051F000 target board about five times a second. All on-chip peripherals can be simulated by the Keil Software μVision Debugger.

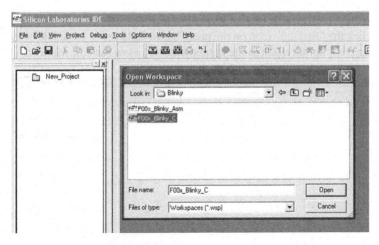

Now you can see that this source C file is added into the project in the project window on the left side of IDE interface as follows.

Click the source code file in the project window and display the code in the edit window. You can skip the code details for the time being.

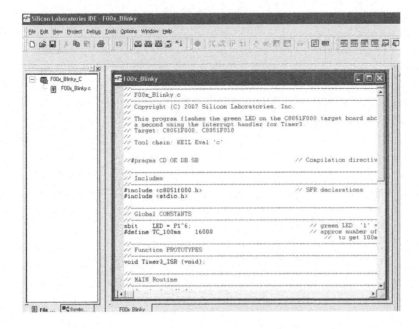

Go to `Project` on the menu bar and select the `build target` option or simply click the "`Build`" icon on the menu bar to build the re-locatable object file. Check the compilation result in the output window below the edit window.

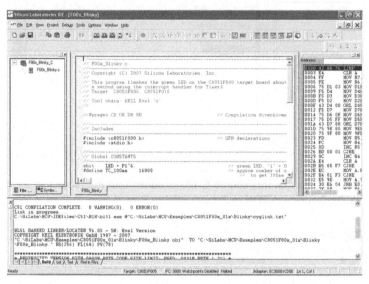

Now you can download the program into the target board by clicking the "Download the Program" icon on the menu bar next to the green circle "Run" icon. This step will generate the absolute executable target image file and load it into the target board.

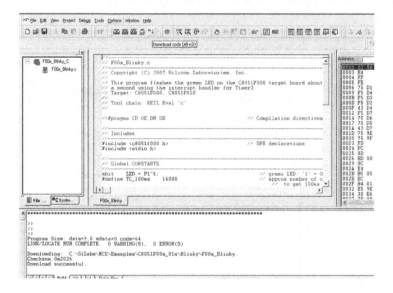

Now you can set up the breakpoints so that you can check the status of the program execution.

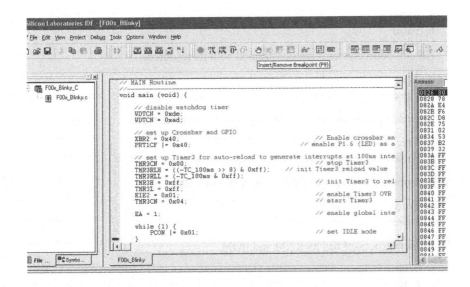

Now you can run the program deployed on the target board by clicking the "Run" icon. Look on the target board and you can see the green LED is blinking.

1.8 Summary

This chapter gives an orientation to embedded systems. It has introduced the hardware and software structure of embedded systems, categories, and applications of embedded systems. Especially, you have learned the constraints and design criteria and challenges in embedded system design and development. Also, the foundational concepts of microprocessors and microcontrollers are discussed. Since this book emphasizes embedded software development, the chapter provided a road map of embedded software design and development including software modeling, software coding, cross-compilation, multi-tasking programming, and RTOS implementation. Two Getting Started labs with the C8051F005DK development kit (with target board) of Silicon Labs and stand-alone C51 Keil software development kit are provided at the end of chapter. These two labs help you get start with embedded system design in both hardware and software aspects.

1.9 Review questions

1. An embedded system must respond to environment change or react to event.

   a. True
   b. False

2. All embedded systems are constrained with its resources.

   a. True
   b. False

3. Embedded systems are general purpose computing devices.

   a. True
   b. False

4. Microprocessor is a special type of microcontroller

   a. True
   b. False

5. A microprocessor has its RAM and ROM.

   a. True
   b. False

6. The MIPS specify the number of C statements executed per second

   a. True
   b. False

7. Embedded software is developed and tested in a cross platform

   a. True
   b. False

8. Most of embedded software are implemented by multi-tasking scheduling.

   a. True
   b. False

9. Embedded systems are always supported by RTOS

   a. True
   b. False

10. The timer is a built-in component of microcontroller for timing control

   a. True
   b. False

11. The embedded code is stored in RAM of microcontroller

   a. True
   b. False

12. The data processed by embedded software is stored in RAM.

   a. True
   b. False

Answers:
1. a   2. a   3. b   4. b   5. b   6. b   7. a   8. a   9. b   10. a   11. b
12. a

1.10 Exercises

1. Practice two embedded C51 programs in the example directory of the C8051F005DK development kit,
2. Practice two embedded C51 programs in the example directory of the Keil development kit,

References

1. 8051 Demo Kit, Getting Started with the 8051 Microcontroller Development Tools, Keil Elektronik GmbH and Keil Software, Inc., 1998
2. Getting Started with µVision2 and the C51 Microcontroller Development Tools, User's Guide 02.2001, Keil Elektronik GmbH and Keil Software, Inc., 2001
3. Silicon Laboratories, Inc. C8051F005, http://www.keil.com/dd/chip/3265.htm, 2008

Chapter 2
Embedded Software Design and Development

Objectives

- Use state Chart in embedded software analysis and design
- Apply time requirement analysis for real-time systems
- Understand the concepts of polling and interrupt
- Understand Multi-tasking Design and RTOS

2.1 Overview

The embedded system software development has the same Software Development Life Cycle (SDLC) just like any other software development, plus special consideration for resource constraints, including CPU, time, memory, operating system, multi-tasking concurrency, and many other non-functional attribute constraints. In order to reduce the time-to-market and guarantee the reliability of the embedded system product, software engineering methodology is recommended for the software design and development. Because the embedded software is not deployed on a general purpose computer system, the embedded software in C/C++ or other high level programming languages must be developed and tested on a cross-platform machine such as a PC, and then loaded to a target microcontroller memory to be tested as shown in Figure 2.1.

For a successful embedded system development, embedded system hardware and software co-design based on the system specification is also very necessary to get the prototype working smoothly. In the co-design phase, software analysts/designers need to work with hardware team members to decide on the type of microcontrollers and microprocessors in accordance with the requirements of the speed and memory, power consumption, the number of I/O devices such as ADC, cost per unit, size and packaging, and others. Also, software development tools must be selected and the partition between software and hardware implementation should be decided in the co-design phase, as well as decisions such as time delay implementation by software program or with a hardware timer.

K. Qian et al., *Embedded Software Development with C*,
DOI 10.1007/978-1-4419-0606-9_2, © Springer Science+Business Media, LLC 2009

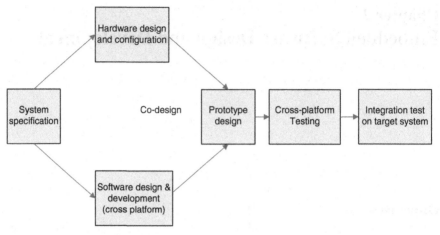

Fig. 2.1 Embedded system co-designs

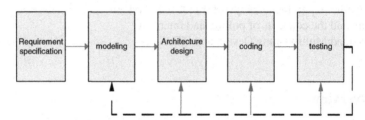

Fig. 2.2 SDLC

The SDLC proceeds in phases consisting of system specification, analysis, design, coding, and testing. The dashed lines indicate the required iteration processes when design changes are needed as shown in Figure 2.2.

The requirements specification provides an unambiguous description of system functionality and non-functional attribute requirements. It is the basis of the initial modeling and design processes. The modeling process analyzes the requirements specification and presents an abstraction model describing the embedded software structure and behavior. It is very beneficial to large complex embedded software design. Software design process/phase provides a blueprint for development implementation, which divides the whole system into subsystem partitions and specifies the relationships between the subsystems. Non-functional requirements are also concerns in software design. Both the modeling process and design process are independent from coding in term of programming methodology and language implementation. Lack of good software modeling and design processes will result in the repetition of the life cycle and will have significant impact on software quality and the time to market.

2.2 Software Requirement Specification

Compared to general purpose software, the non-functional requirements are especially important to all embedded software due to various constraints in resources
and performance. All the quality attributes should be identified in the requirement
analysis process. Quality attributes can be categorized into three groups:

1. Implementation attributes (not observable at runtime)

   - Resource availability: This refers to memory space, power supplier, CPU
     frequency, and RTOS.
   - Maintainability & extensibility: This refers to the ability to modify the system
     and extend it conveniently.
   - Testability: This refers to the degree to which the system facilitates the estab-
     lishment of test cases. It usually requires a complete set of documentation
     accompanied with the system design and implementation.
   - Flexibility: This refers to the ease of modification of a system to cater to
     different environments or problems for which the system is not originally
     designed. Systems developed using the component-based architecture or the
     service-oriented architecture usually possesses this property.

2. Runtime attributes (observable at runtime)

   - Availability: This refers to the ability of a system to be available 24×7. Avail-
     ability can be achieved via replication and careful design to cope with failures
     of hardware, software, or the network
   - Security: This refers to the ability to cope with malicious attacks from outside
     or inside the system. Security can be improved by installing firewalls and
     establishing authentication and authorization processes, and using encryption.
   - Performance: This refers to increasing efficiency such as response time,
     throughput and general resource utilization, which most of the time conflict
     with each other.
   - Usability: This refers to the level of "satisfaction" from a human perspective in
     using the system. Usability includes completeness, correctness, compatibility,
     and user friendliness such as a friendly user interface, complete documenta-
     tion, and help support.
   - Reliability: This refers to the failure frequency, the accuracy of output results,
     the mean-time-to-failure (MTTF), the ability to recover from failure, and the
     failure predictability

3. Business attributes

   - Time to market: This refers to the time it takes from requirement analysis to
     the date the product is released.
   - Cost: This refers to the expense of building, maintaining, and operating the
     system.
   - Lifetime: This refers to the period of time that the product is "alive" before
     retirement.

2.3 Embedded Software Modeling Analysis and Design

2.3.1 Context Diagram

The analysis process starts with the system context analysis, system key tasks, and identification of their relationship. The focus is given to the reactive behaviors of the embedded software. The event behavior features include: periodic or a-periodic events, parallel or serial data processing, synchronous or asynchronous communication, hard real-time or soft real-time response reaction, and others. Based on the system modeling, the design process produces an implementation guideline for developers such as multi-tasking processing architecture.

The context diagram generation may be the first step in the embedded software modeling process. The context diagram is derived from the requirements specification. It provides a preliminary draft of the embedded software and its environment, which shows all events the system interacts with. It specifies elements of a system, data and data flow around the system, and the system internal and external communication.

Here is an example of a multiple room temperature control system specification. The system provides centralized and distributed temperature control functions. A local desired temperature can be set by a room control panel in each individual room or a global temperature can be set at the central control panel. The temperature sensors are installed in each room to monitor the current room temperature. The A/C and furnace are turned on or off by the controller depending on the desired temperature and the current temperature. Each room has a vent driven by a motor to control the air flow so that different rooms may reach different desired temperatures.

Based on Figure 2.3(a), we can derive a preliminary software partition context diagram shown in Figure 2.3(b), which consists of the controller module, keypad module, sensor module, LCD module, vent motor control module, A/C unit control module, furnace control module, etc. This context diagram clearly depicts the input events for this embedded software and the actuators controlled by this embedded software. At this stage, the most important issue is to fully understand the system requirement (functional and non-functional) so that we can decide on the selection of microcontroller, communication mode (serial or parallel communication) with devices, adoption of RTOS, and modeling of the embedded software in the co-design phase.

2.3.2 Finite State Machine (FSM) and State Chart

As we know, system modeling presents an abstraction of the system (a high level description) in software aspects, which helps understanding of the functional requirements in block diagram form, and helps to identify all required software elements and tasks. There are many modeling tools available for modeling the

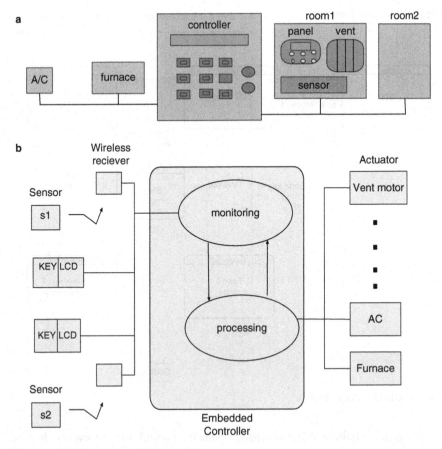

Fig. 2.3 (**a**) HVDC system (**b**) Context Diagram

Fig. 2.4 State Notation

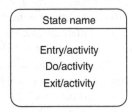

behaviors of embedded system software, such as Universal Modeling Language (UML) and Petri Net. The state Chart diagram is a very popular analysis modeling method for real-time embedded software, which is derived from Finite State Machine (FSM).

A FSM consists of a finite number of states, transitions between the states, and actions to be performed. A state represents a certain behavior which lasts for a period of time while performing tasks or being idle waiting for events. Figure 2.4 is the state notation where you can specify the entrance actions, state actions, and exit actions.

Fig. 2.5 Transition Link   Event (attributes)[guide condition] /reaction

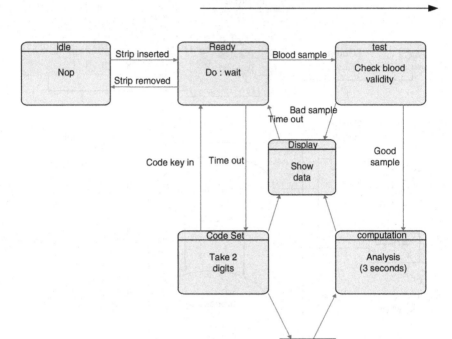

Fig. 2.6 Glucose Meter FSM

A transition indicates a state change guided by conditions or events. It is a response to an event with a set of attributes that moves the system from one state to another state. There may be many transition links from one state to other states with different events or with the same event but different guide conditions. An event can refer to either an internal event (such as timer timeout overflow) or external event (a car detected by sensor). A condition can refer to a set of variable values, and a reaction can refer to reassignment of these variables or to new event creation. Figure 2.5 shows a transition link where the guide condition and reaction are optional.

A FSM diagram can describe many software behaviors, such as a microwave or glucose monitor. Here is a simplified FSM diagram for a glucose monitor which is a typical embedded system.

When the test strip is inserted into the monitor, the system moves to a ready state where it is waiting for the blood sample, and the system moves back to the idle state when the strip is removed. At this time, the patient can set the strip code in two digits and it is saved in the data store. If the blood sample is not enough, the error message is displayed in the display state and system goes back to the ready state to wait for a new blood sample. If the blood sample is valid, it moves to the computation state to analyze the glucose level with the code reference from the data store and reports the result. A FSM can be easily implemented by a program shown next.

Fig. 2.7 A Simple FSM

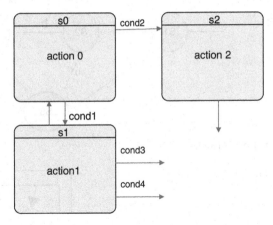

The following fragment describes the behavior of the FSM in Figure 2.7 above:

```
init state S0;
while(1)
{
    switch(state)
    {
        S0: action0;
            if (cond1) state = S1;
            else (cond2) state = . . .;
            break;
        S1: action1;
            if (cond3) state= . . . ;
            else if (cond4) state = . . . ;
            else state = S0;
            break;
        S2: action2;
            if (...) ...
    }
}
```

However, a FSM cannot represent multiple states that are simultaneously active nor describe any nested states within states in a hierarchical structure. It can only be used for a simple system with few states. A simple flat FSM for a counter or validation task is shown in Figure 2.8 where S1-S4 takes inputs and validates them. If the inputs are not valid then the system moves to state S5 to handle exceptions, and then goes back to initial state to start over again. It will be too complicated if the number of states becomes very large.

Figure 2.9 Group these states to make a single nested state S' so that the transition between S' and S is greatly simplified.

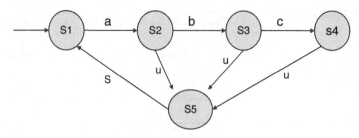

Fig. 2.8 Flat FSM

Fig. 2.9 Nested State Chart

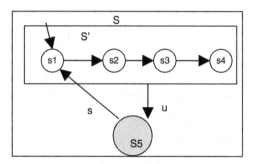

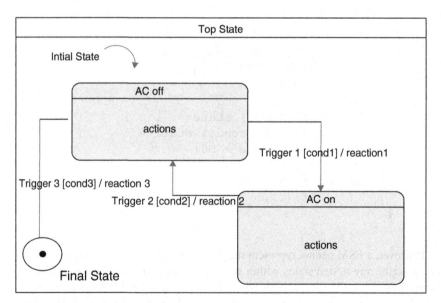

Fig. 2.10 A complete State Chart

In this way, a state can be refined into a set of sub-states until each state is simple enough to have its own responsibility. Figure 2.10 shows the init state (AC-off), final state, and AC-On state in a state Chart diagram.

Fig. 2.11 A simple State
Chart

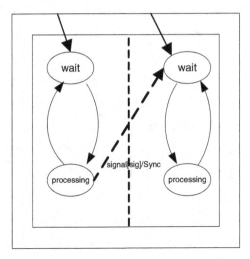

The following diagram, Figure 2.11, demonstrates two concurrent tasks that are active at same time.

Two tasks can be running concurrently with links between them. The dashed links indicate synchronization and message passing communication between tasks, such that one task can notify another task by a signal of job completion or other event. There may also be an external event notification such as an interrupt request from any external event resource.

More complicated logical relationships can be represented by the combination of logic AND (concurrency) and logic OR (selection) in a state Chart. The following diagram exhibits the concurrency behavior and hierarchy structure in a state Chart.

The state A is a super state of the state B and state C, while both states B and C are nested in state A. The state B and state C are separated by a vertical bar, which specifies the concurrency of B and C. The states D and E inside C are also two parallel states, just like the states B and C in state A. The logical relationship between the pair (B, C) and the pair (D, E) is a logical AND, which indicates B and C will be active at same time after state A is entered. It is the same for the states of D and E after state B is entered. Once the state C is entered, the default state is F, and the state F and the state G will be alternately active, so the relationship between F and G is logical OR. This means only one of these two states can be active at any time. The tree on the right side shows the logical relationship in term of concurrency between sibling states and alternate relationship between super-sub states.

A concurrent state can contain one history state and one deep history state. A transition to the history state will resume the state it last had in this state region. A typical application of the history state is for the Interrupt Service Routine (ISR) return, which returns the control to where it left. A history state can have multiple incoming events/actions. It can have at most one outgoing event/action, which points to the "resume" state if the transition occurs for the first time without any history. The regular history state only applies to the level in which it appears, while the deep

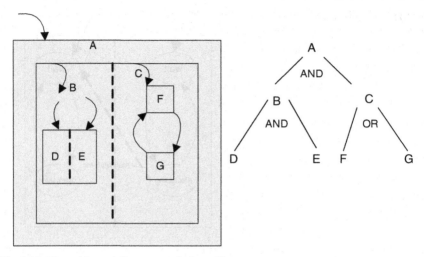

Fig. 2.12 Hierarchies and Concurrency in State Chart

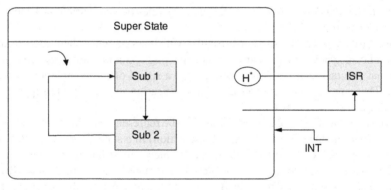

Fig. 2.13 History State

history state entrance applies to the most recently visited state in the deepest level. It is noted as H*.

After completion of interrupts, the control will return to where it left off, as noted by the H states, e.g., a timer can trigger a timeout event which interrupts a task, an ISR handles the event, and the interrupted task resumes afterwards.

The FSM is good for control-oriented system analysis which monitors inputs, controls the transitions by stimulus/events, and takes actions on the states. The state Chart is multitasking-oriented, which overcomes this shortcoming to support the real-time multi-tasking software analysis modeling. Similar to FSM, the state Chart consists of states (including initial and final states), signals (events), transitions with triggers (event and data conditions), and actions (e.g., emitting signals). In addition, it supports state hierarchy, i.e., nested states, and various communications between two active states.

When the state Chart is used, we can assign a concurrent task (a concurrent state) for each important device control so that we can easily divide the whole software design into multiple partitions.

There are many state Chart simulation development tools available in the market. StateMate, SpeedChart, StateFlow, BetterState, VisualVHDL, StateVision, and LabView are well known among these tools. Some other state Chart development tools such as Rational Rose and Rhapsody can even convert the state Chart into actual C or VHDL code.

In summary, the state Chart provides a formal model for reactive dynamic behavior of embedded system, especially for the concurrency behavior. It is a good fit for large system modeling and design, because it has eliminated the state explosion problem.

2.4 Time Requirement Analysis for Real-Time Systems

As you know that most embedded software are *real-time* systems, a waiting task is guaranteed to be given the CPU when an external event occurs. Real-time systems are designed to control devices such as industrial robots, which require timely processing. Such systems must meet timing requirements regardless if they are hard real-time embedded systems or soft real-time embedded systems. Almost all embedded software are multitasking oriented, in which multiple tasks, also known as processes, share common processing resources such as a CPU. With a single CPU, only one task is said to be *running* at any point in time, i.e., the CPU is actively executing an instruction for that task while all others are waiting. The act of reassigning a CPU from one task to another one is called a context switch. Running multiple tasks concurrently can make maximum use of CPU time, reduce the CPU idle time to a minimum degree, and handle urgent requests immediately. A task represents an activity such as a process or a thread. Threads are lightweight processes which share an entire memory space. Thus, threads are basically processes that run in the same memory context. Context switches between threads does not involve changing the memory context. A task can even have multiple threads. The term *task* in this book represents both a process and thread. The multi-tasking design and implementation can separate the design concerns, and divide and conquer the problem domains, but interaction and resource sharing between tasks still bring many design and implementation complexities.

Each task must keep track of its own concerns, and has its own state including its own status, CPU register status, program count, its own memory space and stack, so that the CPU can switch back and forth between these processes/tasks.

What is the timing requirement? When an event request occurs in a reactive embedded system, the target task must respond to the event within a preset time. The Worst-Case Execution Time (WCET) of a task tells us the maximum length of time the task could take to execute. A task often shows a certain variation of execution times depending on the input data or behavior of the environment. The actual

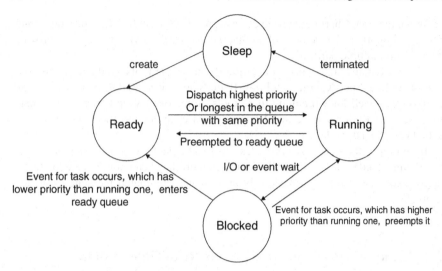

Fig. 2.14 RTX51 Tasks Status Diagram

response time may be shorter that the WCET. Knowing worst-case execution times is of prime importance for the timing analysis of hard real-time systems. There is also a deadline for each task to complete for either periodic events or a-periodic events.

Understanding life cycle of a task is very important for time requirement analysis. Let us examine the multi-tasking 8051 RTX-51. It recognizes four task states; a process is always in one of these states at any given time:

1. READY Tasks which are READY to be run by the CPU are in this state.
2. RUNNING (ACTIVE) Task which is currently being executed by CPU processor. Only one task can be in this state at any time.
3. BLOCKED (WAITING) Task waits for an event or resource.
4. SLEEPING Tasks before they are started or after termination are in this state.

This diagram shows the life cycle of a task in a multitasking environment, where it moves from one state to another state, and completes other tasks for CPU. The task selection for CPU (running state) is determined by a scheduler (also called dispatcher).

The RTX_51 scheduler follows the following rules:

1. The task with the highest priority of all tasks in the READY state is executed first.
2. If several tasks of the same priority are in the READY state, the task that has been ready the longest will be the next to execute.
3. Exception: round-robin scheduling to be discussed soon.

2.4.1 Non-Preemptive Scheduling

Non-preemptive multitasking is a simple task scheduling method for periodic time requirement systems. Such systems are either statically scheduled which most often are periodic systems, or in the form of cooperative multitasking, in which case the tasks can self-interrupt and voluntarily give control to other tasks. Cooperative multitasking is a type of multitasking in which the process currently controlling the CPU must offer control to other processes. It is called "cooperative" because all tasks must work cooperatively. In non-preemptive scheduling, once a task started, it will hold the CPU until it completes, or it may give up the CPU by itself due to lack of resources. It does not need any context switch from a running task to another task. The context switch takes a lot of time to save its current status, including its stack and Program Count (PC) address, so that it can resume its task after it comes back to run on the CPU.

A simplified modeling for a non-preemptive scheduling method can be a cyclic scheduling method where the tasks can be scheduled in a fixed static table off-line.

Assume that the embedded software consists of a set of tasks and all of them have a fixed period. A-periodic events can be estimated by their worst case interval gap between two consecutive task events.

Also, assume that all tasks are independent and WCET are known in advance so that the deadline is at the end of WCET.

You can also schedule the higher priority task before the tasks with lower priority. The advantage of such cyclic scheduling is simple: zero overhead for context switches between processes/tasks; the disadvantage is the inflexibility.

If there are n tasks and the WCET of ith task is c_i, then the period of any task T_i must satisfy

$$T_i >= \sum c_j (j = 1, 2, \ldots, n)$$

Otherwise some task may miss its deadline.

Therefore, software analysis and design should make each task as shorter as possible. For these long tasks you may need to break it into many small pieces.

Here is a cyclic schedule example:

Task	Execution Time	Period
Task1	20ms	50ms
Task2	25ms	100ms

You can find that the period of T1 (50ms) $>$ c1(20ms) + c2(25ms).

20ms(T1)	30ms	20ms(T1)	25ms(T1)	5ms

50   100

The following C code fragment shows the template for the non-preemptive cyclic scheduling implementation. Assume there is a timer set on the period of 50 ms.

```
while(1)
{
    Wait_for_50ms_timer_interrupt;
    do task1;
    Wait_for_50ms_timer_interrupt;
    do task1;
    do task2;
}
```

Round-robin (RR) is one of the simplest time-shared cooperative scheduling algorithms which assigns prefixed time slices to each process in order, handling all processes without priority (equal priority). The task with CPU control will either voluntarily yield the CPU to other task or be preempted through an internal timer interrupt. Round-robin scheduling is both simple and easy to implement, and starvation-free.

Many RTOS support RR scheduling.

Let's take look at an RR example in RTX51 RTOS. Assume there are two counting tasks: job1 and job2 as listed below.

```
int c1, c2;
                                //Round robin scheduling
void job0(void) _task_ 0  //starting task by default
{
    os_create (1);          //make task 1 ready
    while(1)
       c1 ++;
}
void job1(void) _task_ 1
{
    while(1)
       c2 ++;
}
```

The task0 creates task1, and the RTOS will switch CPU between task0 and task1 after task0 starts.

2.4.2 Pre-emptive Scheduling

In reality, a reactive embedded system must respond and handle external or internal events with different urgency. Some events have hard real-time constraints, while the others may only have soft real-time constraints. In other words, some task should be assigned higher priority than other tasks. An important design aspect of real-time software systems is priority-based scheduling, which ensures it will meet critical timing constraints such as deadline and response time. In priority-driven scheduling, the CPU always goes to the highest priority process that is ready. There are many priority-based scheduling algorithms to assign priority to each process in the multi-tasking real-time system. The popular fixed-priority scheduling algorithms are static timing scheduling, Round-robin scheduling and Rate Monotonic Scheduling(RMS), and its deadline based analysis is called Rate Monotonic Analysis(RMA), while the popular dynamic priority-based scheduling is Earliest Deadline First(EDF) scheduling that assigns priorities at runtime, based on upcoming execution deadlines where the priority is time varying rather than fixed.

2.4.3 RMS

Rate Monotonic Scheduling (RMS) is a priority-based static scheduling method for preemptive real-time systems. It is a popular static scheduling algorithm for such systems where the round-robin scheduling analysis fails to meet task deadlines all the time. It can guarantee the time requirement and maximize the schedulability as long as the CPU utilization is below 0.7. It has been proved that the RMA is optimal among all static priority scheduling algorithms. The rate-monotonic analysis assigns shorter period/deadline processes higher priority at design time, assuming that processes have the following properties:

- No resource sharing
  (processes do not share resources, e.g., a hardware resource, a queue, or any kind of semaphore blocking or busy wait non-blocking)
- Deterministic deadlines are exactly equal to periods
- Context switch times are free and have no impact on the model

Once the priority of a task is assigned, they will remain constant for the lifetime of the task.

Let's discuss a RMS scenario. First, look at the scenario with two tasks.

Task	Execution Time	Period(Deadline)	Priority	Utilization
Task1	20ms	50ms	2(high)	40%
Task2	45ms	100ms	1(low)	45%

The task1 must meet its deadline of 50, 100, 150, ... and task2 must meet its deadline at 100, 200, 300, ... Since task1 has a shorter period, it is assigned higher priority such that once it starts it will not be preempted until it completes. The static schedule is shown as follows.

T1(20)	T2(30)	T1(20)	T2(25)	(5)	T1(20)	T2(30)	Continue the same pattern

       50   100   150

At time 50, task2 is preempted by task1 because task1 is ready every 50ms and task1 has higher priority than task2. This schedule guarantees all tasks meet their deadline.

If task2 gets higher priority over task1, then task 1 will miss its deadline at time 50 as seen below.

T2(45)	T1(5)	T1(45)

50

Here is an example of three tasks (processes) listed in the table below.

Task	Execution Time	Period(Deadline)	Priority	Utilization
Task1	4ms	10ms	3(high)	40%
Task2	5ms	15ms	2(medium)	33%
Task3	6ms	25ms	1(low)	24%

Because $T(1) < T(2) < T(3)$ (where T(i) is the period of task i) ,

Therefore $P(1) > P(2) > P(3)$ (where P(i) is the priority of task i).

Also notice that CPU utilization is $4/10 + 5/15 + 6/25 = .40 + .33 + .24 = .94 <$ 100%.

Let's schedule these three tasks according to their priorities:

#1(4)	#2(5)	#3(1)	#1(4)	#3(1)	#2(5)	#1(4)	#3(1)	−3

       10   15   20   25

What happens? At the time of 25ms, task3 miss its deadline by 3ms. Why? It is due to the fact that total utilization rate is 94% which is far beyond the schedulable bound 70%. The schedulable bound is given later.

Let's reduce the utilization rates as follows:

Task	Execution time	Period(Deadline)	Priority	Utilization
Task1	3ms	10ms	3(high)	20%
Task2	4ms	15ms	2(medium)	20%
Task3	4ms	25ms	1(low)	16%

The total CPU utilization is 56% at this time, so let's re-schedule it.

#1(3)	#2(4)	#3(3)	#1(3)	#3(1)		#2(4)		#1(3)		#3(1)	

      10   15   20   25   30

The same pattern will continue after time 30.

One major limitation of fixed-priority scheduling is that it is not always possible to fully utilize the CPU. It has a worst-case schedulable bound of:

$$Un = \sum Ci/Ti(i = 1..n) <= n^*(2^{1/n} - 1)$$

where n is the number of tasks in a system. As the number of tasks increases, the schedulable bound decreases, eventually approaching its limit of $ln\ 2 = 69.3\%$.

Liu & Layland (1973) proved that for a set of n periodic tasks with unique periods, a feasible schedule that will meet deadlines exists if: CPU Utilization $< Un$.

In general, RMS cases can meet all the deadlines if CPU utilization is 70%. The other 30% of the CPU can be dedicated to lower-priority non real-time tasks.

The context switch cost for the RMS is very high, although its CPU utilization is not perfect.

In order to fully make use of CPU time and also to meet all deadlines, we need to use a dynamic priority scheduling algorithm.

2.4.4 Dynamic scheduling with EDF

You know that priority is fixed in the static priority-based scheduling, but the priority of a process can change in a dynamic priority-based scheduling method to increase the CPU utilization and to allow all tasks meet their deadline. The Earliest Deadline First (EDF) assigns higher priority to these tasks that are closer to their deadline at run time. The process closest to its deadline is assigned with the highest priority. The EDF can be applied to scheduling for both periodic and a-periodic tasks if deadlines are known in advance. The advantage of it is its superior CPU utilization, but its disadvantages including high costs on context switches and no guarantees on all deadline requirements.

EDF is not very practical in many cases due to its complexity and is not as popular as RMS.

EDF must recalculate the priority of each process at every context switch time (preemption time). This is another overhead cost in addition to the cost of context switches.

Let's explore a multi-tasking case as follows:

Task	Execution Time(Ci)	Deadline (Period)	Utilization
Task1	4ms	10ms	40%
Task2	4ms	15ms	27%
Task3	5ms	25ms	20%

The total CPU utilization = 87%

T1(4)	T2(4)	T3(2)	T1(4)	T3(1)	T2(4)	T3(1)	T1(4)	T3(1)	T3(5)

0   4   8   10   14   15   19   20   24   25   30

Assume tasks t1, t2, t3 are ready at time 0.

The deadline of t2 are at the time of 10, 20, 30, 40, ..., the deadlines for t2 are at the time of 15, 30, 45, and the deadlines for t3 are at the time of 25, 50, 75, ...

At time 0, t1 has the highest priority, because its next deadline is shorter than the other two.

At time 4, context switch time, t1 is just finished and is not ready, and t2 is closer to its next deadline than t3, so t2 goes first.

At time 8, only t3 is available and so t3 gets its 2 units until time 10, when the t1 is ready again.

At time 10, t1 gets back the CPU and completes at time 14.

At time 14, only t3 is ready and t2 will be ready at time 15, therefore t3 gets another 1 unit CPU time.

At time 15, t2 must run CPU and completes at time 19. T3 gets another one unit CPU time and completes before its deadline of time 25.

At time 20, t1 gets the CPU and runs 4 units time, and then t3 gets another one unit time to complete its execution time.

At time 25, neither t1 nor t2 is ready but t3 is ready for the next round, therefore t3 runs 5 units time.

At the time 30, the cycle will start over again.

Compared to RMS, you can see much more frequent context switches take place during the concurrent executions.

2.5 Multi-Tasking Design Methodology

Almost all real-time embedded systems are real-time reactive, which must react to external events or internal timer events within an expected time limit. After the system time requirement analysis and system modeling, we can start the software design, which will provide a guideline for software coding.

There are two classical modeling patterns for real-time embedded systems. One is a simple explicit loop controlled state Chart for soft real-time operating systems shown in Figure 2.15.

The shortcoming is that when the $task_i$ is waiting for an unavailable resource, the $task_{i+1}$ cannot precede it and so some other tasks may fail to meet the response dead-

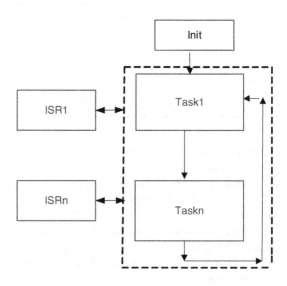

Fig. 2.15 Simple Loop Architecture

line requirement. There is no priority preference among the tasks. The advantage is its simplicity and that no RTOS support is needed.

There are many different ways to schedule and design a multi-tasking real-time system due to the system complexities and time constraint requirements. You can write a task scheduler on your own by polling external events or using external and internal timer interrupts, or use a commercial RTOS.

2.5.1 Polling

The simplest looping approach is to have all functional blocks including the event polling functions in a simple infinite loop like a Round-Robin loop.

```
main()
{
    while(1)
    {
        function1();
        function2();
        function3();
    }
}
```

The functions function1 and function2 may check the external data every 50 ms. The function3 may store the collected data and make some decisions and take actions based on the collected data.

The question is how to control the timing? Without a timer control interrupt due to various reasons such as not enough ports or interrupts available, you can design a time_delay function,

```
void time_delay(unsigned int delay)
{
    unsigned int i,j;
    for(i=0; i<=delay; i++)
    {
        for (j=0; j<=100; j++);
    }
}
```

A function call of time_delay(1) will produce approximately 1 ms for an 8051 running at 12MHz.

You can estimate it in this way: The 8051 runs at 1MIPS, the inner loop has 10 assembly machine instructions (by View − > Disassemble window in µvision) and 100 iterations takes about $100 \times 10µs = 1ms$.

Assume that all function execution times are very short and can be ignored. You can insert a time_delay(50) at the end of each cycle to make the program poll the I/O ports every 50 ms.

```
main()
{
    while(1)
    {
      function1();
      function2();
      function3();
      time_delay(50);
    }
}
```

Here we ignore the execution time of all functions. If the total execution time of these three functions is 10ms, then we can adjust the time delay to 40 ms. In reality, you don't see this implementation very often, because the time control is not accurate and it is not appropriate for any hard real-time systems. For very simple applications with limited timers and interrupt ports, you can still use this design style.

2.5.2 Interrupts

A popular design pattern for a simple real-time system is a division of a background program and several foreground interrupt service functions. For example, an application has a time critical job which needs to run every 10ms and several other soft time constrained functions such as interface updating, data transferring, and data notification. The C51 program template is given as follow:

Foreground:

```
void critical_control
    interrupt     INTERUPT_TIMER_1_OVERFLOW
{
    // This ISR is called every 10 ms by timer1
}
```

Background:

```
main()
{
    while(1)
    {
      function1();
      function2();
      function3();
    }
}
```

This simple background loop with foreground interrupt service routine pattern works fine as long as the ISR itself is short and runs quick. However, this pattern is difficult to scale to a large complex system. For example, the critical time control ISR function itself needs to wait for some data to be available, or to look up a large table, or to perform complex data transformation and computation. In this situation, the ISR itself may take more than 10ms and will miss the time deadline and also breach the time requirements for other tasks.

An alternative solution is to have a flag control variable to mark the interrupt time status and to split the ISR into several sub states as follows.

```c
int timerFlag;      // global data needs a protection
void isr_1 interrupt INTERRUPT_TIMER_1_OVERFLOW
{
    timerFlag = 1;
    // This ISR is called every 10 ms by timer1 set
}
int states ;

critical-control()
{
    static states next_state = 0;
    switch(next_state)
    {
        case 0:
            process1();
            next_state=1;
            break;
        case 1:
            process2();
            next_state=2;
            break;
        case 2:
            process3();
            next_state=0;
            break;
    }
}
main()
{
    Init();
    while(1)
    {
        if (timerFlag)
        {
            critical_control();
            timerFlag=0;
```

```
        }
        function1();
        function2();
        function3();
    }
}
```

A rule of thumb for the timer interval is always to make the interval short enough to ensure the critical functions get serviced at the desired frequency.

So far, the discussion is given on simple real-time applications. For a large and complex real-time system with more than dozen concurrent tasks, you need to use a RTOS to make priority-based schedule for multi-tasking jobs.

2.5.3 RTOS

RTOS makes complex, hard real-time embedded software design much easier. The RTOS-based model diagram is shown in Figure 2.16. The links between tasks can represent the synchronization signals, data exchanges, or even a timeout notification between tasks.

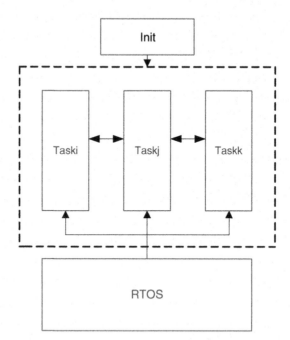

Fig. 2.16 Parallel Architecture

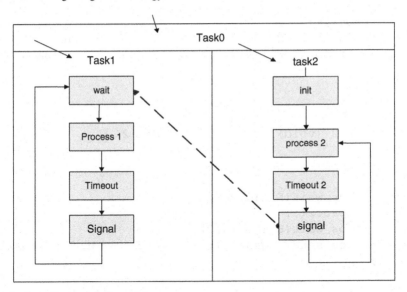

Fig. 2.17 A simple state Chart diagram

A RTOS is a background program which controls and schedules executions and communications of multiple time constrained tasks, schedules resource sharing, and distributes the concerns among tasks. There are a variety of commercial RTOS available for various microcontrollers, such as POSIX (Portable Operating System Interface for Computing Environments) and CMX-RTX. A RTOS is widely used in complex, hard real-time embedded software. Assume you have an init master task that starts two tasks that need to run forever. These two tasks are relatively independent, e.g., the task1 is a main control task and task2 monitors an external event and notifies it to the task1. You can design these two tasks in a parallel mode in a state Chart diagram shown in Figure 2.17.

Here is the 8051 RTX51 implementation of the above application model for you to get your first taste of the RTOS.

```
#include <reg51.h>
#include <rtx51.h>

void task1 (void) _task_ 1
        //task1 is assigned a priority 0 by default
        //4 priority levels: 0-3 in RTX51
{
   while(1)
   {
     os_wait(K_SIG,0,0);// wait in blocked state
                        // for signal to be activated
                        // to a ready state
```

```
        proc1();
        os_wait(K_TMO,30,0); // wait for timeout
        os_send_signal(2);    // send signal to task 2
    }
}


void task2 (void) _task_ 2    //Task 2
{
    while(1)
    {
        os_wait(K_SIG,0,0);
        proc2();
        os_wait(K_TMO,30,0);
        os_send_signal(1);    //send a signal to task1
    }
}


void start_task (void) _task_ 0 _priority_ 1
                //task 0 with higher priority 1
{
    system_init();
    os_create_task(1);        //make task1 ready
    os_create_task(2);        //make task2 ready
    os_delete_task(0);        //make task0 itself sleep
}


void main (void)
{
    os_start_system (0);             //start up task0
}
```

The detailed discussion will be given in the RTOS chapter 5.

2.6 Software Design Issues

2.6.1 Task Interactions

In many cases, synchronization and inter-process communication are very necessary. Most tasks have to interact with other tasks in their executions. They can interact simply by exchanging messages synchronously with parameter message passing or asynchronously with message queues; they can coordinate themselves by synchronization in such way that task A waits until it receives a signal from task B before proceeding; they can interact implicitly through resource sharing, such as global data so that one task can get data updated by another task.

Due to the concurrency situation, the shared data must be protected by mutual exclusion access control in order to prevent any malfunction on the shared data.

In other words, the relationship between concurrent tasks may be independent, cooperative, or competitive.

2.6.2 Resource Sharing

2.6.2.1 Data Sharing

Many processes/tasks need to share same data items. For example,

```
int c =0;

//Task a:

while(1)
{
   int i;

   i=c;       //line 1
   i++;       //line 2
   c-i;       //line 3
}

   //Task b:

while(1)
{
   int i;

   i=c; //line 4
   i--; //line 5
   c=i; //line 6
}
```

If two tasks are running concurrently with such scheduling: Line 1, 4, 2, 5, 3, 6, the value of global variable c will be -1 instead of 0, because the effect of line 3 is overridden by line 6. This indicates that the global data c should be protected, which can be done by a lock or semaphore in order to guarantee mutual exclusion and avoid such a race condition. The mutual exclusion only allows one process to get access to the shared data at a time, and all other processes are locked out until the current one leaves the critical section and unlock the lock. The implementation technology includes low level system supported primitives: semaphores or high level synchronization primitives: monitors, or others. Message passing in explicit data transferring through send and receive primitives is another way.

A semaphore is a protected entity token for restricting access to shared resources in a multitasking environment. By the semaphore mechanism, resources can be shared free of conflicts between the individual tasks. If the resource is already in use, the requesting task is blocked until the token is returned to the semaphore by its current owner.

A simple binary semaphore is called a mutex. A counting semaphore is a counter for a set of available resources, rather than a locked/unlocked flag of a single resource. The synchronization resource sharing by semaphores are often called *wait* and *signal*, or *acquire* and *release*, or *pend* and *post* a semaphore.

Semaphores can only be accessed using two atomic operations (request and release the shared resource) which should not be interrupted once they are started. Almost all RTOS support semaphore mechanisms in the following ways: the atomic *p* operator requests the semaphore of a resource, and the atomic *v* operator releases the semaphore as follows.

```
p(Semaphore s) // Acquire Resource
{
  wait until s > 0, then s -= 1;
}

p(Semaphore s) // Release Resource
{
  s += 1;
}

init(Semaphore s, int v)
{
  s := v; // v is the number of available resources.
          // If there is only one resource, s is
          // initialized as 1.
}
```

2.6.2.2 Code Sharing

In the embedded software, many subprograms such as interrupt service routines are invoked by multiple tasks concurrently, and these programs may be called recursively, which require such programs to be reentrant. A reentrant function can safely be called from multiple threads simultaneously, the execution of the function can be interrupted, and it can be called again, e.g., by another task (program), without affecting each other. That is, the function can be re-entered while it is already running.

If a function contains static variables or accesses global data, then it is not reentrant.

The static variables of a function maintain their values between invocations of the function. When concurrent multiple tasks invoke this function, a race condition occurs. The same race condition may take place when multiple tasks invoke the same function. Each attempts to modify that global variable, which is not protected.

A function is considered *reentrant* if the function cannot be changed while in use. Reentrant code avoids race conditions by removing references to global variables and modifiable static data. In other word, all data with a reentrant function must be atomic so that the code can be shared by multiple concurrent tasks without a race condition. In addition to the atomic data requirement, a reentrant function should work only on the data provided to it by the caller, should not call any non-reentrant functions, and should not return any address to a static or global data.

In the following example, neither functions f1 nor f2 are reentrant.

```
int global = 0;

int f1()
{
   static s1 =1;
   global += 1;
   s1 += 1;
   return global + s1;
}

int f2()
{
   return f() + 1;
}
```

The function f1 depends on a global variable global and a static variable s1. Thus, if two tasks execute it and access these two variables concurrently, then the result will vary depending on the timing of the execution due to the race condition. Hence, f1 is not reentrant, and neither is f2 because it calls the non-reentrant function f1.

```
int f3(int i)
{
   int a;
   a = i + 1;
   return a;
}

int f4(int i)
{
   return f(i) + 1;
}
```

Now both f3 and f4 are re-entrant functions at this time, because the f3 function only uses either atomic variables or the data provided by the caller and the f4 function calls the reentrant function f3.

If any non-reentrant function needs to share the common data in the concurrent execution, mutual exclusion needs to be enforced. The semaphore for critical sections is one of the common practices.

The RTX51 RTOS provides up to eight binary semaphores. The semaphores allow the following pair of operations:

- Wait for token:os_wait()
- Return (send) token: os_send_token()

E.g., here is a C51 fragment using semaphores

```
os_wait (K_MBX + SEM_1, 255, 0);// Wait for semaphore

// put critical section code here; It may be a non-
// reentrant function or code accessing a shared data

os_send_token (SEM_1); //release semaphore

os_send_token (SEM_1);
```

It is also used to initialize the semaphore token for the multi-tasking environment initialization where the semaphore SEM_1 is defined as an integer of value 1-8.

2.7 Lab Practice: A Traffic Light Control System Modeling and Design

In this lab, we will model and design a simplified automated traffic light control system in the street intersection. The C51 code of a similar system is included in the Keil development kit. We will focus on the system modeling and design process in this lab. Its implementation will be in the RTOS chapter.

There are three lights: Red, Green, and Yellow in sequence. The time duration of each light is predetermined. For modeling and design purposes, we have one light group (R, G, Y) for each street direction and one pedestrian self-service button and walk permit indicator in each direction. A pedestrian can push the button to request the walk permit and system will switch the walk light from stop to walk. There are two car detection sensors: one in each direction to sense for approaching car. If a coming car approaches in one direction and no car in the other direction, it will notify the system to switch the light to let the approaching car go.

Figure 2.18 shows the environment of the traffic light control system in one direction.

The following context diagram only lists the components in the direction of north bound and east bound. The sensor1 and sensor2 are used to detect car arrivals in

Fig. 2.18 Street Environment
of the Traffic Light Controller

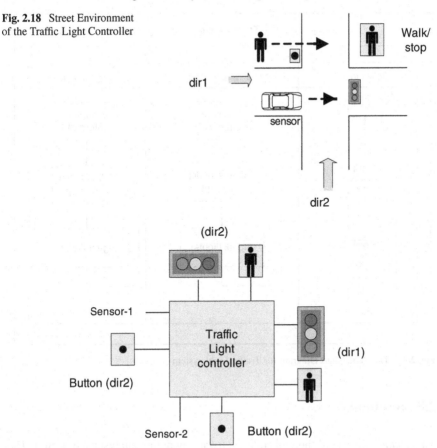

Fig. 2.19 The Context Diagram

these two directions and trigger the interrupts. The button1 and button2 will make
the walk permit request via external interrupts. The two kinds of actuators are the
walk/stop light and the Red-Yellow-Green traffic light. You can derive your state
Chart diagram from the context diagram based on the input devices where the
embedded system gets data or signal from and the actuators on which the system
must have control over and take action upon.

After you analyze the context diagram, you may decide to have one task for
button input and one task for car detect input, but neither of them can decide the
light changes by themselves, because the system must consolidate the traffic lights
and walk permit lights. You can have a third task called lights task, which has an
infinite loop in the sequence of Red => Green => Yellow with predefined intervals
in case of no car arrival request or pedestrian crossing request. Once the light task
gets requests from the other two tasks, it can alter the normal light display sequence
to satisfy the requests. The state Chart diagram in Figure 2.20 is one of the models
you may get. The implementation of this model will be given in chapter 5.

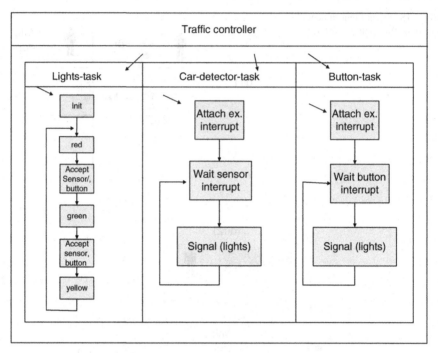

Fig. 2.20 The State Chart Diagram for Traffic Light system

2.8   Summary

This chapter discussed the embedded software modeling analysis and design. The state Chart diagram is one of the graphic modeling tools to explore the embedded system's behavior and presents an abstraction model for the software design. The non-functional requirements such as time constraints for real-time embedded software must be satisfied due to the functional requirements. A simple, real-time embedded system can be scheduled by Round-Robin scheduling, but many hard real-time embedded software with multiple concurrent tasks need more advanced scheduling algorithm supported by RTOS. The RMS is a popular time analysis method for static priority-based multitasking scheduling where the shortest task is always assigned with highest priority in the pre-emptive scheduling. Multiple tasks need to share resources, and shared resource protection becomes an embedded software design concern. The semaphore token used for concurrent access to shared resources are discussed to avoid the race condition. The reentrant functions shared by multiple tasks to allow recursive invocation are another common issue in the embedded software design. In the software SDLC, a sound embedded software analysis and design build a solid foundation for real-time embedded software development coding and testing.

2.9 Review Questions

1. The transition link in a state Chart can specify the event, condition, and action.

   a. True
   b. False

2. Two states with logic AND can only be run CPU one after another.

   a. True
   b. False

3. Two states with logic OR can run CPU concurrently.

   a. True
   b. False

4. A history state can be used to represent the interrupt resume point.

   a. True
   b. False

5. The action noted in a state is same as the action noted in the transition.

   a. True
   b. False

6. In Round-robin scheduling each task can be assigned with different time slice.

   a. True
   b. False

7. RMS is used to analyze the dynamic priority-based multi-tasking scheduling.

   a. True
   b. False

8. EDF is used to analyze the static priority-based multi-tasking scheduling.

   a. True
   b. False

9. The priority is based on the task execution time in RMS.

   a. True
   b. False

10. In EDF the priority of a task is determined on how close the task is to its deadline at run time.

    a. True
    b. False

11. There is no context switch cost in RR scheduled multi-tasking.

    a. True
    b. False

12. Each task module in embedded software model must be an infinite loop.

    a. True
    b. False

    Answers:
    1. a   2. b   3. b   4. a   5. b   6. b   7. b   8. b
    9. a   10. a   11. b   12. b

2.10 Exercises

1. Give a complete analysis modeling and design of the simplified temperature controller with RED and GREEN LED indicators and keypad for high and low bound setting project in this chapter.
2. Redesign the traffic light control system project given in this chapter using state Charts. Add following features:

   • The system allows you to set a time range for a normal daily working period. (ex: 6:00am –10:00pm)
   • Beyond this time period, the traffic lights blink yellow in both directions.

3. List all non-functional requirements for the simplified temperature LED system.
4. List all non-functional requirements for the traffic light controller system.
5. Perform RMS analysis on this time requirement:

   Task1: execution time: 25 ms, period: 50 ms.
   Task2: execution time: 40 ms, period: 100 ms.

6. Perform RMS analysis on this time requirement:

   Task1: execution time: 3 ms, period: 10 ms.
   Task2: execution time: 4 ms, period: 15 ms.
   Task3: execution time: 5 ms, period: 20 ms.

7. Perform EDF analysis on this time requirement:

   Task1: execution time: 3 ms, deadline: 10 ms.
   Task2: execution time: 4 ms, deadline: 15 ms.
   Task3: execution time: 5 ms, deadline: 20 ms.

8. Run the Ex1 RTX51Tiny example provided by the Keil development kit.
9. Draw a state Chart for the above example.
10. Run the Ex2 RTX51Tiny example provided by the Keil development kit.
11. Draw a state Chart for the above example.

References

1. D. Harel, State Charts: A visual Formalism for Complex Systems, Science of Computer Programming, 1987
2. Rajesh Gupta, mesl.ucsd.edu - /gupta/cse237b-f07/Lectures/, 2007
3. Michael Point, Embedded C, Addison Wesley, 2002
4. C51 Primer, www.esacademy.com/automation/docs/c51primer/
5. Embedded software design tutorial, www.freertos.org/tutorial/solution1.html, 2007
6. RTX51 Tiny User's Guide, http://www.keil.com/support/man/docs/tr51/
7. μVision® User's Guide, http://www.keil.com/support/man/docs/uv3/

Chapter 3
8051 Microcontroller

Objectives

- Understand the 8051 Architecture
- Use SFR in C
- Use I/O ports in C
- Programming with Timers
- Programming with external and serial interrupts

3.1 Overview

The Intel 8051 is a very popular general purpose microcontroller widely used for small scale embedded systems. Many vendors such as Atmel, Philips, and Texas Instruments produce MCS-51 family microcontroller chips.

The 8051 is an 8-bit microcontroller with an 8-bit data bus and a 16-bit address bus. The 16-bit address bus can address a 64K (2^{16}) byte code memory space and a separate 64K byte data memory space. The 8051 has 4K on-chip read-only code memory, and 128 bytes of internal Random Access Memory (RAM) organized in Harvard Architecture, the details of which will be discussed in the memory section. The 8051 has two timers/counters, a serial port, 4 general purpose parallel input/output ports, and interrupt control logic with five sources of interrupts. Besides internal RAM, the 8051 has various *Special Function Registers* (SFR) such as the accumulator, the B register, and many other control registers.

There are 34 8-bit general purpose registers in total. The ALU performs one 8-bit operation at a time. It has two 16-bit timers and supports 3 internal interrupts (one serial) and 2 external interrupts. It comes with 4 8-bit bi-direction I/O ports (3 of them are dual purposed). Some 8051 chips come with UART for serial communication and ADC for analog to digital conversion.

The Keil C51 compiler is an implementation of the C language ANSI standard specifically for 8051 processors, which contains all the necessary C extensions for 8051 microcontroller programming. All the embedded software code in this book is written in C51 language.

K. Qian et al., *Embedded Software Development with C,*
DOI 10.1007/978-1-4419-0606-9_3, © Springer Science+Business Media, LLC 2009

3.1.1 8051 Chip Pins

There are 40 pins on the 8051 chip. Most of these pins are used to connect to I/O devices or external data and code memory. The 4 I/O ports take up 32 pins (4 × 8 bits) plus a pair of XTAL pins for the crystal clock, a pair of Vcc and GND pins for the power supply (the 8051 chip needs +5V 500mA to function properly), a pair of timer pins for timing controls, a group of pins (EA, ALE, PSEN, WR, RD) for internal and external data and code memory access controls, and one Reset pin for reboot purpose. Figure 3.1 shows a pin out diagram of the typical 8051 chip. The curry brackets on the ports give the alternate functions of the pins.

Let's briefly discuss the group of pins (EA, ALE, PSEN, WR, and RD) and port 0 and port 2 in Figure 3.2.

The EA' (External Access) pin is used to control the internal or external memory access. The signal 0 is for external memory access and signal 1 is for internal memory access.

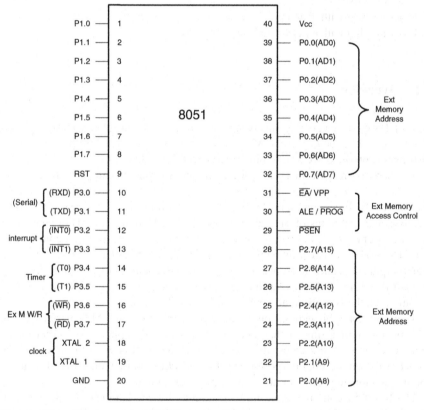

Fig. 3.1 Pin out Diagram of the 8051 Microcontroller

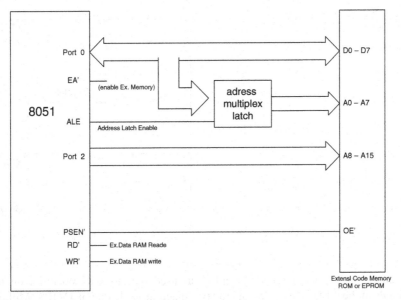

Fig. 3.2 The Pin Connection for External Code and Data Memory

The PSEN' (Program Store Enable) is for reading external code memory when it is low (0) and EA is also 0.

The ALE (Address Latch Enable) activates port 0 joined with port 2 to provide the 16-bit external address bus to access the external memory. The ALE multiplexes the P0 port: 1 for latching address on P0 as A0–A7 in the 16 bit address buss, 0 for latching P0 as data I/O.

That is why P0.x is named ADx, because P0 is multiplexed for address bus and data bus at different clock times. WR' only provides the signal to write external data memory and RD' provides the signal to read external data and code memory.

This diagram only shows the connections for external code memory.

You can see from the pin out diagram above that a microcontroller is a complete computer manufactured on a single chip, which can then be embedded within dedicated devices for a specific application.

3.1.2 System Clock and Oscillator Circuits

The 8051 requires an external oscillator circuit. The oscillator circuit usually runs around 12MHz. In other words, the crystal generates 12M pulses in one second. The pulse is used to synchronize the system operation in a controlled pace. A machine cycle is the minimum amount time a machine instruction must take. Some instructions require multiple machine cycles, such as those instructions with a memory operand which needs multiple memory accesses. An 8051 machine cycle consists of 12 crystal pulses (clock cycles). The first 6 crystal pulses (clock cycles) is used

Fig. 3.3 External Crystal
Oscillator for the 8051

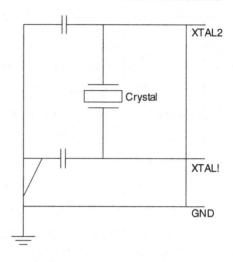

Fig. 3.3 External Crystal
Oscillator for the 8051

to fetch the opcode and the second 6 pulses are used to perform the operation on the operands in the ALU. This gives an effective machine cycle rate of 1MIPS (Million Instructions Per Second). The frequency of a crystal oscillator for the 8051 can be up to 48MHz. Figure 3.3 shows the pins of XTAL1, XTAL2, and GND for connecting the external crystal oscillator.

3.1.3   8051 Internal Architecture

After the review of the 8051's pin layout, you may know how these pins are connected to the internal components of the 8051 microcontroller. Figure 3.4 shows a basic internal architecture of 8051 and also maps the pins of four I/O ports to the internal buses (data, address, and control) that connect CPU and memory components within the chip.

You know that the CPU has many important registers. The Program Count (PC) always holds the code memory location of the next instruction.

The CPU is the heart of any computer, and is in charge of computer operations. It fetches instructions from the code memory into the Instruction Register (IR), analyzes the opcode of the instruction, updates the PC to the location of the next instruction, fetches the operand from the data memory if necessary, and finally performs the operation in the Arithmetic Logic Unit (ALU) within the CPU. The B register is a register just for multiplication and division operations, which requires more register space for the product of multiplication and the quotient and the remainder of division. The immediate result is stored in the accumulator register (Acc) for the next operation, and the Program Status Word (PSW) is updated depending on the status of the operation result, such as Carry-Out.

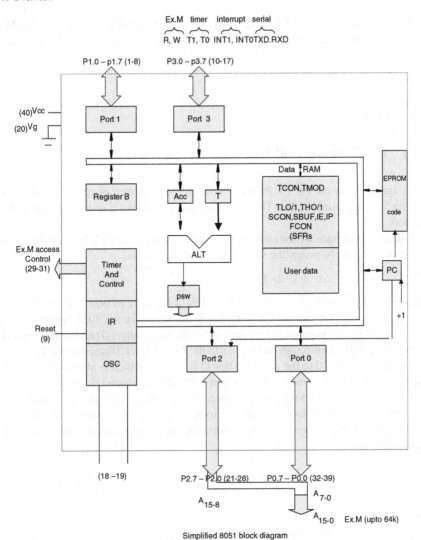

Simplified 8051 block diagram

Fig. 3.4 8051 Internal Architecture

There also are many additional CPU registers not included in the diagram, such as the address register, data buffer register, Stack Pointer (SP) register for stack operations, Data Pointer (DPTR) register for indirect memory data access, and general registers R0-R7 that are accessible to assembly language.

All the CPU and memory components are connected by the buses (address bus, data bus, and control bus). The control bus provides the operational control signals synchronized to the oscillator frequency (12 pulses per second).

You can find a group of Special Function Registers (SFR) in the data RAM. Most of them are accessible to the C51 program. We will discuss SFRs later in this chapter.

3.2 Ports

3.2.1 Port Reading and Writing

There are 4 8-bit ports: P0, P1, P2 and P3. All of them are dual-purpose ports except P1 which is only used for I/O. The following diagram shows a single bit in an 8051 I/O port.

When a C program writes a one byte value to a port or a single bit value to a bit of a port, just simply assign the value to the port as follows:

```
P1 = 0x12; or P1^2=1;
```

where P1 represents the 8 bits of port 1, and P1^2 is pin #2 of port 1 of the 8051 as defined in the reg51.h include file of C51, a C dedicated for the 8051 family. When data is written to the port pin, it first appears on the latch input (D) and is then passed to the output (Q) and through an inverter to the Field Effect Transistor (FET).

If you write logic 0 to the port pin, this Q is logic 0, which is inverted to logic 1 and turns on the FET. It makes the port pin connected to ground (logic 0).

If you write logic 1 to the port pin, then Q is 1, which is inverted to logic 0 and turns off the FET. Therefore, the pin is at logic 1 because it is connected to Vcc.

You can see that the written data is stored in the D latch after the data is written to the port pin.

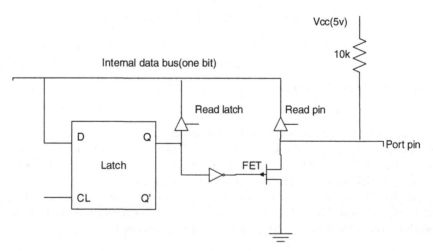

Fig. 3.5 Single Bits in I/O Port

However, you must initialize the port for reading before reading from it. If the latch was logic 0, then you will always get 0 regardless of the data in the port pin, because it is grounded through the FET gate. Therefore, in order to read the correct data from a port or a port pin, the last written logic (stored in latch D) must be $0 \times$ FF (8 bits) or 1 (single bit). E.g., you read the entire P1 port or single bit of P1 port in this way:

```
unsigned char x; bit y;
P1 = 0xFF;     //port reading initialization
x = P1;        //read port
y = P1^2;      //read bit
```

3.2.2 The Port Alternate Functions

PORT P1 (pins 1 to 8): The port P1 is a port dedicated for general purpose I/O. The other ports P0, P2 and P3 have dual roles in addition to their basic I/O function.

PORT P0 (pins 32 to 39): When external memory access is required, port P0 is multiplexed for address bus and data bus and can be used to access external memory in conjunction with port P2. P0 acts as A0–A7 in the address bus and D0–D7 for port data, as shown in Figure 3.2 and Figure 3.3. It can be used for general purpose I/O if no external memory is present.

PORT P2 (pins 21 to 28): Similar to P0, the port P2 can also play a role (A8–A15) in the address bus in conjunction with port P0 to access external memory, as seen from Figures 3.2 and 3.3.

PORT P3 (pins 10 to 17): In addition to acting as a normal I/O port, the port P3 plays some other very important roles. P3.0 can be used for the serial receive input pin ($R \times D$) and P3.1 can be used for the serial transmit output pin ($T \times D$) in a serial port, P3.2 and P3.3 can be used as external interrupt pins (INT0' and INT1'), P3.4 and P3.5 can be used for external counter input pins (T0 and T1), and P3.6 and P3.7 can be used as external data memory write and read control signal pins (WR' and RD') for memory access. These signals will be discussed again when we discuss the interrupt, timer, and serial communication.

Figure 3.6 gives a simplified port layout of an 8051 microcontroller. The input devices like the keypad, sensor, and an encoder which generates pulses are connected to the chip on the left side, while the output devices like the LED and a motor are connected on the right side.

Note that the port 1, port 2, and port 3 have internal built-in weak pull-up resistors but port 0 does not have it. If you want to attach a push button switch to port 0, then a pull-up resistor is required. Assume that the simple switch button is connected to a pin of port 1 so it does not need a pull-up resistor.

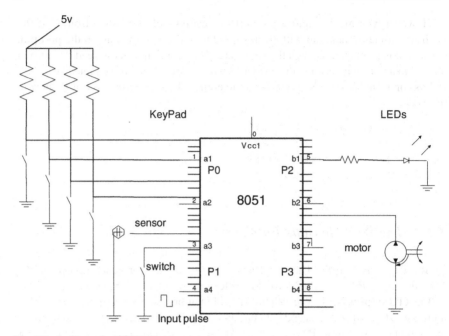

Fig. 3.6 An Example of 8051 Port Layout

3.3 Memory and SFR

3.3.1 Memory

The 8051 code (program) memory is read-only, while the data memory is read/write accessible. The program memory (stored in EPROM) can be rewritten by the special programmer circuit.

The 8051 memory is organized in a Harvard Architecture. Both the code memory space and data memory space begin at location 0×00 for internal or external memory, which is different from the Princeton Architecture where code and data share the same memory space. The advantage of the Harvard Architecture is not only doubling the memory capacity of the microcontroller with the same number of address lines, but also increasing the reliability of the microcontroller, since there are no instructions to write to the code memory which is read-only. There are separate instructions to read from external data memory and code memory. The following diagram shows the 8051 memory structure.

In this model, the data memory and code memory use separate maps by a special control line called Program Select Enable (PSEN'). This line (i.e., when PSEN' = 0) is used to indicate that the 16 address lines are being used to address the code memory. When this line is '1', the 16 address lines are being used to address the data memory. The 8051 has 256 bytes of internal addressable RAM, although only the first 128 bytes are available for general use by the programmer. The first 128 bytes

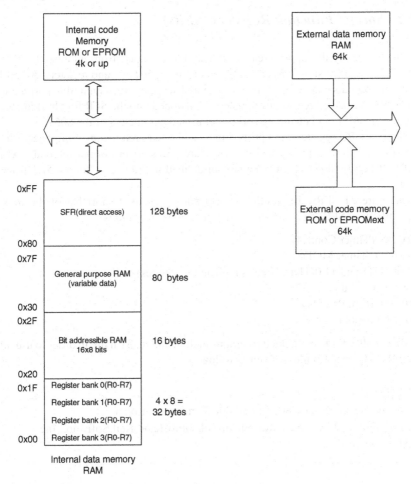

Fig. 3.7 8051 Memory Structure

of RAM (from 0×00 to $0\times7F$) are called the direct memory, and can be used to store data.

The lowest 32 bytes of RAM are reserved for 4 general register banks. The 8051 has 4 selectable banks of 8 addressable 8-bit registers, R0 to R7. This means that there are essentially 32 available general purpose registers, although only 8 (one bank) can be directly accessed at a time. The advantage of using these register banks is that it saves time on context switches for interrupted programs to store and recover their status. Otherwise push and pop stack operations are needed to save the current state and to recover it after the interrupt is over. The default bank is bank 0.

The second 128 bytes are used to store Special Function Registers (SFR) that the C51 program can configure and use to control ports, timer, interrupts, serial communication, and other tasks.

3.3.2 Special Function Registers (SFRs)

The SFRs occupy the upper area of addressable memory, from address 0×80 to $0 \times FF$. This area consists of a series of memory-mapped ports and registers. All port inputs and outputs can be performed by get and set operations on a SFR port name such as P3. Also, different status registers are mapped into the SFR for checking the status of the 8051, and changing some operational parameters of the 8051.

All 8051 CPU registers, I/O ports, timers and other architecture components are accessible in 8051 C through SFRs. They are accessed in normal internal RAM (080H–0FFH) by 8051 C, and they are all defined in the header file *reg51.h* listed below.

There are 21 SFRs. In addition to I/O ports, here is a short list of the most frequently used SFRs to control and configure 8051 operations:

- TCON (Timer Control)
- TMOD (Timer MODe)
- TH0/TH1 and TL0/TL1 (Timer's high and low bytes)
- SCON (Serial port CONtrol)
- IP (Interrupt Priority)
- IE (Interrupt Enable)

Almost all 8051 C embedded programs include the reg51.h file in order to use all the SFRs. The reg51.h file is given as follows.

```
/*------------------------------------------------------------
REG51.H
Header file for generic 80C51 and 80C31 microcontroller.
Copyright (c) 1988–2001 Keil Elektronik GmbH and Keil Software, Inc.
All rights reserved.
------------------------------------------------------------*/

/* BYTE Register */
sfr P0 = 0×80;
sfr P1 = 0×90;
sfr P2 = 0×A0;
sfr P3 = 0×B0;
sfr PSW = 0×D0;
sfr ACC = 0×E0;
sfr B = 0×F0;
sfr SP = 0×81;
sfr DPL = 0×82;
sfr DPH = 0×83;
sfr PCON = 0×87;
sfr TCON = 0×88;
sfr TMOD = 0×89;
```

```
sfr TL0 = 0×8A;
sfr TL1 = 0×8B;
sfr TH0 = 0×8C;
sfr TH1 = 0×8D;
sfr IE = 0×A8;
sfr IP = 0×B8;
sfr SCON = 0×98;
sfr SBUF = 0×99;

/* BIT Register */
/* PSW */
sbit CY = 0×D7;
sbit AC = 0×D6;
sbit F0 = 0×D5;
sbit RS1 = 0×D4;
sbit RS0 = 0×D3;
sbit OV = 0×D2;
sbit P = 0×D0;

/* TCON */
sbit TF1 = 0×8F;
sbit TR1 = 0×8E;
sbit TF0 = 0×8D;
sbit TR0 = 0×8C;
sbit IE1 = 0×8B;
sbit IT1 = 0×8A;
sbit IE0 = 0×89;
sbit IT0 = 0×88;

/* IE */
sbit EA = 0×AF;
sbit ES = 0×AC;
sbit ET1 = 0×AB;
sbit EX1 = 0×AA;
sbit ET0 = 0×A9;
sbit EX0 = 0×A8;

/* IP */
sbit PS = 0×BC;
sbit PT1 = 0×BB;
sbit PX1 = 0×BA;
sbit PT0 = 0×B9;
sbit PX0 = 0×B8;
```

```
/* P3 */
sbit RD = 0×B7;
sbit WR = 0×B6;
sbit T1 = 0×B5;
sbit T0 = 0×B4;
sbit INT1 = 0×B3;
sbit INT0 = 0×B2;
sbit TXD = 0×B1;
sbit RXD = 0×B0;

/* SCON */
sbit SM0 = 0×9F;
sbit SM1 = 0×9E;
sbit SM2 = 0×9D;
sbit REN = 0×9C;
sbit TB8 = 0×9B;
sbit RB8 = 0×9A;
sbit TI = 0×99;
sbit RI = 0×98;
```

Let us discuss the sbit register variables of these SFRs defined in reg51.h that are often used in embedded C program.

1. TCON (Timer/Counter Control Register) SFR for timer control

bit 7	bit 6	bit 5	bit 4	bit 3	bit 2	bit 1	bit 0 (88H)
TF1	TR1	TF0	TR0	IE1	IT1	IE0	IT0

TF0/TF1: Timer0/1 overflow flag is set when the timer counter overflows, reset
by program

TR0/TR1: Timer0/1 run control bit is set to start, reset to stop the timer0/1

IE0/IE1: External interrupt 9/1 edge detected flag
1 is set when a falling edge interrupt on the external port 0/1,
reset(cleared) by hardware itself for falling edge transition-activated INT; Reset by code for low level INT.

IT0/IT1: External interrupt type (1: falling edge triggered, 0 low level triggered)

2. IE (Interrupt Enable Register) SFR used for interrupt control

bit 7	bit 6	bit 5	bit 4	bit 3	bit 2	bit 1	bit 0(A8H)
EA		ET2	ES	ET1	EX1	ET0	EX0

EX0/EX1: (1/0) Enables/disables the external interrupt 0 and the external
         interrupt 1 on port P3.2 and P3.3
ET0/ET1: (1/0) Enables/disables the Timer0 and Timer11 interrupt
         via TF0/1
ES: (1/0) Enables/disables the serial port interrupt for sending and
         receiving data
EA: (1/0) Enables/disables all interrupts

3. IP (Interrupt Priority Register) SFR used for IP setting

bit 7	bit 6	bit 5	bit 4	bit 3	bit 2	bit 1	bit 0
		PT2	PS	PT1	PX1	PT0	PX0

PX0/1:   External interrupt 0/1 priority level
PT0/1/2: Timer0, Timer1, Timer2 (only for 8052) interrupt priority level
PS: Serial port interrupt priority level

4. PSW (Program Status Word) SFR for CPU status

bit 7	bit 6	bit 5	bit 4	bit 3	bit 2	bit 1	bit 0
CY	AC	F0	RS1	RS0	OV		P

P: parity check flag
OV: ALU overflow flag
RS0/RS1: Register bank specification mode
00: bank 0 (00H-07H); 01: bank1; 10: bank 2; 11: bank 3(18H-1FH)
F0: User defined lag
CY: ALU carry out
AC: ALU auxiliary carry out

5. P3 (Port 3) SFR used for I/O and other special purposes

bit 7	bit 6	bit 5	bit 4	bit 3	bit 2	bit 1	bit 0
RD	WR	T1	T0	INT1	INT0	TxD	RxD

Addition to I/O usage, P3 can also be used for:

RXD/TXD: Receive/Transmit serial data for RS232

INT0, INT1: External interrupt port inputs

T0, T1:   Alternative Timer 0/1 bit

WR/RD: Write/Read control bits used for external memory

If external RAM or EPROM is used, ports P0 and P2 are used to address the external memory.

Other port SFRs such as P0, P1, P2 are mainly used for data I/O.

6. TL0/TL1 SFRs: Lower byte of Timer 0/1, used to set the timer interrupt period.
   TH0/TH1 SFRs: Higher byte of Timer 0, used to set timer interrupt period
   Some SFRs such as TMOD and PCON don't have pre-defined sbits in reg51.h, and the bit configurations of these SFRs will be discussed in the places where they are used.

7. TMOD (Timer Mode Register) SFR (not bit addressable)

bit 7	bit 6	bit 5	bit 4	bit 3	bit 2	bit 1	bit 0
Gate	C/T	M1	M0	Gate	C/T	M1	M0

Note: bit 0-3 for Timer0 and bit 4-7 for Timer1

Gate Control.

0 = Timer enabled (normal mode)

1 = if INT0/INT1 is high, the timer is enabled to count the number of pulses in the external interrupt ports (P3.2 and P3.3)

C/T = Counter/Timer Selector

0 = count internal clock pulse (count once per machine cycle = oscillator clock/12)

1 = count external pulses on P3.4 (Timer 0) and P3.5 (Timer 1)

Working as a "Timer", the timer is incremented by one every machine cycle. A machine cycle consists of 12 oscillator periods, so the count rate is 1/12 of the oscillator frequency.

Working as a "Counter", the counter is incremented in response to a falling edge transition in the external input pins. The external input is sampled once every machine cycle. A "high" sample followed by a low sample is counted once. In addition to the "Timer" or "Counter" selection, Timer 0 and Timer 1 have four operating modes.

The Timer 0 has two FSRs called TL0 and TH0 and the Timer 1 has TL1 and TH1 respectively. TL0/1 are used to store the low byte and TH0/1 are used to store the high byte of the number being counted by the timer/counter.

In mode 0, only TH0/1 is used as an 8-bit Counter. The timer will count from the init value in the TH0/1 to 255, and then overflows back to 0.

If interrupt is enable (ET0/1 = 1) then an overflow interrupt is triggered at this time, which will set TF0/1 to 1.

If used as a timer, its rate is equal to the oscillator rate divided by (12×32).

M1	M0	Mode Control
0	0	(Mode 0) 13 bit count mode
0	1	(Mode 1) 16 bit count mode
1	0	(Mode 2) Auto reload mode
0	0	(Mode 3) Multiple mode

Note: Mode 0–2 are the same for both Timer 0 and Timer 1, but mode 3 is not.

If used as a counter, the counting rate equals to the oscillator rate divided by 32.

Mode 1 is the same as Mode 0, except that the Timer runs with both 16 bits of TH and TL registers together and it will count to 65535 and then overflow back to 0.

If used as a timer, its rate equals to the oscillator rate divided by 12.

If used as a counter, the max counting rate equals to the oscillator rate divided by 24.

Mode 2 configures the Timer register as an 8-bit Counter (TL0/1) with automatic reload from TH0/1 after overflow. Overflow from TL0/1 not only sets TF1, but also reloads TL0/1 with the preset value of TH0/1 automatically.

Mode 3 is not very popular, so we skip it.

Here is a timer/counter configuration example in C51.

```
//0X52 = 01010010₂ enable timer 0 in mode 2,
//counter 1 in mode 1

TMOD = 0X52;
```

Here we set the Timer/counter1 as a counter in mode 1 with 0101_2 and set the Timer/counter0 as a timer in mode 2 with 0010_2. The mode 1 of the counter can let the counter count the input pulses up to 65,535 and then overflows back to 0. If the T1 (P3.5) pin is connected to an encoder which produces one pulse each revolution of a motor, then we can use TH1 and TL1 to calculate total input pulses in the port pin P3.5 by TH1*256 + TL1 in a specified period of time controlled by the timer 0. In this way, we can conclude how fast the motor is running and take actions against it if necessary.

The timer 0 is set in mode 2, which is an auto reload mode. You can set TH0 and TH1 to control the timeout period for calculating the rotation rate of the motor.

After time out from timer 0, the TH1 and TL1 must be cleared to 0 to start over the pulse counting.

Here is another example to show how to produce a 25 ms timeout delay using Timer 1. 25,000 machine clock cycles take 25ms because one machine cycle = 1 μs in a 12MHz crystal oscillator 8051.

```
// Clear all T1 control bits in TMOD.
TMOD &= 0x0F;
// set T1 in mode 1 and leave T0 unchanged
TMOD |= 0X10;
```

```
ET1 = 0;          //don't need interrupt
TH = 0X9E;        //0X9E = 158
TL = 0X62;
                  //0X62 = 98, 158 x 256 + 98 = 40536
                  // 65536 - 25000 = 40536
TF1 = 0;          //reset timer 1 overflow flag
TR1 = 1;          // start timer1
// The loop will go 25ms until the timer 1
// overflow flag is set to 1
while (TF1 != 1);
   TF1 =0;        //reset TF1
```

You cannot use any bit symbol in TMOD because it is not bit addressable. You must use bit-wise operations to set TMOD.

8. PCON (Power Control Register) SFR (not bit addressable)

bit 7	bit 6	bit 5	bit 4	bit 3	bit 2	bit 1	bit 0
SMOD	–	–	–	GF1	GF2	PD	IDL

SMOD (serial mode) 1 = high baud rate, 0 = low baud rate
GF1, GF2 flags for free use
PD: 1 = power down mode for CMOS
IDL: 1 = idle mode.
Ex. PCON $|$ = 0 × 01;
// to set the IDL bit 1 to force the CPU in a power save mode
// the operator is a shorthand bit wise logical OR operator
The Acc, B, DPH, DPL, SP SFRs are only accessible by assembly languages such as

9. SCON (Serial Port Control Register) SFR

bit 7	bit 6	bit 5	bit 4	bit 3	bit 2	bit 1	bit 0
SM0	SM1	SM2	REN	TB8	RB8	TI	RI

REN: Receiver enable is set/reset by program
TB8: Stores transmitted bit 8(9th bit, the stop bit)
RB8: Stores received bit 8(9th bit, the stop bit)
TI: Transmit Interrupt is set at the end of 8th bit (mode 0)/ at the stop bit (other modes) indicating the completion of one byte transmission, reset by program
RI: Receive Interrupt is set at the end of 8th bit (mode 0)/at the stop bit (other modes) indicating the completion of one byte receiving, reset by program
RI and TI flags in the SCON SFR are used to detect interrupt events. If RI = 1, then a byte is received at the RxD pin. If TI = 1 then a byte is transmitted from the T×D pin.

SM0	SM1	Serial Mode	Baud Rate	Device
0	0	0 (Sync.) half duplex,	Oscillator/12 (fixed)	8-bit shift register
0	1	1(Async) full duplex	Set by Timer 1	8-bit UART
1	0	2(Sync) half duplex	Oscillator/64 (fixed)	9-bit UART
1	1	3(Async) full duplex	Set by Timer 1	9-bit UART

We focus on mode 0 and mode 1, because mode 2 and mode 3 are not often used.

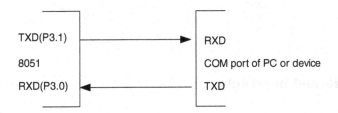

The built-in Universal Asynchronous Receiver/Transmitter (UART) integrated circuit can support serial full duplex asynchronous communication over a computer or peripheral device.

In mode 0, 8051 T×D plays the role of a synchronous clock signal and R×D is used for both receiving and transmitting data, meaning that the mode 0 is a half duplex synchronous serial working mode. The frequency of the T×D clock is 1MHz (1/12 of 12MHz) and the cycle period is $1 \mu s$.

The mode 1 works with UART without synchronous clock. In other word, it is an asynchronous full duplex serial communication mode. There are start and stop bits surrounding a byte of data during the transmission.

The baud rate of serial communication is measured in bps (bits/sec). The typical standard serial baud rates are 1200, 2400, 9600, and 19200 bps. The baud rate is determined by the overflow rate of Timer 1. By default, the baud rate = 1/32 of overflow rate of Timer 1 (if SMOD of PCON is 0).

How do we configure Timer 1 to get the desired overflow rate? Just set Timer 1 in its auto reload mode 2.

The loaded value of TH1 is determined by this formula for the 12MHz 8051:

TH1 = 256 − 1000000 / (32* (desired baud))

For example, in order to get the 19200 bps

TH1 = 256 − 1000000/32/19200 = 256 −2 = 254 = 0xFE

TH1 = 253 -> baud rate 9600 bps
TH1 = 243 -> baud rate 2400 bps
TH1 = 230 -> baud rate 1200 bps

If you set the SMOD bit of the PCON SPR, you can double the baud rate. For example, if SMOD = 1 then baud rate = 19200 bps if TH1 = 253.

The SBUF SFR is a serial buffer data register used to store the received or transmitting data in byte. The SBUF usage is shown below.

```
char c;

c = 0x41;

SBUF = c; // send 'A' to serial output line

c = SBUF; // get a char from serial line
```

3.4   SFRs and Interrupts

As we discussed before, an interrupt is an internal or external event that suspends a program and transfers control to an event handler or ISR to handle the event. After the service is over the control is given back to the suspended program to resume its execution. The microcontroller in an embedded system connects to many devices and needs to handle service requests from devices all the time. That is why so many SFRs are used to deal with interrupts.

The 8051 supports 3 types of interrupts: external interrupts, timer/counter interrupts, and serial interrupt and supports five interrupt sources: 2 external (INT0 and INT1), 2 Timers (TF0 and TF1), 1 Serial (SI).

You can classify Registers for function to as follows:

1. Enable interrupts

   IE SFR enables interrupts individually and globally

   EX0/EX1: Enable external interrupt INT0/INT1
   ET0/ET1: Enable Timer 0/Timer1 interrupt
   ES: Enable serial interrupt
   EA: Enable global interrupt

   Set the bit to 1 to enable its interrupt, such as EA = 1; or reset to 0 to masks that interrupt, such as EA = 0;

2. Interrupt Flags

   The interrupt flags are set to 1 when the interrupts occur.
   IE0/IE1 in TCON - For External Interrupts
   TF0/TF1 in TCON - For Timer Interrupts
   T1/R1 in SCON - For Serial Interrupts

The flag 1 indicates the interrupt's occurrence and the flag 0 indicates no interrupt.

3. Interrupt Priority

There are two types of interrupt priority:
User Defined Priority and Automatic Priority
User Defined Priority

The IP register is used by users to define priority levels. The high priority interrupts can preempt a low priority interrupt. There are only two levels of interrupt priorities. E.g.,

```
// The external interrupt INT0 at port P3.2 is
// assigned a high priority.

EX0 = 1;
// The external interrupt INT1 at port P3.3 is
// assigned a low priority.

EX1 = 0;
```

Automatic Priority
In each priority level, a priority is defined as follows:
INT0, TF0, INT1, TF1, SI.

```
EX0 = 1;
```

For example, if two external interrupts are set at the same priority level, then INT0 has precedence over INT1.

3.4.1 External Interrupts

An external interrupt is triggered by a low level or negative edge on INT0 and INT1, which depends on the external interrupt type setting. Set up an external interrupt type by IT0 and IT1 of the TCON SFR. E.g.,

```
IT0 = 1; // set INT0 as Negative edge triggered
IT1 = 0; // set INT1 as Level Triggered
```

The external interrupt source may be a sensor, ADC, or a switch connected to port P3.2 (INT0) or P3.3 (INT1). You use IE0/IE1 to test the external interrupt events: Ex. If IE0 = 1, then the INT0 interrupt takes place. Note that if an external interrupt is set to low level trigger, the interrupt will reoccur as long as P3.2 or P3.3 is low that makes the code difficult to manage.

You can enable external interrupts by setting EX0/EX1 of the IE SFR. E.g.,

```
EA = 1;
EX0 = 1; //enable external interrupt INT0
```

If the interrupt is level activated, then the IE0/1 flag has to be cleared by user software as follows

```
EX1 = 0;
```

You don't need to reset edge-triggered external interrupts.

The following C51 fragment makes the INT1 external interrupt ready on port P3.3 pin:

```
EA =1;
EX1 =1;
IT1 =1;
```

3.4.2 Timer/Counter Interrupts

This unit can be used as a counter to count external pulses on the P3.4 and P3.5 pins or it can be used to count the pulses produced by the crystal oscillator of the microcontroller.

Timer Interrupt is caused by Timer 0/ Timer1 overflow.
TF0/1: 1 = Condition occurred
Enabled using IE
ET0/1 = 1, EA = 1

For example,

```
TMOD = 0X12; // set timer 1 in mode 1
             // timer 0 in mode 2.
EA = 1;      // enable global interrupt
TH1 = 15;    // Make timer 1 overflow every 240 clock
TL1 = 15;    // cycles (240us). 240=256-25
ET0 = 1;     // enable timer 0
TR0 = 1;     // start timer0. Timer 0 overflows after
             // 65535 clock cycles.
ET1 = 1;     // enable timer 1
TR1 = 1;     //start timer 1
```

3.4.3 Serial Interrupts

Serial communication with Universal Asynchronous Receive Transmit (UART) protocol transmits or receives the bits of a byte one after the other in a timed sequence on a single wire. It is used to communicate with any serial port on devices and computers. The serial interrupt is caused by completion of a transmission or reception of a byte of data.

The transmit data pin (T×D) is at P3.1 and the receive data pin (R×D) is at P3.0.

All communication modes are controlled through SCON, a non bit-addressable FSR. The SCON bits are defined as SM0, SM1, SM2, REN, TB8, RB8, TI, and RI. You use timers to control the baud of asynchronous serial communication, which is set by TMOD and TCON as we discussed before.

Now, let's practice full duplex asynchronous serial communication in mode 1 to simultaneously transmit and receive data.

```
#include <reg51.h>
main()
{
  char c;

  // set timer1 in auto reload 8 bit timer mode 2
  TMOD=0x20;

  // load timer 1 to generate baud rate of 19200 bps
  TH1 = 0xFD;
  TL1 = 0XFD;

  // set serial communication in mode 1
  SCON=0x40;

  // start timer 1
  TR1 = 1;

  while(1)
  {
    // enable reception
    REN = 1;

    //wait until data is received
    while((SCON & 0X02) == 0);

      // same as while(RI==0);
      // reset receive flag
      RI=0;

    // read a byte from RXD
    c = SBUF;

    // disable reception
    REN = 0;
```

```
    // write a byte to TXD
    SBUF = c;

    // wait until data transmitted
    while(SCON & 0X01TI==0);
      //same as while(TI==0);
      // reset transmission flag
      TI=0;
    }
  }
```

3.5 Summary

This chapter explores the internal architecture of the 8051 microcontroller and its interface. The Harvard Architecture for separation of code and data memory is discussed. The detail and usage of 8051 SFRs, especially the timer control SFRs such as TMOD, TCON and serial control SFR such as SCON, the interrupt control registers such as IE are discussed. The configurations of external interrupt, timer/counter interrupt, and serial communication interrupt with C51 are demonstrated. You should have a better understanding on how to use 8051 to connect and control external devices such as sensors, switches, LEDs, LCDs, and keypads. Also, you should have learned how to design and handle the timing clock issue for embedded systems.

This chapter is a foundation for the next chapter on the embedded system software development and programming in C.

3.6 Review Questions

1. The 8051 can support up to 5 interrupts.

   a. True
   b. False

2. The 8051 memory is organized in Harvard Architecture.

   a. True
   b. False

3. 8051 SFRs are located in the internal RAM of 8051.

   a. True
   b. False

4. Not all 8051 SFRs are bit addressable.

   a. True
   b. False

5. Both code memory space and data memory space begin at address 0x00.

   a. True
   a. False

6. The 8051 machine cycle period is equal to 12 oscillator clock periods.

   a. True
   b. False

7. A machine instruction requires at least one machine cycle in the 8051.

   a. True
   b. False

8. The port 0 and port 2 of 8051 can be used either for parallel or serial I/O.

   a. True
   b. False

9. The Timer/counter pins are P2.2 and P2.3.

   a. True
   b. False

10. The external interrupt pins are p2.0 and p2.1 pins.

    a. True
    b. False

11. The EA pin is used to enable 8051 interrupts.

    a. True
    b. False

12. The ALE pin is used to multiplex port 2 for either data port or address bus.

    a. True
    b. False

13. Before reading from a pin of a port, the last write to that pin must be 1.

    a. True
    b. False

14. The usable data RAM for C program in 8051 is less than 128 bytes.

    a. True
    b. False

15. The MIPS of the 8051 is 12.

    a. True
    b. False

    Answers:
    1. a   2. a   3. a   4. a   5. a   6. a   7. a   8. b
    9. b   10. b   11. b   12. a   13. a   14. a   15. a

3.7 Exercises

1. Configure timer 0 interrupt rate period to 50ms.
2. Configure the serial port baud rate to 19200 bps.
3. Configure the INT0 to low level interrupt.
4. Configure the INT1 to falling edge interrupt.
5. Set the INT0 at high priority and INT1 at low priority
6. What is the maximum external RAM space of the 8051?
7. What is the maximum program RAM space of the 8051?
8. Which two pins must be activated in order to access external ROM?
9. Which interrupt is used to count the incoming pulses?
10. What SFRs are used for serial communication?
11. How many SFRs are not bit addressable?
12. How do you make the CPU be idle?

References

1. 8051 Tutorial, www.8052.com
2. 8051 datasheet, http://www.pjrc.com/tech/8051/datasheets.html

Chapter 4
Embedded C Programming with 8051

Objectives

- Explore C51 extension to ANSI 8051
- Discuss the C51 Interrupt Service Routine(ISR)
- C51 programming fundamentals

4.1 Overview

This chapter introduces 8051 C programming. The 8051 C is designed for programming the 8051 microcontroller. It is both an extension and subset of ANSI C. It is assumed that the readers of this book have basic C programming knowledge. The ANSI C syntax is given in Appendix A for your reference. The difference in programming with 8051 C compared to ANSI C programming are all about the microcontroller architecture such as I/O ports, memory, CPU registers, timers and interrupts. Everybody knows C is the closest to assembly language and is a better choice for large and complex system software, device drivers, or embedded software. However, it is still platform independent so that ANSI C may not be the best choice for the time critical or resource critical software project. It is difficult to write projects in machine dependent assembly language because the programmer must know all the hardware details, and it is difficult to do debugging, testing, and maintenance. The 8051 C is between the C standard language and "51" family assembly language. It will be much easier for a C programmer to switch to 8051 C because he/she only needs to learn the extensions to the language and to deal with missing parts of the standard library. Assembly instructions can be embedded into 8051 C programs if it is necessary. Most microcontrollers have a dedicated C compiler available just like the 8051 C for "8051" family microcontrollers. This chapter will discuss the C extension related hardware so that you will have a better understanding of the foundation of the 8051 microcontroller before you do coding in 8051 C.

K. Qian et al., *Embedded Software Development with C*,
DOI 10.1007/978-1-4419-0606-9_4, © Springer Science+Business Media, LLC 2009

4.2   Memory in 8051 C Programming

4.2.1   8051 Memory Types

The biggest difference of 8051 C from standard ANSI C is its ability to access the architectural components of the 8051 microcontroller such as I/O, interrupts, CPU registers and memory. Most embedded system software has very limited data and program size. The 8051 separates the data segments from the code segments in memory. The register related data, interrupt service data, stack data and any frequently accessed data are kept in on-chip internal memory but the code and large data structures such as arrays and lookup tables are kept in EPROM or extended RAM off-chip memory. Because of the memory constraint in the 8051 microcontroller, 8051 C allows C programmers to decide which memory segment to assign the data items to. In order to make best use of 8051 memory in the embedded system, you need to know the memory configuration very well. The capacity of on-chip memory is very limited (256 bytes). The on-chip memory is faster but more expensive while the extended RAM can be up to 64K byte which is slower but cheaper. First, let's explore the 8051 memory organization and its types.

There are five typical memory types used for data memory in 8051 C: data, idata, bdata, xdata and pdata. There is one typical code memory type for code, but you can also assign large, constant data items in the code type segment (64kB).

Figure 4.1 shows the 8051 memory architecture.

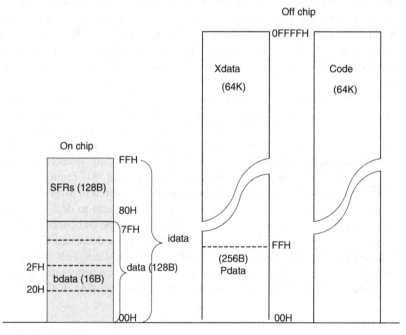

Fig. 4.1 The 8051 Memory Space

The **data** type memory is a 128 byte on-chip memory segment with an address starting at 000H(0) and ending at 07FH(127). This directly accessible internal memory segment is mostly used to store frequently used variables in the program such as parameter variables, temp variables, function variables and especially interrupt service variables which must be quickly accessible otherwise program performance will be affected.

From 080H(128) to 0FFH(255) in RAM is the Special Function Register (SFR) memory segment which are used to control timer/counter, Acc, interrupts, and I/O ports. You will see the detailed discussion of SFRs in next the section.

Within the **data** segment there is a 16-byte special segment called **bdata** with an address from 020H to 02FH which is bit addressable. Each individual bit in this segment has its unique bit address for fast access and manipulation. E.g.,

```
unsigned char bdata aByte;
// The aByte is stored in bdata segment.
aByte ^1 = 0;              // The bit 0 is reset
aByte ^1 = 1;              // The bit 1 is set
```

The **idata** segment (128 byte) is the second memory segment at 080H-0FFH available in the extended on-chip RAM for the 8052. It is indirect accessible. In other words, it must be accessed with the indirect address mode (address is held in a register).

The **xdata** segment (64KB) from 00000H-0FFFFH (65,535) is available on off-chip RAM which augments the internal memory. E.g.,

```
int xdata x,y;
// x and y are stored in off-chip external RAM.
```

The paged **pdata** segment is within the first 256 bytes of the **xdata** which accommodate up to 256 bytes for data variables although it is not as efficient as internal memory access.

The code segment (64kB) available on off-chip external EPROM is used for program storage. It can also be used to store constant data such as lookup tables and other large but less frequently changed data. E.g.,

```
unsigned char code myStr = "This is a long constant
data";
```

This constant data is stored in the code memory.

4.2.2 Memory Models

With memory models you can simply determine the default memory type used for function parameters and variables declared with no explicit memory type. You may also override the default memory type by explicitly declaring variables with specified memory types.

The three memory models are listed below:

SMALL

In the small memory model all variables default to the internal data memory of the 8051.

This is the same as if they were declared explicitly by the **data** memory type. The small mode data access is the fastest because the direct memory access is used on the on-chip RAM, but is limited to 128 bytes (256 bytes for 8052). You always try to use small memory in your application unless it can not work out before trying other two memory models. C 8051 programmers with a single 8051 chip can only use the SMALL memory model unless external memory is utilized.

COMPACT

In the compact memory model all variables default to one page (256 bytes off-chip) of external data memory. This is the same as if they were explicitly declared as the **pdata** memory type. The programmer can still access internal data memory. The compact mode data access is slower than the small mode access because byte registers R0 and R1 (@R0, @R1 in assembly) are used to indirectly address the data which can only reach $2^8 = 256$ bytes.

LARGE

In the large model all variables default to external off-chip **xdata** memory (up to 64k bytes). The data in this model as if were explicitly declared as the **xdata** memory type (64k). The memory access is slower than the small and compact models because it uses 2 bytes data pointer (DPTR) to address the external memory.

You can use the **#pragma** directive in your C program to specify the memory model. The default memory model is SMALL.

In the following example, the compiler is directed to use the LARGE memory model but each individual data variable can override the LARGE memory model (default to xdata type) by explicit specification with data type or bdata type.

```
#pragma LARGE

// override data1 to data type
unsigned int data data1;

int data2;              // default xdata type
bit bdata bit1;         // override bit1 to bdata type
```

4.3   Data Types of 8051 C

The standard data types of ANSI C are listed below:

- char (sign char, unsigned char)
- int (signed short, signed int, unsigned int, signed long, unsigned long)

- enum
- struct
- float (not available in the Keil evaluation kit)

The data structure types such as enum, struct, array and the pointer types of all basic data types (except bit type) are also supported in 8051 C.

You already know the 8051 memory constraints, especially for the internal data memory. It's crucial for you to think of data types when you declare a variable. For example, you always declare variable with unsigned short int type if the data range is between 0 and 65,525. If you use long type instead it will take 4 bytes memory space instead of 2 bytes unless the variable need to hold a bigger number.

In addition to above types the 8051 C accommodates 4 more types:

Type	Usage	Bits	Range
bit	Holds a binary value(0/1)	1	0/1
sbit	bit addressable bit in SFR	1	0/1
sfr	8-bit SFR in RAM	8	0–255
sfr16	16-bits SFR in RAM such as DPTR	16	0–65,535

The bit type may not be used for pointer type which is different from other types in standard C. The sfr type is a special type in 8051 C representing an 8-bit special register in memory.

The sbit type is an 8051 special single bit type pointing to a bit in a specific special function register.

For example, you declare a sbit variable as follows:

bit x;   //Normal bit variable x;
sbit myBit = P1^7;   // The myBit represents the MSB(bit 7) of the port #1.

A sbit variable must point to a specific bit in an SFR in its declaration. You cannot simply initialize a binary value in its declaration. After the sbit variable points a bit in an SFR, you can set or get the value of that bit in the SFR.

For example, use a sbit variable as follows:

myBit=1;   // set the MSB of port#1 to 1
myBit=~myBit;   // reverse the MSB of port#1
x=mybit; // read the MSB of port#1 to 1 and assign a bit variable x ,assume
// the last writing to this bit of the port 1 was 1 which is required by 8051

But you need to remember that all sfr type variables must be declared outside of any functions because all sfrs can not be accessed indirectly. Actually the sft type plays a role of pointer pointing to the SFR area. The sfr type can not be used as a pointer type. Here is an example of sfr type variable declaration

```
//0X24 is a bit in bit addressable BDATA area.

sbit myBit = 0x24;
```

```
main()
{
while(1)
myBit = !myBit;
}
```

You notice that the variable myBit is declared outside any functions due to its sfr type.

Let us write our first embedded C program with a loop. The loop will read the value of Port 1, write it to Port 2, delay for a while, cut the value by half and display the new value again in Port 1. Repeat the loop until the value of Port 1 is 0. The initial value of Port 1 is 127.

You have seen that P0-P3 ports are used to input from or output data to I/O devices.

When you read data from a port or a bit of the port, you need to set in reading mode by writing 1's to all bits of the port or that bit before reading. The actual input data come from some input device connected to the port and the bit of the port. The input device can be a keypad, a switch, or a button.

Here is an example which reads data from one port and writes data to another port.

```
#include <reg51.h>
unsigned int temp;
void DELAY_Wait(unsigned int);

void main(void)
  {
    while (1)     //Foregoing Loop
    {
      P1 = 0XFF; // set P1 reading mode
P1 = 0X7F; //set P1 to initial value 0x7F (127 decimal)

      while(P1 > 0) //Repeat the loop until P1 = 0
      {
      DELAY_Wait(30); //delay for about 30 ms

      P2 = P1;     //read the Port 1, write it to Port 2

      temp = P2;   //copy the value into a variable

temp >>= 1; //cut temp to half by bitwise shift right

      P1 = temp; //assign the new value to Port 1

      }     //end while (P1>0)
      }
    }
```

```
void DELAY_Wait(unsigned int x)
{unsigned int i, j;
for(i =0; i <= x; i++) {
    For (j =0; j<= 120; j++);
    }
}
```

The sfr type variables P1 and P2 are defined in the *reg51.h* header file. They point to 0X90 and 0XA0 in SFR RAM, respectively. The program did explicitly set the read mode for P1 but actually the initial value 0x7F sets the 7 bits of P1 in read mode already before next reading.

The following screen shots from the Keil toolkit shows the snap shots of the first iteration of the inner loop execution in above program. Note that an embedded program must loop forever and never exit because no operating system is available to return to.

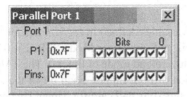
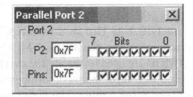

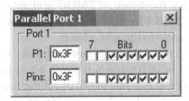

Now, let us use a simple example to check how to use other SFRs defined in *reg51.h*. You may often use Timer 0 or Timer 1 in any time constraint embedded software design.

How to configure and initialize Timers? How do the Timers work?

Assume that an embedded system requires Timer 0 Interrupt Service Routine (ISR) to be executed every 200 clock cycles to do two jobs:

Keep track of the execution count

Blink the LED connected to the pin # 7 (bit 7) of the port 1.

You have a static variable *count* which increments once when the ISR is executed as follows. The interrupt handler number for the ISR of timer 0 is 1.

```
static unsigned long count = 0;

void timer0_ISR (void) interrupt 1
{
   Count ++;
   myBit = !myBit;
}
```

The main program sets Timer 0 as an 8-bit timer with auto-reload in mode 2. The Timer 0 overflows and fires the interrupt when Timer 0 reaches 256. Timer 0 is auto reloaded with 56 in mode 2. All these timer interrupts will be discussed again in the interrupt section.

```
#include <reg51.h>
void main (void) {
// Set "0010₂" mode for Timer 0 for 8-bit timer with auto-reload
TMOD = 0x02;
TH0 = 56;               // Set TH0 to 56, generate one overflow every 200
                        // counts (256-56)
ET0 = 1;                // Enable Timer 0 Interrupts
EA = 1;                 // Enable global interrupt
TR0 = 1;                // Run Timer 0
while (1);              // infinite loop.
}
```

Here the ET0, EA, TR0 are all sbit type variables defined in *reg51.h* header file.

As discussed in last chapter the TMOD is an 8-bit Timer Mode SFR. Bit 0 and bit 1 of TMOD are used to specify the overflow reload mode of timer 0. The TMOD SFR is used to control the mode of operation of both timers. Each bit of the SFR specifies how to run a timer. The high four bits (bits 4–7) are for Timer 1 whereas the low four bits (bits 0–3) are for Timer 0. See the details of TMOD in chapter 3.

This code only uses the timer 0. The 0X02 has 4 lower bits of 0010_2 for timer 0 setting. the mode 2 (10_2) uses 8-bit timer/counter (with auto-reload).

The left most 0 in 0010_2 resets Gate bit to make the timer run regardless of the state of INT0/1. The second left most 0 bit in 0010_2 resets the C/T bit to make timer/counter 0 as a regular timer. The right most two bits in 0010_2 set the timer 0 in mode 2 so that the Timer 0 will overflow every 200 clock cycles (256-56 = 200), because the initial count is set in the higher 8 bits of TH0.

Assume the 8051 CPU runs at 12 MHz (12M clocks/second) and each timer increment takes 12 clock cycles, hence each timer increment takes 10^{-6} seconds. The rate of interrupt is $1/(200*10^{-6}) = 5$ KHz. In other words, Timer 0 overflows every 0.2 ms, and will call the Timer 0 ISR to increment the overflow count and toggle bit 7 of port 1.

4.4   Functions

4.4.1   Interrupt Functions

As we discussed above, an interrupt is a triggered event that temporarily suspends the foreground program and lets another background program called an interrupt service routine (ISR) or interrupt handler to deal with the event.

An interrupt driven system can do multiple tasks simultaneously. It allows the system to respond to an event and handle the event asynchronously. After the ISR completes its job, control returns to the foreground program.

Most embedded system software is time critical so programmers adopt the interrupt (event) driven approach instead of inefficient busy polling like the following code:

```
While(TF0 != 1) { . . . }

Or while( p7^1 == 0){ . . . }
```

Here the program continuously checks all "service request flags", waiting for the events to occur. Once it finds a request, it services the device and keeps polling. In an interrupt driven program, the main foreground program can handle other things without wasting time waiting for the event.

In an interrupt system, when the CPU is informed of an interrupt, it first completes its current instruction and saves the Program Counter (PC) and current status on the stack. The CPU then fetches the ISR address (interrupt vector) and puts it into the PC and runs the ISR until it reaches the RETI instruction. After that, the CPU pops up the old PC from the stack and resumes the interrupted program. Most embedded systems are interrupt driven since the interrupt can not be predicted in advance. Meanwhile, the CPU is free to do other things.

Figure 4.2 shows how a foreground program is interrupted by a level 1 interrupt and the CPU switches the control to its ISR0. Somehow during the execution of ISR0 another level 1 interrupt occurs which interrupts the ISR0. After ISR1 completes, ISR0 is resumed and in turn the original program is resumed.

Here is a simple interrupt application with an external interrupt #2 which is connected to p3^2 (bit 3 of pin 2 for INT0, see *reg51.h*). Once there is an interrupt caused by a edge trigger, the interrupt 0 event is fired and ISR *myISR ( )* is called.

```
#include <reg51.h>

void myISR() interrupt 0
{
  . . .
}

main()
{
EA = 1;     // enable global interrupt
EX0 = 1;    // enable external interrupt 0
IT0 = 1;    // 0 level triggered, 1 edge triggered
while(1)
{
  . . .
}
}
```

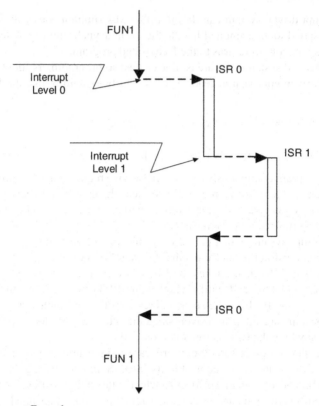

Fig. 4.2 Interrupt Example

The 8051 supports 5 Interrupt Sources:

The next table shows these 5 interrupts with their associated interrupt handler numbers. All ISR functions must specify its interrupt handler number so that the CPU can find its corresponding vector space and jump to the ISR location to execute the ISR.

Interrupt Number	Interrupt Type	Event Flag	Vector
0	Ex. INT0(P3.2)	IE0	0003H
1	Timerc0(P3.4)	IF0	000BH
2	Ex. INT 1(P3.3)	IE1	0013H
3	Timer1(P3.5)	IF1	001BH
4	Serial(P3.0, P3.1)	RI/TI	0023H

Let's review the interrupt related SFRs one more time which were discussed in last chapter.

IE (Interrupt Enable) SFR

EA(Global)   N/A   N/A   ES(SI)   ET1   EX1   ET0   EX0

Enable external interrupt: EX0/1 = 1, EA = 1
Enable timer interrupt: ET0/1 = 1, EA = 1
Enable SI serial interrupt: ES = 1, EA = 1

IF (Interrupt Flags) SFR

TCON SFR and its individual bits

TF1	TR1	TF0	TR0	IE1	IT1	IE0	IT0

External Interrupts style:

IT0/IT1: 1 -> Negative edge triggered, 0 = Level Triggered

External Interrupt flag:

IE0/IE1: 1 -> Indicating external event occurred

For timer setting:

TR0/TR1: 1 -> start timer, 0 -> stop timer

For Timer overflow flags:

TF0/TF1: 1-> timer overflow

The 8051 implements two types of interrupt priority: User Defined Priority and Automatic Priority. IP SFR is used to set the interrupt priorities.

IP (Interrupt Priorities) SFR

			PS(SI)	PT1	PX1	PT0	PX0

PX0/PX1: 1 -> higher interrupt priority for external interrupt 0/1, 0 -> lower priority
PT0/PT1: 1 -> higher interrupt priority for Timer interrupt 0/1, 0 -> lower priority
PS: : 1 -> higher interrupt priority for serial port interrupt 0/1, 0 -> lower priority

For example:

```
PX0 =1;     //external interrupt 0 high priority
```

In the same priority level, a fixed sequence order is pre-defined in a sequence of INT0, TF0, INT1, TF1, SO.

A lower priority ISR can be interrupted by a higher priority ISR, but a lower priority ISR can not interrupt a higher priority ISR. For example, if we configure the 8051 so that all interrupts are of low priority 0 except the serial interrupt at level 1. With this configuration, the serial interrupt can always interrupt the system, even if another interrupt is currently executing. However, if a serial interrupt is executing, no other interrupt can interrupt the serial interrupt routine since the serial interrupt routine has the highest priority.

Here is the complete example of a Timer 0 ISR which is connected to the interrupt number 1(INT1 – To interrupt)

```
#include <reg51.h>

unsigned int count;

void myRT0() interrupt 1
{
TF0=0;    //Timer 0 overflow flag
count++;
}

main()
{
// timer 0 in mode 2(8 bits), counts up to 256

TMOD = 0x02;

//reload value, 256-56=200, Overflows every
                // 200 CPU clocks
TH0 = 56;
TF0 = 0;
ET0 = 1;        // enable Timer 0 interrupt
EA = 1;         // enable global interrupt
TR0 = 1;        // start timer 0

While(1);       // wait for INT
}
}
```

An interrupt function has a "using" attribute to specify the register bank. The "using" attribute tells the compiler to switch register banks on entry to an interrupt routine. The 8051 has a register bank of eight general-purpose registers (R0–R7). Due to the time spent on the stack for saving the status and risk of stack damage while switching to an ISR, the 8051 provides four register banks you can use. Register bank 0 is used by default; the registers R0 to R7 are used extensively for the temporary storage of library routines and for locals. Register banks 1, 2, or 3 are best used by ISRs to avoid saving and restoring registers on the stack and to avoid the risk of stack damage because the same priority interrupts can share a register bank. Here is the syntax of ISR declaration with the "using" attribute,

```
void <ISR_name>(void)
interrupt <interrupt_handler__number>
[ using <register_bank> ]
```

The "using" attribute in an ISR definition above is optional. Small interrupt routines are not recommended to use the "using" attribute, since they use the default register bank 0. Complex and time critical interrupts which call other functions must use the "using" attribute. Here is a simple example of an ISR for Timer 0 using register bank #2.

```
unsigned int count;

void timer0 (void) interrupt 1 using 2
{
if (++count == 1000)
count = 0;

}
```

4.4.2 Reentrant Functions

The interrupt activity is needed in almost all embedded software. In embedded system software, a function may need to call itself recursively, or to be interrupted by another function which calls the same function indirectly, or to be shared by multiple processes simultaneously. The interrupted function must save its status including the Program Counter(PC) and values of all register and local variables so that the function can be resumed correctly later. The normal C51 function can not be invoked recursively because the context data is stored in a fixed memory location and the recursive calls will corrupt the stack data area. This requires such functions to be reentrant. The extension of *reentrant* function is used to force the compiler to make a separate stack area for each instance of the function so that the function will always work correctly regardless of the circumstances. The cost of the reentrant function is the consumption of the memory space.

A normal 8051 C function does not guarantee such features because it can not protect its own current status well when it switches. The reentrant function extension attribute allows you to declare functions to be reentrant. The stack for a reentrant function is simulated in internal or external memory depending on the memory model.

The first example given here is a function A() interrupted by a ISR which calls this function A() recursively so that the function A() should be declared as a reentrant function.

```
A(int x) reentrant
{
//actions;
}

Void myINT (void) interrupt 2
{
   A(10);
}

Main()
{
while(1)
{ int i;
   i = 5;
   A(i);
   . . .
}
```

The second example is a table lookup function shared by multiple processes.

```
char data[] ={'A', 'B', 'C'};
char lookup(int i) reentrant
{
char x;
x = data[i];
return (x);
}
```

This function may also be interrupted by another ISR which calls this function as well so that this lookup function is declared as a reentrant function.

The next example is another simple reentrant function which calls itself within the function.

```
void recursive(unsigned int value) reentrant
{if (value>0) recursive(--value);
}
```

If a reentrant function calls another function, the latter must also be reentrant as well.

4.4.3   Real Time Function

In chapter 2 you have seen some RTX examples in real time operating system. The C51 provides the _task_ and _priority_ keywords to the function extensions where the _task_ tells the function as a real time task function and _priority_ tells the priority level of the task if task is run in a priority-based multi-tasking scheduling environment.

For example:

Void myFuction (void) _task_ 2 _priority_ 3.

You can define up to 256 real time functions numbering from 0 to 255. You can specify up to 5 priority levels from 0 to 4.

The detail usage of real time function is given in the chapter 5.

4.5   Pointers

As you know the C provide generic pointer type which is used to define pointers.

For example, a swap function swaps two variables as follows:

```
void swap(int *x, int *y)
{ int z ;
  z = *x ;
  *x=*y ;
  *y = z ;
}


swap(&a, &b);
```

If a = 2 and b = 3 before swap function is called then a = 3 and b = 2 after you call this function. The pointers point to the location of ant type data variables in the memory except the bit and sbit types in C51. The value of the pointers is the memory address instead of the value of data.

Here the pointers x and y are generic pointers stored in internal data memory of the 8051. However you can specify a specific area the pointers are stored by a memory type specifier such as

```
int * xdata ptr1; // generic pointer ptr1 stored
                  //in xdata memory
int * data ptr2;  // generic pointer ptr2 stored
                  //in data memory
```

You can also restrict a pointer to always refer to a specific memory area by a memory type specifier as a memory-specific pointer. The memory-specific pointers are more efficient than the generic pointers in terms of access speed and memory consumption.

```
unsigned long int code *pter1;//points to unsigned long
                                //int data in code area
  unsigned char xdata *ptr2;   //points to unsigned char
                                //data in data area
    char data *ptr3; //points to char data in data area
```

4.6   Mix C and Assembly Code

You have known the trade off between C and assembly language in the embedded software development. In some cases you can take advantage of assembly code to call an assembly routine from your C program or embed assembly code inline in your C program. For example, some particular standard assembly functions are available to use, some time critical task needs to be written in assembly for fast execution, or you need to access SFRs or memory-mapped I/O devices directly using assembly code. It is not very difficult to call assembly code from C and vice-versa because the C51 provides the mechanisms to do so.

You can use pair of inline assembly directive #pragma ASM and #pragma ENDASM to include the assembly code in your C program in the following example.

```
#include <reg51.h>
void sub(unsigned char x);
void main()
{ . . .
sub(10);
  . . .}
sub(unsigned char x)
{
#pragma ASM
mov A, #x //or use R7 register to get the value of
           //parameter and put in Acc
mov @R0, A // put it in buffer
#pragma ENDASM
}
```

Next example shows how to call an assembly code from C51 program.

```
extern void a_func(unsigned int x);
void main()
{
int y;
y =_func();
}
```

Create a separate C file with the definition of a_fun() as follows:

```
#pragma SRC   //let C compiler generate a .src file
              //instead of obj file
unsigned int a_func(unsigned int x)
{ return x-1; //this may be a fake statement,
              //the purpose of it to generate a skeleton
              //for your true assembly code replacement
}
```

Then use c51 compiler command to compile this C file with option of src to generate the assembly source code in a .src file.

Modify the source code in assembly to fit your need and rename it to .a51 file and use a51 command assemble it into objective code.

Finally, link this object code with the object code from the main program to get the target code.

4.7 Modular Programming in C

It is clear that a single source file or "module" is sufficient to hold the entire C program.

Modular programming, however, is a "divide and conquer" software design and programming technique which breaks up a large program into manageable subprogram units such as functions and subroutines. Each module represents a separation of concerns which improves software maintainability and reusability by enforcing logical boundaries between modules.

As an embedded system is composed of several modules, each with a unique function, so the embedded software system is built from a number of discrete tasks and then finally assembled into a complete, working software.

A modular program consists of a main module and many auxiliary modules, such as device drivers in embedded software systems. In reality each module is a separate source file. If you need to revise or update functions in one module, you only need to work on that file containing the function. For example, most embedded systems have an initialization and configuration function called init() which is included in one of the modules. Each individual module is much shorter than the entire program, hence it is much easier to read and understand.

Modular programming also helps debugging and testing programs and reduces the likelihood of bugs. Local scopes of variables in modules and smaller size of the individual modules make it easier to understand the effects and impacts of changing a variable.

Modular programming in C is to organize a program in multiple files. There is a main module which contains the main() function. This is the entrance of the entire program and many other modules in formats of C source code files or header files.

First, you must decide how to divide your program into multiple files or modules. For example, you can make each interrupt service subroutine as a separate module, same as other interrupt handlers.

Next, after you determine all modules you need to decide how to interface with each other. In other words, you need to decide the visibilities of the variables and functions in each module. For these private data variables or helper functions, you should define them as private visibility by C static scope to make them accessible within the module file where they are defined. For most functions, data variables and data types, you need to make them public to expose to all other modules that need to access or share and reuse these resources.

4.7.1 Scope of Functions and Variables

In a multi-module C program, one module may need to call functions defined in other modules. Multiple modules may share some data, and some data may need to be transferred from one module to other modules. The scope of data and functions must be specified properly to avoid data and program corruption.

A typical 8051 application consists of many modules in multiple source files where each has a number of functions accessing variables in RAM. Each function has some temporary variables which will be used to store intermediate process values for internal use, but some functions need to access global variables shared by multiple functions. Let's check the accessibility of data and functions in the following example.

C uses the extern keyword to make an external reference to a variable or function residing in other modules.

The keyword static is used to specify the scope of variable of function to be the enclosing module.

A variable defined outside any function is treated as a global variable which is often used for main program and interrupt service routines to share or exchange data.

You can find that the variable "a" is defined outside any function in *main.c* so that it can be accessed everywhere in this module and can also be seen from any other module which makes an external reference to this variable.

The *main.c* module makes an external reference to *exfunc()* defined in module1.c so that *exfunc()* can be called within this module.

The scopes of variables "b" and "c" are within the *main()* function because they are defined inside the *main()* function.

```
main.c:

int a ;
extern int exfunc(int) ;
```

```
int func( int x)
{
return(x*x);
}

main()
{
Int b;
int c;
b = exfunc(c);
a = func(b);
}
```

MODULE1.c

```
extern int a;
int exfunc(int x)
{
int d ;
static int count ;
count++ ;
d = x * a ;
return(d) ;
}
```

The *module1.c* makes an external reference to the global variable *a* to use it in *exfunc()*. The local variable *count* is defined as a static variable so that it will remember its value after the *exfunc()* function call exits. When the *exfunc()* function is called again, the count variable will operate on its previous kept value, which is different from local variables in a function that doesn't keep their data once the function exits.

Although we can organize a multi-module C program in this way, it is not in a well structured manner. The tied and complicated connections between modules make maintenance work very difficult. When you develop a large and complex embedded system software with its own Real Time Operating System (RTOS), you should use a better approach to organize the program structure. The Object Orientation (OO) is a very popular software design and programming approach, but it may cause more memory overhead and increased time consumption. For a time and space critical embedded system, OO may not be the best approach. In the next few sections we will discuss how to use header files to better organize a C program in a multi-file structure.

4.7.2 Header Files

You already reviewed the delay.h header file in the LED *toggling* example. You can place public (global) parts of a module in a header (.h) file. This header is included by other files that use its corresponding module. The *main* model includes the *reg51.h* and *delay.h* in order to use port #1 defined in *reg51.h* and call delay function defined in *delay.h* in the *toggling* example. A header file typically contains global variable definitions, typedef of data type declarations and function prototypes. This insures that the module and all the files that use the module agree on data types, global data, and functions.

It is also common for one header to include other headers. If both header files include a common header file and a C source code file includes these two header files, it will cause a compiler error due to multiple declarations of a type or macro. The conditional compilation directive of the C preprocessor directives can be used to solve this kind problem as seen in the toggling example. The following example illustrates the solution:

```
delay.h

#ifndef _DELAY_
#define _DELAY_

/* body of header */

#endif
```

This directive checks to see if the identifier is not currently defined. If the _DELAY_ identifier has not been defined by a **#define** statement, then the code immediately following the command will be compiled. This prevents any duplicated inclusion.

Notice that for a function, the header file can only contain the prototype of a function, but never contains its complete implementation code. The header plays a decoupling role between the function implementation in its source file and the function execution in the destination file where the function is called.

4.7.3 Multi-module C Programming

We know the header file plays a role of interface between the modules with data and function definition and the modules referencing these data and functions. Here is a simple example with two modules connected by a header file.

The main program has an infinite loop calling a function *f()* which is defined in another module named module1. The *MyHeader* file provides a constant identifier PI, a type definition of "Real" and a function prototype of *f()*.

```
main.c

#include "MyHeader.h"

void main( void )
{
   int x;

   while(1){
   f(x);}

}
```

```
MyHeader.h

#ifndef _MYHEADER_H
#define _MYHEADER_H

#DEFINE PI 3.14259
typedef double Real;

void f( Real );      // external function prototypes

#endif
```

```
module1.c

#include <stdio.h>
#include <math.h>
#include "MyHeader.h"

void f( int x )
{
   int i;
   for (i=1; i<x; i++) circle(i);;
}
// internal scoped function
static void circle( Real R )
{
   Static count;                  //static variable
   count ++;
   Printf("%f %d", PI*sqr(R), count);

}
```

Because neither *main.c* nor module1.c has the _MYHEADER_H identifier defined, the header file will be included and compiled.

This program will keep printing the area of a circle associated with a count label until you stop it.

For a large embedded system it is not practical to have a single header file incorporated in each source file regardless of whether the incorporated files need them or not.

A good practical solution is to generate module-specific include header files as shown in the next diagram. Each module is paired with its corresponding header file.

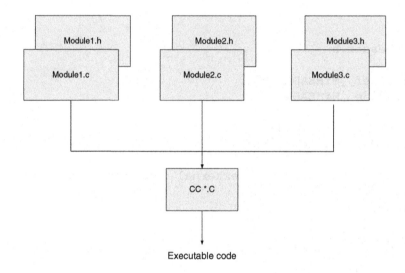

The header file consists of two parts:
Part 1: original data, type, macro definitions and function prototypes used for host modules
Part 2: external references to the items listed in part1 for referencing modules
The template for module1.c is shown below:

```
#ifdef _module_ //_module_ is a identifier used for
                //conditional compilation

// part1
#else

//part2

#endif
```

Assume there are two modules, *module1.c* and *module2.c*.
The *module1.c* is shown below.

```
#define _module1_
#include <module1.h>
#include <module2.h>
```

.

.

.

```
function1(){ . . . };       //function1 definition
```

.

.

.

```
function2();                     //call function2
```

The corresponding *module1.h* is shown below.
#ifdef _module_ //_module_ is a identifier used for

```
                         // conditional compilation

function1();                     // prototype of function2

#else

extern function1();

#endif
```

The *module2.c* is shown as below.

```
#define _module1_
#include <module1.h>
#include <module2.h>
```
.
.
.

```
Function1(){ . . .; function2(); }
// call function2 in the definition of function1
```

The header file for *module2.c* is listed below.

```
#ifdef _module2_ //_module_ is a identifier used for
                 //conditional compilation

function2(); // prototype of function2

#else

extern function2();

#endif
```

Although both header files are included in both modules, the original function prototype declarations are compiled in the host modules and external references are compiled in the referencing modules by the conditional compilation directives in the header files.

4.8   Lab: Debug and Test Embedded C Program with the Keil µVision3

This "hello world" type program toggles the MSB (Most Significant Bit – the bit 7) of Port 1 on the 8051. If an LED is connected to this port, then the LED will be toggled on and off about every 0.5 second and will be flashing at a 1Hz rate.

Step 1: Creating Projects

Create a new project named *MyFirstProj* as shown in lab of chapter 1 and save it in a directory called *embedded_8051_c* on the C drive. The new created project contains a default target, Target1, and file group name.

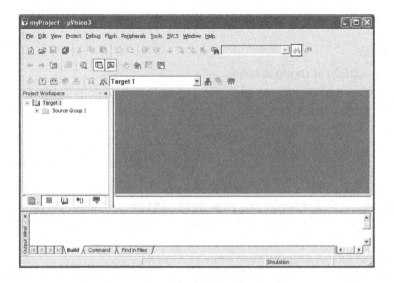

Step 2: Source Code Preparation

You can create a new source file with the menu option File –> New. This opens an empty editor window where you can enter your source code. The µVision3 enables C color syntax highlighting when you are editing.

You save your file with File – >Save As. We are saving our example file under the name MAIN.C.

Here is the code list of *main.c*:

```
#Pragma SMALL
//8051 registration configuration file
#include <reg51.h>
#include "delay.h"// to reference the delay() function
                  // defined in delay.c module
sbit x=P1^7;            //Let x represent MSB of port
#1(bit 7)
main()
{
while(1)               //Forever loop
{
x=!x;                  // Tog MSB of Port 1
delay(500);}           // Delay about 500 ms
}
```

Save this file in the same directory where the project is. Once you have created your source file, you can add this file to your project. The µVision3 offers several ways to add source files to a project. For example, you can select the file group in the Project Window –> Files and right click to open a local menu. The option Add Files opens the standard files dialog.

Select the file main.c you have just created.

You can also simply right click on Source Group 1 of Target 1 in the Project Window to add the main.c to the source group of the project.

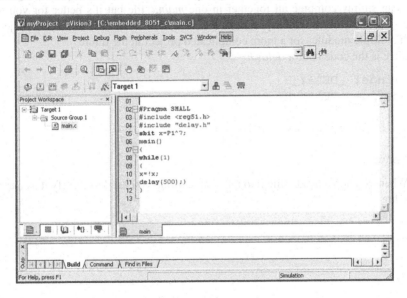

Follow the same steps to create and save the *delay.c* file.

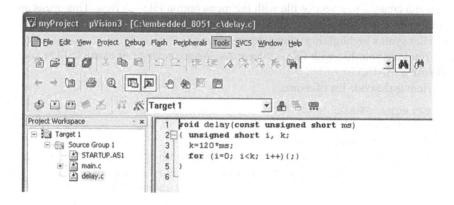

Here is the C source code of *delay.c*

```
void delay(const unsigned short ms)
{ unsigned int i, k;
  k=100*ms;
  for (i=0; i<k; i++){;}
}
```

There is no precise formula available to calculate the exact number of above loops to generate one ms delay. We need to try and adjust the parameters to make it close to what is expected. We know the simulator runs at 1 MIPS (one machine instruction takes 10^{-6} seconds). We estimate that each loop takes about 10 machine codes which results in about 1000 instructions in each loop $(100*10 = 1000)$. If we call delay(1) then it will generate about 1 ms delay.

The last file is the header file *delay.h* which contains the conditional include directive in order to avoid duplicate definitions. Actually, for this simple C program, you can simply combine all together in one *main.c* file but it's better for you to know how to write modular programs and how to use the Keil to build a project with multiple modules for a more complicated project in the future.

Here is the code list for *delay.h*

```
#ifndef _DELAY_H
#define _DELAY_H

void delay(const unsigned ms);

#endif
```

When you add a header file into the source group you need to specify it as a text type file.

After you add all three files to the resource group of the project by right clicking the source group and selecting the files to add the project window lists all the added files in the source group.

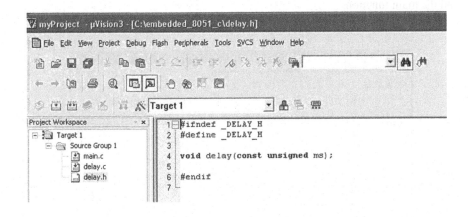

Step 3: Building Projects

Go to Project -> Build Target to build the application. If there are any syntax errors, The Keil μVision3 will display errors and warning messages in the Output Window. A double click on a message line opens the source file at the correct location in the μVision3 editor window.

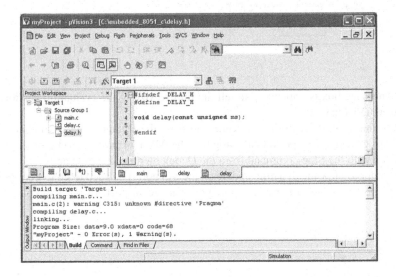

Step 4: Debugging and testing the project

Once the program is compiled and linked, you can test it with the Keil μVision3 debugger. In μVision3, use the Start/Stop Debug Session command from the Debug menu or toolbar. The μVision3 initializes the debugger and starts program execution till the main function.

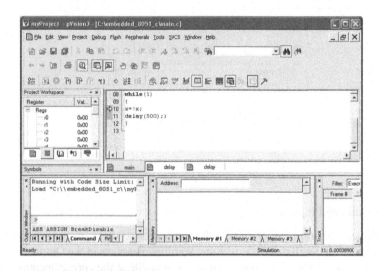

A message box is popped up to tell the limited size of the evaluation version of the Keil μVision3.

Run the program with the Go command from the Debug menu or toolbar. The program executes and periodically toggles the MSB of port 1. You can stop the program with the Stop command from the Debug menu or the toolbar.

In order to view the dynamic update on the I/O port, you need to go to Peripheral -> I/O port to select a particular port you want to inspect. In our example, it is port 1.

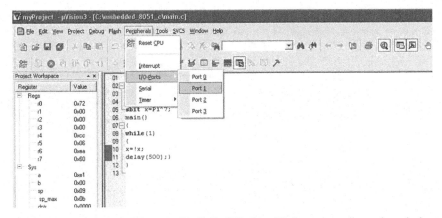

You also need to go View -> Periodic Window Update, to activate the window update so that you see the dynamic changes of the data in the port.

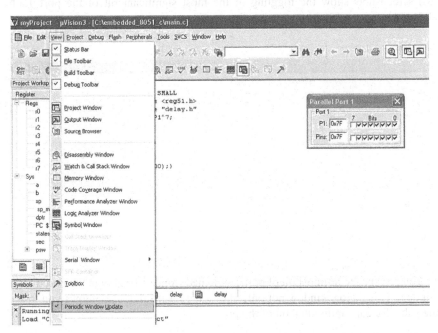

Now it's ready to go. Select Debug -> Go to run the application. In order to see the toggling of the P1^7 you can run the program in the step by step mode using the "step over" option in the debug menu or click the "step over" icon on the tool menu bar as shown in the next screen.

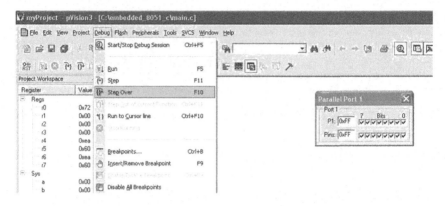

The yellow arrow is always moving forward one statement at a time. The next two screenshots show the toggling of the most significant bit of the port 1 on 8051 chip.

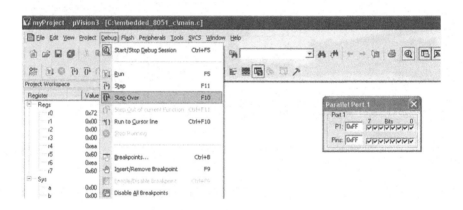

You can see the leftmost bit of port 1 switched from 1 to 0 now in the port dialog window. This dialog window not only shows the results, but also allows you to set the value for each individual bit of the port.

4.9 Practice Examples

In the last section you learned how to use the Keil μ Vision3 cross-compiler development toolkit to develop a simple embedded C application. In this section, you will use this toolkit to practice some examples.

Example 1: Development of an application that move data from one port to another port with the Keil

This practice demonstrates how embedded software reads data from the port 2 and transforms this data to the port 1.

```c
#include <reg51.h>
void main (void)
{
unsigned char temp;      // temp variable for port values

P2 = 0xFF;               // Setup P2 for Input

while (1)
  {
  temp = P2;             // Read P2 into temp
  temp <<= 1;
  P1 = temp;             // Write temp to P1
  }
}
```

After the first iteration of the loop you will see the value in P1 is 1-bit shifted left of the value of the port 2 as follows.

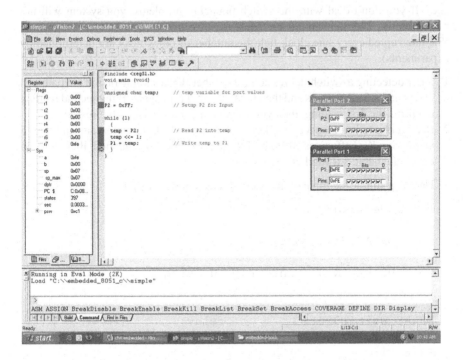

You can use the Toolbox buttons in the debugger to change the value of P2 and monitor the changed data in P1 from the Port 1 and Port 2 dialogs in the Peripherals Menu.

Example 2: Development of an external interrupt application

The sbits INT0 (P3.2) and INT1 (P3.3) are used to produce external interrupts in flag IE0 and IE1 of SFR TCON. INT0 and INT1 are sampled once each machine cycle and polled in the next machine cycle. To ensure proper sampling, an input on INT0/1 must hold for at least one machine instruction cycle (12 clock cycles).

$(IT0/1 = 0)$ is configured for low-level interrupt trigger and $(IT0/1 = 1)$ is configured for negative edge interrupt trigger when high on INT0/1 in one machine cycle followed by a low in the next machine cycle.

If the external interrupt is low-level triggered $(IT0/1 = 0)$, the external source must hold the request active until the requested interrupt is actually generated. Then it must deactivate the request before the ISR is completed or another interrupt will be generated.

Many embedded system requires mechanical switch-reading operations such as turn on or turn off a light switch, press and release a button on a keypad. When you turn on or turn off a switch, there will be a bounce (repeating on and off for a short period of time) instead of an ideal state of on/off (high voltage/low voltage). If you don't deal with the switch bouncing problems, you system will not run correctly. There are many strategies to solve this problem. You can have an ISR interrupted every one clock tick(the number of clock ticks are determined by experiments).

1. After detecting a switch depression (remember the key value on the keypad, ex.) and wait for 5 clock ticks and then read the input port again. If the second reading confirms the first reading, then you can assume the key is really pressed.
2. Read and confirm 5 successive key presses at 1 clock tick intervals, and then 5 successive Key off states. If both of these conditions are satisfied, then you can conclude that it is a valid key press.

Here is a simple example of an external interrupt with INT0.

```
#include <reg51.h>

void DELAY_Wait(unsigned int);

void P3_EX_INT0() interrupt 0 using 2

{
DELAY_Wait(1000);        // delay
P1 <<= 1;
P2 = P1;
}
```

```
main()

{

P1= OXFF;   // set P1 in read port mode
P2 = 0X00;
EX0 = 1;    // enable INT0 on P3.2
IT0 = 0;    // (edge triggered(1), level triggered(0)
EA = 1;     // global interrupt enable

while(1);

}

void DELAY_Wait(unsigned int x)
{unsigned int i, j;
for(i =0; i <= x; i++) {

    for (j =0; j<= 120; j++);
    }
}
```

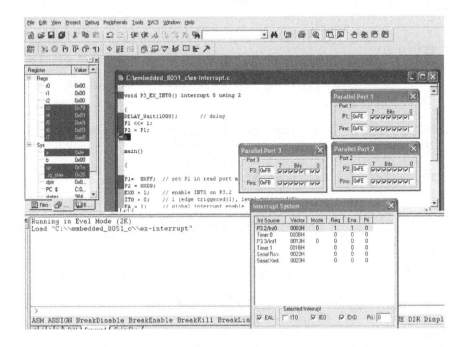

Example 3: Development of a Timer Driven Application (16 bit timer program reload)

Assume that you need to produce an interrupt every 20 ms with Timer 0 to control some device or take certain actions. How to configure Timer 0?

The Timer 0 has two 8-bit SFRS: TH0 and TL0. Once the timer starts running it continually increment it count at the rate of 1M increment per second (assume you are using 12 MHZ 8051 with crystal oscillator at 12 cycles per instruction (i.e., 1 MIPS).

The combined 16 bits of TH0, TL0 can hold up to 65535 counts and it will fire an overflow once it reaches $65536 \left(2^{16}\right)$ counts. How many timer increment counts are there within 20.

The number of timer increments $= (20ms/1000ms)^{*} 10^{6} = 20000$

So the initial value for Timer setting should be 65536-20000 = 45536. Split this number into two bytes as follows:

$$TH0 = 45,536/256 = 177 = 01011001b = 0 \times 59$$
$$TL0 = 45,536\%256 = 224 = 01110000b = 0 \times 70$$

Here is the main program and timer 0 ISR.

```
#include <reg51.h>
static int count;         // the number of timer 0

void myINT(void) interrupt 1
{

TF0 = 0;
TR0 = 0;              //stop Timer 0
                      // This ISR is called every 20 ms
count++;

TH0 = 0X59;          // must reload timer 0 in mode 1
TL0 = 0X70;

TR0 = 1;             // restart Timer 0
}

                              // interrupts(overflows)
Main()
{
TMOD = 0x01;          //set timer 0 in mode1 (16 bits mode)

ET0=0;                        // disable Timer 0 interrupt
```

```
TH0 = 0X59;                  // initialize timer 0
TL0 = 0X70;

TF0 = 0;                     // clear Timer0 Overflow flag
ET0 = 1;                     // Enable timer 0 interrupt
TR0 = 1;                     // start Timer 0
EA = 1;                      // Enable global interrupt
while(1);                    // infinite loop


}
```

After you build the project for this program, do the following:

Click the Start Debug from the Debug menu
Right click on the line "count++; " to set up a breakpoint to watch the variable *count*. A timer dialog will open from the peripheral menu and be placed on the right side to monitor the changes.
Next, you select the Watch & Call Stack Window item from the View menu to open Watch window
Right click on the variable *count* to select Add "count" to Watch Window.
Pick #1 Window

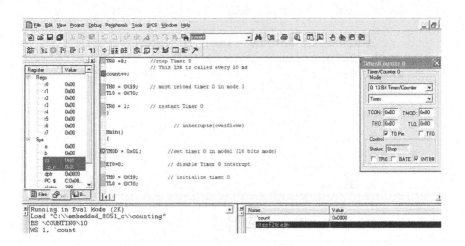

Monitor the change of variable count after you run the debugger again. The variable counter is incremented by 1 after the timer 0 interrupts and the ISR is called again.

Example 4: "Hello world" with serial port

```
#include <REG51.H>
#include <stdio.h>

main () {

    SCON = 0x50; //serial mode 1, 8-bit UART,

        // baud rate set by timer 1, enable rcvr
    TMOD |= 0x20; //timer 1 in mode 2, 8-bit auto-reload
        TH1 = 2;    //reload value for timer 1 1200 baud
        TR1 = 1;    //run timer 1
        TI = 1;     //set for interrupt,
                    //send first char of UART

    while (1) {

    P1 ^= 0xFF;    //toggle P1 just for testing

    printf ("Hello world!\n");
                //display "Hello World!" on monitor
    }
}
```

After building the project for this simple serial port application program, do the following:

Start the debugger from Debug menu
Select the Periodic Window Updates from the View menu
Open the Port 1 and serial Port from Peripheral menu
Select Run from the Debug menu
Open the Serial Window #1 from the View menu

You will see the output as follows.

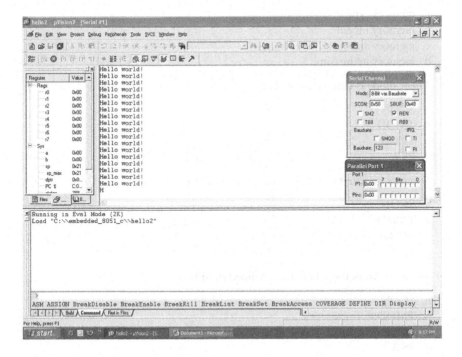

4.10   Summary

This chapter has introduced the basic concepts of embedded software programming in 8051 C. It has covered the 8051 C extensions of the data types, I/O port access and the five interrupts (timer, external, and serial). Interrupt functions and reentrant functions were also discussed.

You noticed that an embedded program always has a loop that executes forever. It never exits because there is no underlying operating system to return to.

This chapter also discussed the multi-module structure for large and complex embedded system software. A step-by-step guide to the Keil μ Vision3 toolkit was introduced and the practice examples were demonstrated and tested.

4.11   Review Questions

1. Large memory model defaults to

   a. xdata
   b. idata
   c. pdata
   d. code

2. #PRAGMA directive is used to define memory in

   a. memory type
   b. memory model
   c. memory size
   d. memory addressing

3. Timer mode is defined in SFR of

   a. SCON
   b. TMOD
   c. TCON
   d. PSW

4. External interrupt type IT0/1 are defined in SFR of

   a. SCON
   b. TMOD
   c. TCON
   d. PSW

5. Timer interrupt flags TF0/1 are defined in SFR of

   a. SCON
   b. TMOD
   c. TCON
   d. PSW

6. TR0/1 are used to

   a. start/stop timers
   b. enable, disenable timers
   c. for timer mode configuration
   d. None

7. TH0, TL0 are used for

   a. either auto-reload or program-reload of timer 0
   b. only for auto-reload
   c. only for program-reload
   d. both of them are 16 bits

8. External interrupts are defined in

   a. P3.2
   b. P3.3
   c. P1
   d. P2

9. Level 1 priority interrupt ISR can interrupts a level 0 priority interrupt ISR

   a. true
   b. false

10. A reentrant function can not call a non-reentrant function.

    a. true
    b. false

11. An embedded program always has a loop and executes forever because there is no underlying operating system to return to.

    a. true
    b. false

12. The statement sbit myBit = 0; is a legal statement in 8051 C

    a. true
    b. false

Keys to the review questions:
1. a 2. b 3.b 4. c 5. c 6. a 7. a 8. a,b 9. a 10. a 11. a 12. b

4.12 Programming Exercises

1. Develop the following programs with the Keil μ Vision3 toolkit and test them.
2. Write a reentrant Factorial function and a main program to calculate the factorial value of a given positive integer number.
3. Write a table lookup reentrant function which is executed by multiple programs at same time.
4. Write an External interrupt ISR for INT0 which is triggered by an edge signal.
5. Write a Timer 1 ISR on mode 1 which can produce a 1 second time delay in a 12 MHZ CPU microcontroller.
6. Write a program to move a byte data in direct RAM (below 128b) to the port 1.
7. Write a program to toggle the pin 1.2 every 50 ms.
8. Write a "Hello world!" program to display the greeting every 1 second.
9. Write a program to count the Timer 0 (default set) overflows in 1 second.

References

1. C and the 8051, 4th edition, Thomas W Schultz, Wood Island Prints, 2008
2. Embedded C, Michael J Pont, Addison-Wesley Professional, 2002
3. 8051 Demo Kit, Getting Started with the 8051 Microcontroller development Tools, http://www.adatronik.com.pl/files/IDE/keil/dm51.pdf

Chapter 5
Real-Time Operating Systems

Objectives

- Multitasking scheduling
- Inter-task communication
- RTX51-Tiny RTOS programming
- Benefits of using RTOS

5.1 Overview

A Real-Time Operating System (RTOS) is a piece of software that sits between the hardware and user-generated code. In other words, the RTOS provides an abstraction layer that hides the details of the processor from the application software. Figure 5.1 shows how the layers relate to each other. Since it is smaller than a full-blown OS, we often call this a kernel or an executive process. In this chapter, we will focus on the RTX51, a commercial RTOS developed by Keil designed specifically for the 8051 family of microcontrollers.

Let's start from the top with the application software. In the real-time system, this layer is split up into tasks, which are generic computational blocks with timing restraints, and synchronization and communication relationships with each other. This should be described in the design process. Generally, each device is represented by its own task.

As discussed before, a task's timing restraint tells us the Worst-Case Execution Time (WCET), or the deadline for execution. Additionally, most tasks require data or signals to be passed to other tasks, they cannot run in isolation. They are aware of the existence of other tasks, but cannot directly affect them. This is the role of the RTOS layer.

There is only one task running at any time, since only one processor is available. The RTOS is responsible for scheduling when tasks get to run by performing context switches and transitioning tasks between one of four states:

- READY: The task is ready to run and is waiting for control of CPU
- RUNNING (ACTIVE): The task is currently being executed

K. Qian et al., *Embedded Software Development with C*,
DOI 10.1007/978-1-4419-0606-9_5, © Springer Science+Business Media, LLC 2009

Fig. 5.1 The RTOS sits on
top of hardware, acting as an
abstraction layer

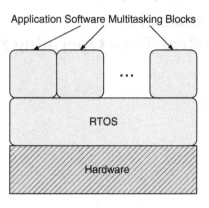

Application Software Multitasking Blocks

- BLOCKED (WAITING): The task is waiting for an event to occur or a resource to become available
- SLEEPING: The task is not ready to run. This happens when the task is not yet created, or after a task has terminated or been deleted

All declared tasks start in the SLEEPING state. In the RTX51 RTOS introduced later, the main() function is generally responsible for making task number 0 ready and starting the RTOS. A simplified version, RTX51-Tiny, automatically readies task 0 and jumps into the RTOS, bypassing the main() function. Possible transitions between states are detailed in Figure 5.2. State changes are performed by the RTOS based on the task scheduler or system calls.

1. Tasks can move from SLEEPING to READY generally through an RTOS system function called from a different task.
2. Tasks that are READY can be selected for execution by the RTOS, moving it into the RUNNING state. This depends on the RTOS and the scheduling algorithm. For example, RTX51 always runs the task with the highest priority that has been waiting the longest time. There can only be one running task at a time, and the previous running task is moved to the READY or BLOCKED state.
3. A task in the RUNNING state can be moved to the READY state if it runs out its time slice, or if a higher priority tasks is ready to run.
4. Tasks waiting for an event (timeout, signal, semaphore, etc.) can be moved from BLOCKED to READY once that event occurs.
5. A task in the RUNNING state can be BLOCKED if it is told to wait for an event to occur. If the event is immediately satisfied, then the task will continue execution and never enter the BLOCKED state.
6. A task waiting for an event can move directly to the RUNNING state if that event occurs and it has higher priority than the currently running task.
7. Tasks are moved from the RUNNING state to SLEEPING state once it has completely finished execution.

Fig. 5.2 The four task states
and possible paths to move
between them

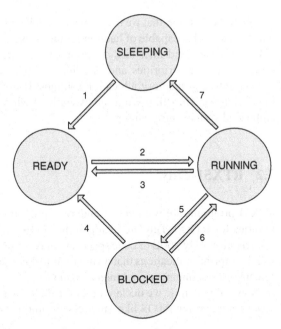

One of the simplest ways a scheduler can handle multiple tasks is through pre-defined time switching. Most RTOS require at least one hardware timer, such as Timer 0 on the 8051. This type of scheduler would do task switching only at timer interrupts or ticks. For example, a timer might be set such that every 10ms the RTOS will go and update a set of tables that keep track of task information such as task state, interval count, and timeout count, and subsequently decide on which task to run. However, long tick intervals could lead to missed task deadlines.

Additionally, the scheduler can look for interrupts from other sources, or it can be called from system functions. In this way, the RTOS is no longer limited to task switching only at the tick interval.

But why not just reduce the tick interval so it can meet all the deadlines? Switching out of the running task to the RTOS is not cheap, at minimum we must push the return address onto the program stack, and neither is updating the task tables. Reducing tick interval would lead to immense processor overhead and hurt efficiency.

Using an RTOS makes writing multitasking embedded systems easier by standardizing task definition, context switching and other commonly used functions. It is responsible for:

- scheduling task runtime
- providing software timer
- resource sharing
- intertask communication
- dynamic memory allocation

The RTX51 RTOS that we use comes in a Full and royalty-free Tiny version. This real-time kernel is capable of handling round-robin and pre-emptive task switching, interrupt events, and inter-task communication. The Tiny version supports everything except task priorities and pre-emptive task switching, messaging routines, semaphores, and memory allocation routines. RTX51-Full has since been discontinued, but we will still use it as an example of what such an RTOS provides to the embedded systems programmer.

5.2 RTX51-Tiny

RTX51 programs are written in standard C programming language. The necessary libraries for RTX51-Tiny are available in the PK51 Professional Developer's Kit. Tiny requires only 900B of code space and makes use of Timer 0. It was designed for small footprint applications that do not require advanced features such as messaging, semaphore, and memory pool management.

Now let's see how we declare tasks for RTX51. You will see how taking advantage of a prewritten RTOS like TinyOS can simplify system and software design.

```
#include <rtx51tny.h>
int counter1;
void task0 (void) _task_ 0 {// RTX51 begins task 0
    counter1 = 0;              // initialize counter
    os_create_task (1);        // make task 1 ready
    os_delete_task (0);        // stop task 0 (init is
                               // completed).
}
void task1 (void) _task_ 1 {
    while (1) {                 // infinite loop
        counter1++;            // increment counter 1
    }
}
```

Declaring a task is similar to declaring a C function, with the addition of the '_task_' attribute. Each task must be assigned a number, from 0–255 under RTX51 Full or 0–15 under Tiny. Tasks cannot take or return any parameters except void. In this case, the task name is 'task0'. Whenever we start an RTX51-Tiny program, it will automatically start task in 0. Thus at first, task 0 is in the RUNNING (ACTIVE) state, while all other tasks are in the SLEEPING state. To start other tasks, we have to use the system function 'os_create_task' to mark them READY. Alternatively, we use the 'os_delete_task' function to mark tasks as SLEEPING. The uVision debugger refers to sleeping tasks as DELETED. Check Table 5.1 below for a list of often used RTX51 functions.

Table 5.1 List of RTX51 most used system functions.

Function	Description
isr_send_signal	Send a signal to a task (call from interrupt)
os_attach_interrupt*	Assign task to interrupt source
os_clear_signal	Delete a previously sent signal
os_create_task	Move a task to execution queue
os_create_pool*	Define a memory pool
os_delete_task	Remove a task from execution queue
os_detach_interrupt*	Remove interrupt assignment
os_disable_isr*	Disable 8051 hardware interrupts
os_enable_isr*	Enable 8051 hardware interrupts
os_free_block*	Return a block to a memory pool
os_get_block*	Get a block from a memory pool
os_send_message*	Send a message (call from task)
os_send_signal	Send a signal to a task (call from task)
os_send_token*	Set a semaphore
os_set_slice*	Set the RTX51 system clock slice
os_wait	Wait for an event
oi_reset_int_mask*	Disables interrupt sources external to RTX51
oi_set_int_mask*	Enables interrupt sources external to RTX51
os_check_mailbox*	Returns information about the state of a specific mailbox
os_check_mailboxes*	Returns information about the state of all mailboxes in the system.
os_check_semaphore*	Returns information about the state of a specific semaphore
os_check_semaphores*	Returns information about the state of all semaphores in the system

* These functions are not available for the TinyOS kernel

Fig. 5.3 Simple task declaration and flow chart

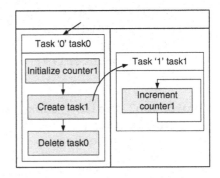

The function of this code snippet is laid out in the flow chart in Figure 5.3. We see that task 0 is responsible for setting the initial value of counter1 and then starting task 1 while stopping task 0. Task 1 has an infinite while loop to update the value of counter1. Most of your task functions will contain an infinite loop in some form or another.

So far the example displayed only one running task. Let's see how we can implement round-robin, cooperative, and pre-emptive multitasking using RTX51.

5.3 Task Scheduling

5.3.1 Round Robin Multitasking

Round-robin multitasking is the default for RTX51-Tiny. The time slice is based off the system clock and is defined during compile. All tasks to be scheduled in this fashion must also be of priority 0, which is the default priority.

```
#include <rtx51tny.h>
int counter0;
int counter1;
int counter2;
void job0 (void) _task_ 0  { // RTX51 begins in task0
    counter0 = 0;                 // initialize counters
    counter1 = 0;
    counter2 = 0;
    os_create_task (1);           // start task 1
    os_create_task(2);            // start task 2
    while (1) {                   // infinite loop
        counter0++;               // increment counter 0
    }
}
void job1 (void) _task_ 1 {
    while (1) {                   // infinite loop
        counter1++;               // increment counter1
    }
}
void job2 (void) _task_ 2 {
    while (1) {                   // infinite loop
        counter2++;               // increment counter2
    }
}
```

This time, task 0 was not stopped, but enters an infinite loop after starting the other two tasks. Thus there are three running tasks for the Tiny to control. Let's use the µVision debug mode to watch the progression of these three counters over time, and keep track of the execution queue for priority 0.

Notice that when the program first starts, tasks 1 and 2 are in the SLEEP-ING(DELETED) state, before being created. The debug tasklist window also shows which task is currently RUNNING.

Since there is only one task, the RTOS always chooses job0 to run again after its time-slice ends. Figure 5.4 shows how the execution queue would look in this situation, and how job0 stays in the RUNNING state.

After running each task once, you can see that all the counters progress at approximately the same rate. RTX51 always chooses the task that is READY and has been waiting to execute for the longest time.

Figure 5.5 shows how the tasks move between the execution queue and RUNNING state. After task 0 runs out its time slice, the RTOS switches to task 1. The execution order goes from task 0 to task 1, task 2, and back to task 0.

Fig. 5.4 Status of execution queue right after RTOS initialization

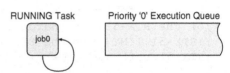

RUNNING Task   Priority '0' Execution Queue

Fig. 5.5 Status of execution
queue while all 3 tasks are
active

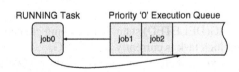

In RTX51-Full, we can dynamically set the number of processor cycles in a clock
tick using the 'os_set_slice' function. For Tiny, the length of the time slice is set using
parameters in the 'Conf_tny.A51' file as shown below.

```
;RTX-51 TINY Hardware-Timer
;===========================
;
;With the following EQU statements the initialization
;of the RTX-51 TINY Hardware-Timer can be defined
;(RTX-51 TINY uses the 8051 Timer 0 for controlling
;RTX-51 software timers).
;
;  Define the register bank used for the timer
;  interrupt. Default is Registerbank 1
```

```
INT_REGBANK    EQU    1
;
;   Define Hardware-Timer tick time in 8051 machine
;   cycles.
INT_CLOCK      EQU    10000 ; default is 10000 cycles
;
;   Define Round-Robin Timeout in Hardware-Timer ticks.
;   default is 5 Hardware-Timer ticks.
;    0 disables Round-Robin Task Switching
TIMESHARING    EQU    5
```

By default, hardware timer is configured to overflow every ten thousand cycles, and each time slice is defined as five timer overflows. In total, each task is getting 50,000 processor cycles, minus the time spent switching between tasks. If we assume the microprocessor runs at a speed of 20MHz, then each slice would be approximately 2.5ms.

5.3.2 Cooperative Multitasking

The other scheduling method supported by RTX51-Tiny is cooperative multitasking. Configure the program to execute in cooperative scheduling mode by setting the TIMESHARING variable to 0 in the 'Conf_tny.A51' file. The RTOS will no longer automatically cycle through READY tasks. Task switches are only performed when the running task voluntarily gives up control of the processor.

Execution flow can be coordinated using 'os_wait', 'os_send_signal', and 'os_clear_signal' system calls among others.

```
#include <rtx51tny.h>
int counter0;
int counter1;
void job0 (void) _task_ 0 { // RTX51 begins in task 0
    os_create (1);           // make task 1 READY
    while (1) {               // infinite loop
        // increment counter
        if (++counter0 == 0) {
            // signal task 1
            os_send_signal (1);
            // wait for signal; releases
            // CPU control
            os_wait (K_SIG, 0, 0);
        }
        os_wait (K_TMO, 1, 0);  // wait for 1 tick
                                // give up CPU
```

```
    }
}
void job1 (void) _task_ 1 {
    while (1) {                        // infinite loop
            os_wait (K_SIG, 0, 0); // wait for signal
                                   // give up CPU
            // increment counter 1
            counter1++;
            os_send_signal (0);    // signal task 0
    }
}
```

In the above example, counter 0 is continuously incremented and checked for overflow condition. A wait-for-timeout command separates every counter increment by one system clock tick. Upon overflow, task 0 sends a signal event to task 1 and then relinquishes control using a wait-for-signal. The inter-task communication section has a more in-depth discussion of signaling events. The statechart in Figure 5.6 shows how the tasks have to signal back and forth.

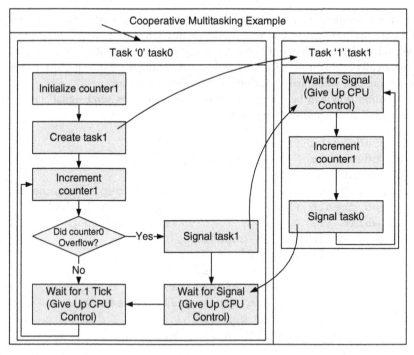

Fig. 5.6 Statechart for a cooperative multitasking program with two tasks

5.3.3   Priority-Driven Preemptive Multitasking

Preemptive task scheduling is only available for RTX51-Full, since Tiny does not support task priorities. Tasks can be assigned a priority of 0 through 3, with 0 the lowest priority. The RTOS always tries to run the highest priority task, so when a higher priority task becomes available, it will immediately perform a context switch. Declare task priority by adding a '_priority_' parameter.

```
void job1 (void) _task_ 1 _priority_ 1 {
    ...
```

Preemption is necessary in some circumstances. Consider what happens in a round-robin system when the running task sends a signal event to a waiting task. The soonest the RTOS can switch tasks is at the end of the time slice, potentially causing a missed deadline. Let's modify our counter example for pre-emptive multitasking.

```
#include <rtx51tny.h>
int counter0;
int counter1;
void job0 (void) _task_ 0 _priority_ 0 {
    // RTX51 starts off in task 0
    os_create (1);                      // start task 1
    while (1) {                         // infinite loop
            // increment counter 0
            if (++counter0 == 0)
                    // signal task 1
                    os_send_signal (1);
        os_wait (K_TMO, 1, 0);        // wait for 1 tick
    }
}
void job1 (void) _task_ 1 _priority_ 1 {
    while (1) {                         // infinite loop
            os_wait (K_SIG, 0, 0);     // wait for signal
            // increment counter 1
            counter1++;
    }
}
```

Figure 5.7 shows the statechart diagram for a preemptive system. Notice the difference is that task0 no longer needs to block itself after signaling task 1. While task 1 is waiting for signal, task 0 is the highest priority task ready to run. When the RTOS receives the signal to task 1, it immediately stops task 0 and hands over execution control to the higher priority task. As long as task 1 is ready, it will maintain control of the processor. Figure 5.8 shows where each task is at every step of the program. Tasks not shown are considered blocked.

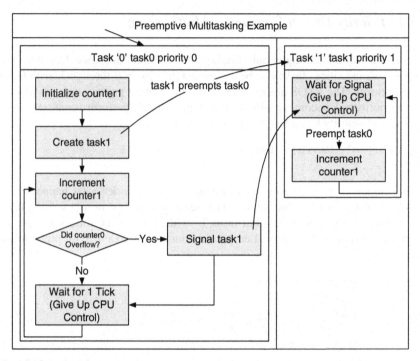

Fig. 5.7 Statechart for preemptive multitasking system

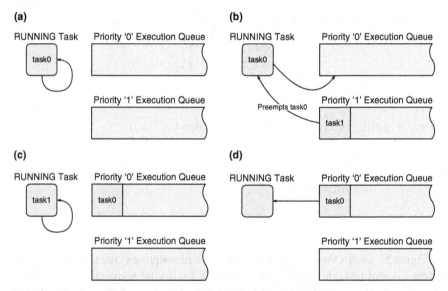

Fig. 5.8 The state of the execution queues (**a**) while task1 is blocked (**b**) when task1 preempts task0 (**c**) while task1 is active and (**d**) when task1 waits for signal

5.4   RTOS Events

5.4.1   Signal Event Based Communication

Signals are one way to carry out inter-task communication. They are the fastest method of communication because no actual information is exchanged. Most simply, a signal is just a single-bit flag attached to each task by the RTOS. In RTX51, tasks send signals to each other using the 'os_send_signal' function. They can also clear a task's signal flag with 'os_clear_signal', including their own. Signaling is important for coordinating execution flow amongst tasks.

```
void task1 (void) _task_ 1 {
    ...
    os_clear_signal (1);         // clear task 1 flag
    os_wait (K_SIG, 0, 0);   // wait for signal
    ...
}
```

Signals are sent by the 'os_send_signal' to the designated task number. If the target task is already in the BLOCKED state, the RTOS will unblock the task and clear the signal flag. If otherwise the flag is already set before a wait-for-signal command, then the task does not ever enter the BLOCKED state and continues to execute. We can use the 'os_clear_signal' to prevent this situation as above. Tasks can send and clear signal for any other task, including itself. Only one signal can be saved per task, and any extra signals are ignored.

5.4.2   Message Event Based Communication

Message passing is another form of inter-task communication that is available for RTX51-Full but not Tiny. Broadly speaking, a message is a set of data that gets transferred from sender to receiver task through message queues or mailboxes. This can be in the form of a shared memory buffer or separate transmit/receive buffers.

In RTX51, messages are 16-bit data values or a pointer to data buffer that can be sent to one of eight total mailboxes. These are not tied to a single task. Instead, tasks and interrupt functions can freely use any mailbox.

Transmitting messages is done through the 'os_send_message' function.

```
int message;
...
// send data in variable 'message' to mailbox 2;
// timeout after 10 ticks
os_send_message (2, message, 10);
```

If the message cannot be sent, because the mailbox is full or some other error, then the task is set to BLOCKED state until either it goes through or timeout occurs.

Tasks can be set to wait for a messaging event using the K_MBX parameter with 'os_wait'. It is generally paired with a timeout condition as well.

```
// wait for message in mailbox 3 and store
// in &message; or timeout in 10 ticks
os_wait (K_MBX + K_TMO + 3, 10, &message);
```

5.4.3 Semaphores

RTX51-Full provides eight binary semaphores to help prevent resource sharing conflicts between tasks. They can be accessed using the 'os_wait' and 'os_send_token' functions. Valid semaphore values are from 8–15.

```
// wait for token from semaphore 14
os_wait (K_MBX + 14, 0, 0);
// protected task functions
...
// finished with semaphore, return token
os_send_token (14);
```

If the semaphore token is immediately available, the task will not enter the waiting state, and will continue execution. Otherwise it is blocked until the token is freed.

5.4.4 Attaching Interrupts to Tasks

Tasks can also wait for hardware interrupt events. This feature is not available on Tiny. Hardware interrupt vectors can be assigned to RTOS tasks using the 'os_attach_interrupt' and 'os_detach_interrupt' functions.

```
void task1 (void) _task_ 1 {
    // attach interrupt 14 (Timer 3 overflow)
    os_attach_interrupt (14);

    while (1) {
        // wait for interrupt
        os_wait (K_INT, 0, 0);
        ...
    }
}
```

Each interrupt source can only be assigned to one task. However, multiple interrupts can be assigned to a single task. In other words, a task can wait for several interrupts to occur.

Attaching an interrupt does not automatically set the interrupt enable flag in the processor hardware. In fact, the relevant flags are only enabled when a task begins waiting for an interrupt event using 'os_wait'.

5.5   When to Use RTOS

Given any project, how do you tell if you should use an RTOS, or write the code from scratch? There are many advantages to using an RTOS, such as standardized system calls and ease of programmability, but you must also consider some things like code size and processor overhead.

RTOS standardization of commonly used functions such as task declaration, task switching, and inter-task signaling among others, allows the programmer to avoid the difficulty of implementing these from scratch. The code becomes easy to read and debug, making it easier to have multitasking, especially as the number of tasks increase and each task requires its own time-constraint.

Of course, it goes without saying that writing an identical implementation from scratch can result in better performance by using assembly coding tricks and the like. For example, generic task switching is a fairly resource-intensive process. We can write a custom task switch function for each possibility, but that would require a large amount of effort and would sacrifice program modularity.

In large projects with multiple programmers, modularity is important so that the work can be divided into more manageable parts. This improves the code's readability and makes the debug process faster.

But what about very small systems? Indeed using an RTOS might not be ideal for such situation, and may even hurt overall system performance. Each tick, each system call, the RTOS eats up processor cycles to perform its maintenance functions. For ultra-small systems, this could result in significant overhead, and it would be a better option to forgo an RTOS in order to achieve the slimmest or fastest running implementation.

5.6   Practice Labs

Lab 1: Traffic Light Control System with Vehicle Detection and Pedestrian Push-to-Walk Request by RTOS

Purpose:
The purpose of this lab is to create a control system using the commercial RTOS RTX51-Tiny that can control vehicular and pedestrian traffic in two directions. It must also be able to handle input from pedestrian push-to-walk buttons and car

detection sensors placed below the street for improving traffic efficiency. The system will have multiple tasks running in round-robin fashion

1. Write a real-time system using the RTOS RTX51-Tiny for the 8051.
2. Use interrupt service routines (ISR) to process push-to-walk buttons and car detection sensors.

Assignment:
In this lab, you will do the following:

1. Understand how to write RTOS programs for SiLabs C8051F005SDK evaluation board in the μVision IDE.
2. Write tasks and ISRs to control an efficient traffic light control system.
3. Use μVision IDE debugger to simulate the real-time system.

In section 2.7, we detailed a multitasking RTOS responsible for controlling an automatic traffic light system at a street intersection for both vehicles and pedestrians. This example will be written using RTX51-Tiny, which does not support attaching external interrupts to tasks. Note that to compile this code, you must have the PK51 Professional Developer's Kit. The C51 evaluation package does not contain RTX51-Tiny!

Ten outputs are assigned to handle the Red-Yellow-Green lights and Stop-Walk lights for both directions. The push-to-walk button is handled by an external interrupt. The inputs and outputs are defined for building a hardware model using the SiLabs C8051F00SDK evaluation board.

The flow of traffic at the intersection is based on a simple timing scheme. Figure 5.9 shows how the traffic lights progress from one phase to the next. Pedestrians get to walk only when automobile traffic flowing in the same direction has the green light. They can also request to reduce the wait time for the 'walk' signal by pressing the push button. Similarly, detected cars stopped at the intersection could cause the red phase to be shortened if there is no cross traffic.

The light cycle has a total of eight phases that are continuously looped. Two of those phases can be shortened by input from the detectors or buttons. Figure 5.10 shows a simplified statechart diagram. In total, the system is separated into four tasks run in round-robin fashion: Init, Lights, Detector, and Button.

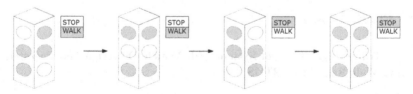

Fig. 5.9 Vehicle and pedestrian traffic light phases

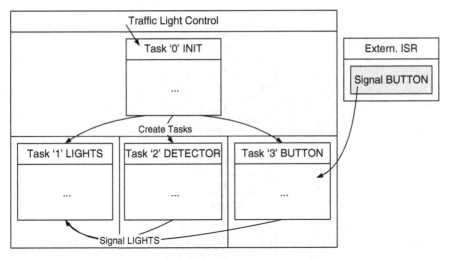

Fig. 5.10 Overall statechart diagram for traffic light control system

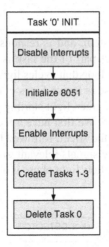

Task 0 is responsible for initializing the 8051 hardware and for creating the other three tasks. Global interrupts are first disabled so that there are no timing issues. The Init task gets deleted at the end, since we only need to initialize once.

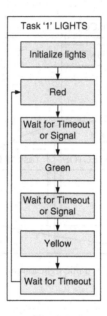

Task 1 is the meat of the system, and is responsible for transitioning between each traffic light phase. The first part of the task is initialization of all the lights, done before entering the infinite loop that cycles light phases.

The length of time each phase is active for is controlled by a wait-for-timeout. Cars moving in direction 1 get a green light starting in phase 1. There are two wait commands controlling this phase. We first have a fixed time delay, long enough so a pedestrian can make it across the street, followed by a wait-for-timeout or signal event. To ensure we only capture signals relevant to this red light cycle, the Lights signal flag is cleared first. The yellow light phase is always constant, so there is only a wait-for-timeout condition.

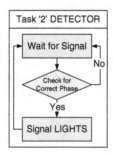

Task 2 is responsible for signaling the Lights tasks when vehicular conditions call for a shorter red light phase. It polls the sensors and signals Lights if a direction has cars waiting at a red light and there is no cross-traffic.

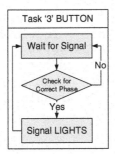

Task 3 is similar to the Detector task, but for pedestrians. Since we cannot attach external interrupts directly to tasks, we instead use an ISR to signal the task. A signal is only sent if we are in the correct phase when the button press is received.

Program:

```
//----------------------------------------------------//
//                                                    //
// TRAFFIC.C: Vehicle and pedestrian traffic          //
//     light controller using RTX51-Tiny RTOS         //
//                                                    //
//----------------------------------------------------//

#include <c8051f000.h>      // sfr definitions
#include <rtx51tny.h>       // RTX-51 tiny functions
#include <stdio.h>          // standard I/O

#define INIT        0
#define LIGHTS      1
#define DETECTOR    2
#define BUTTON      3

sbit dir1_red    = P1^2;    // red light output
sbit dir1_yellow = P1^1;    // yellow light output
sbit dir1_green  = P1^0;    // green light output
sbit dir1_stop   = P1^3;    // stop light output
sbit dir1_walk   = P1^4;    // walk light output
sbit dir1_button = P1^5;    // push button input
sbit dir1_detect = P1^6;    // car detector input

sbit dir2_red    = P2^2;    // red lamp output
sbit dir2_yellow = P2^1;    // yellow lamp output
sbit dir2_green  = P2^0;    // green lamp output
sbit dir2_detect = P2^6;    // car detector input
```

```
//-------------------------------------------------------//
//            Task 0 'init': Initialize                  //
//-------------------------------------------------------//
void init (void) _task_ INIT {
     EA = 0;            // disable interrupts
     WDTCN = 0xde;      // disable watchdog
     WDTCN = 0xad;      //

     OSCXCN = 0x00;     // disable external clock
     OSCICN = 0x07;     // set internal clock 16MHz

     XBR2 = 0x40;       // enable crossbar
     PRT1CF |= 0x1F;    // set P1.0 -- P1.5 as push-pull
     PRT2CF |= 0x1F;    // set P2.0 -- P2.5 as push-pull
     EA = 1;            // enable interrupts

     os_create_task (LIGHTS);
     os_create_task (DETECTOR);
     os_create_task (BUTTON);
     os_delete_task (INIT);
}

//-------------------------------------------------------//
//      Task 1 'lights': Cycle through phases            //
//-------------------------------------------------------//
void lights (void) _task_ LIGHTS {
     dir1_red = 0;
     dir1_yellow = 0;
     dir1_green = 1;
     dir1_stop = 0;
     dir1_walk = 1;

     dir2_red = 1;
     dir2_yellow = 0;
     dir2_green = 0;

while (1) {
         // Phase 1 -- Direction 1 green light
         dir1_yellow = 0;
         dir1_green = 1;
         dir1_stop = 0;
         dir1_walk = 1;
         dir2_red = 1;
         dir2_yellow = 0;
         os_clear_signal (LIGHTS);
```

```
            os_wait (K_TMO, 100, 0);
            os_wait (K_TMO + K_SIG, 255, 0);

            // Phase 2 - Direction 1 yellow light
            dir1_yellow = 1;
            dir1_green = 0;
            dir2_red = 0;
            dir2_yellow = 1;
            os_wait (K_TMO, 255, 0);

            // Phase 3 - Direction 2 green light
            dir1_red = 1;
            dir1_yellow = 0;
            dir1_stop = 1;
            dir1_walk = 0;
            dir2_yellow = 0;
            dir2_green = 1;
            os_clear_signal (LIGHTS);
            os_wait (K_TMO, 100, 0);
            os_wait (K_TMO + K_SIG, 255, 0);

            // Phase 4 - Direction 2 yellow light
            dir1_red = 0;
            dir1_yellow = 1;
            dir2_yellow = 1;
            dir2_green = 0;
            os_wait (K_TMO, 255, 0);
        }
    }
//----------------------------------------------------//
//       Task 2 'detector': Handles detection of      //
//             vehicles at the intersection.          //
//----------------------------------------------------//
void detector (void) _task_ DETECTOR {
    while (1) {
        if (dir1_red && dir1_detect && !dir2_detect)
                os_send_signal (LIGHTS);
        if (dir2_red && dir2_detect && !dir1_detect)
                os_send_signal (LIGHTS);
    }
}
//----------------------------------------------------//
//       Task 3 'button': Handles button presses      //
//          by pedestrians waiting to cross.          //
//----------------------------------------------------//
```

```
void button (void) _task_ BUTTON {
    while (1) {
            os_wait (K_SIG, 0, 0);
            if (dir1_red && dir1_button)
                    os_send_signal (LIGHTS);
    }
}


//-----------------------------------------------------//
//                     Button ISR                      //
//-----------------------------------------------------//
void buttonISR (void) interrupt 17 {
    os_send_signal (BUTTON);
}
```

Simulation:

1. Start the μVision IDE and open the project file Traffic.uv2
2. Enter debug mode by going to **Debug->Start/Stop Debug Session**
3. Add the outputs to **Watch Window 1** by entering the following on the command line in the **Command** tab of the **Output Window:**

```
WS 1, dir1_red
WS 1, dir1_yellow
WS 1, dir1_green
WS 1, dir1_stop
WS 1, dir1_walk
WS 1, dir2_red
WS 1, dir2_yellow
WS 1, dir2_green
```

4. Add some buttons to simulate a car detect or a push-to-walk button press event with the following commands:

```
signal void detect1 (void) {
    P1 |= 0x40;
    twatch ('Clock*0.05);
    P1 &= ~0x40;
}
```

```
signal void detect2 (void) {
    P2 |= 0x40;
    twatch ('Clock*0.05);
    P2 &= ~0x40;
}
signal void button (void) {
    P1 |= 0x20;
    twatch ('Clock*0.05);
    P1 &= ~0x20;
}
```

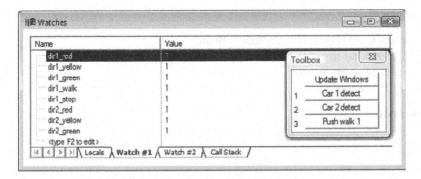

5. Run the program by going to **Debug -> Run**, and see what happens when you press the buttons in different light phases.

Lab 2: LCD Temperature Monitor by RTOS

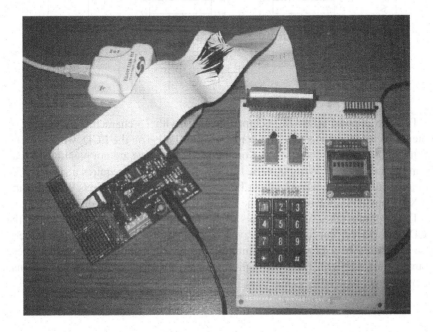

Purpose:

The purpose of this lab is to control a HD44780 LCD panel with the 8051 microprocessor, and display temperature information from the onboard temperature sensor sampled through an ADC. The 8051 will also take input from a keypad, allowing the user to set maximum and minimum temperature bounds.

Assignment:

In this lab, you will do the following:

1. Communicate and control a HD44780-based LCD.
2. Use the ADC to take measurements from the onboard temperature sensor.

Equipment:

1. SiLabs C8051F005SDK Evaluation Board
2. (1) HD44780-based 16 character by 2 line LCD panel
3. (1) 10kΩ potentiometer
4. (12) 10kΩ resistor

Schematic:

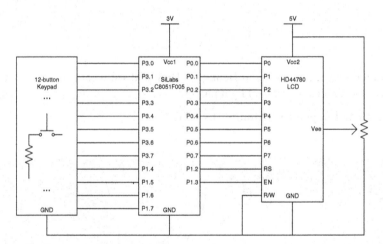

This lab uses an HD44780-compatible LCD with 16 characters by 2 lines. A potentiometer is connected to the contrast control V_{EE} on the LCD, while the rest of the inputs are connected to ports on the 8051. Since we are not planning to read from the LCD, the R/W input is tied to ground. The LCD requires a separate 5V voltage source. The evaluation board uses a 3V source. The code is written using RTX51-Tiny and implemented on the SiLabs C8051F005SDK evaluation board.

This program takes measurements from the temperature sensor and updates the LCD with the current temperature every couple milliseconds. The temperature is also compared to a predefined minimum and maximum. If it lies outside these bounds, then an alarm LED will light up. Figure 5.11 shows the system response in every state.

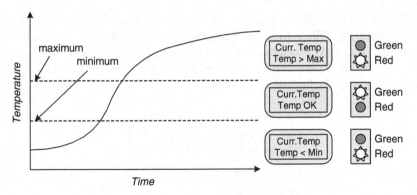

Fig. 5.11 Temperature monitor behavior

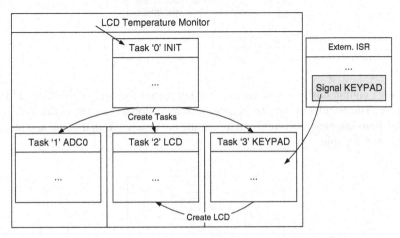

Fig. 5.12 Overall statechart diagram for LCD temperature monitor

Finally, the user can use a keypad to change the minimum or maximum temperature values. Figure 5.12 shows a simplified state chart diagram for our system. The program is split up into four tasks: Init, Adc0, Lcd, and Keypad.

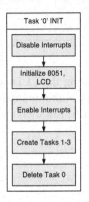

Task 0 sets the ADC to perform conversions when the ADBUSY flag is set (it is normally 0). The conversion is completed once ADBUSY is cleared by the processor. This task also initializes the LCD, which consists of three functions that activates the display and cursor, clears the display area, and sets 8-bit, 2-line operation. Lastly, the Init task deletes itself.

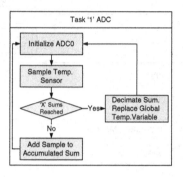

Task 1 continuously takes samples of the temperature sensor and adds it to a local variable. The number of samples is controlled by a global constant. In this case it is set for 4096 samples. The average temperature is extracted from the sum and placed in a global variable.

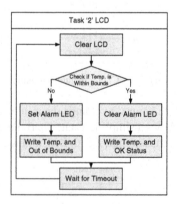

Task 2 is responsible for updating the LCD with current information. It also checks the temperature against the minimum/maximum bounds and updates the LEDs accordingly. The task is set to run a couple of times per second using the wait-for-timeout command.

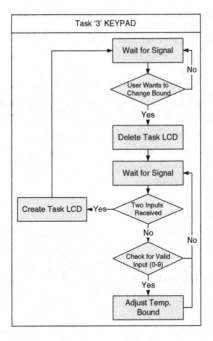

Task 3 is run when the keypad ISR sends a signal denoting the detection of a valid, debounced keypress. If the user presses '*' or '#', the task stops the Lcd task from refreshing the display, and instead shows a prompt for inputting the new minimum or maximum temperature bound, respectively. When it is done, the Lcd task is restarted, and the display is refreshed against the new temperature boundaries.

Program:

```
temperature.c:
//----------------------------------------------------//
//      TEMPERATURE.C: Temperature monitor system    //
//          implemented using RTX51-Tiny RTOS for the //
//          SiLabs C8051F005SDK                       //
//----------------------------------------------------//

#include <c8051f000.h>  // SFR declarations
#include <rtx51tny.h>   // RTX51-Tiny functions
#include "lcd.h"
#include "keypad.h"

#define INIT    0
#define ADC     1
#define LCD     2
#define KEYPAD  3
```

```
//-----------------------------------------------------//
//        16-bit SFR definitions                       //
//-----------------------------------------------------//
sfr16 ADC0 = 0xBE;        // ADC0 data
sfr16 TMR3RL = 0x92;      // Timer3 reload value
sfr16 TMR3 = 0x94;        // Timer3 counter

//-----------------------------------------------------//
//        Global Constants                             //
//-----------------------------------------------------//
#define INT_DEC 4096

sbit GLED = P1^0;
sbit RLED = P1^1;

//-----------------------------------------------------//
//        Global Variables                             //
//-----------------------------------------------------//
float result;
int keyInput;

int minTemp;
int maxTemp;
int minmax;

int quotient;
int update;
int counter;

//-----------------------------------------------------//
//        Task 0 'init': Initialize                    //
//-----------------------------------------------------//
void init (void) _task_ INIT {
    EA = 0;              // disable interrupts
    WDTCN = 0xDE;        // disable watchdog timer
    WDTCN = 0xAD;

    OSCXCN = 0x00;       // external oscillator off
    OSCICN = 0x07;       // internal oscillator set
                         // 16MHz

    XBR2 = 0x40;         // enable xbar weak pull-up
    PRT0CF |= 0xFF;      // enable LCD data port
    PRT1CF |= 0x0F;      // enable RS/EN and LEDs
    PRT1CF |= 0xF0;      // enable keypad ports
```

```
PRT3CF |= 0xFF;

ADC0CN = 0x01;          // disable ADC0, conversion
                        // on write of 1 to ADBUSY,
                        // data is left-justified
REF0CN = 0x07;          // enable temperature sensor,
                        // on-chip VREF, VREF output
                        // buffer
AMX0CF = 0x08;
AMX0SL = 0x0F;          // select int. temp. sensor
ADC0CF = 0x80;          // ADC0 conv. clock = CLK/16
ADC0CF &= ~0x07;        // set PGA gain = 1
ADC0CN |= 0x80;         // enable ADC0

TMR3CN = 0x02;          // Stop Timer3; Clear TF3;
                        // use SYSCLK as timebase
TMR3RL = -16000;        // Init reload values
TMR3   = 0xffff;        // set to reload immediately
EIE2 |= 0x01;           // enable Timer3 interrupts
TMR3CN |= 0x04;         // start Timer3
EA = 1;                 // enable interrupts

LCD_Init ();            // initialize LCD

minTemp = 20;
maxTemp = 40;

os_create_task (ADC);
os_create_task (LCD);
os_create_task (KEYPAD);
os_delete_task (INIT);
}

//----------------------------------------------------//
//   Task 1 'adc0': ADC temperature measurements    //
//----------------------------------------------------//
void adc0 (void) _task_ ADC {
    long accumulator = 0;
    int count = INT_DEC;

    while (1) {
            ADBUSY = 1;          // start ADC conversion
            while (ADBUSY) {
            }
            accumulator += ADC0;
```

```
            count--;
            if (count == 0) {
                    result = accumulator >> 12;
                    result = (result/131072*5-
                                0.776)/0.00286;
                    count = INT_DEC;
                    accumulator = 0;
            }
    }
}


//--------------------------------------------------//
//      Task 2 'lcd': Update LCD                    //
//--------------------------------------------------//

void lcd (void) _task_ LCD {
    while (1) {
            LCD_Clear ();
            LCD_Move (0,3);
            writeTemp (result);
            writeCelsius ();
            LCD_Move (1,3);
            if (result < minTemp) {
                    writeMinFail ();
                    GLED = 0;
                    RLED = 1;
            }
            else if (result > maxTemp) {
                    writeMaxFail ();
                    GLED = 0;
                    RLED = 1;
            }
            else {
                    writeNoFail ();
                    GLED = 1;
                    RLED = 0;
            }
            os_wait (K_TMO, 255, 0);
    }
}


//--------------------------------------------------//
//      Task 3 'keypad': Handle keypad input        //
//--------------------------------------------------//
void keypad (void) _task_ KEYPAD {
```

```
while (1) {
      os_wait (K_SIG, 0, 0);
      if (KeypadGetKey () >= 10) {
            os_delete_task (LCD);
            if (KeypadGetKey () == 10)
                  minmax = 0;
            else
                  minmax = 1;
            LCD_Clear ();
            LCD_Move (0,3);
            LCD_Write (0x53);          // 'S'
            LCD_Write (0x65);          // 'e'
            LCD_Write (0x74);          // 't'
            LCD_Write (0x20);          // ' '
            LCD_Write (0x4D);          // 'M'
            if (minmax == 1) {
                  // write text for Set Max Temp
                  // and clear variable
                  LCD_Write (0x61); // 'a'
                  LCD_Write (0x78); // 'x'
                  maxTemp = 0;
            }
            else { // write text for Set Min Temp
                  // and clear variable
                  LCD_Write (0x69); // 'i'
                  LCD_Write (0x6E); // 'n'
                  minTemp = 0;
            }
            LCD_Move (1,3);
            LCD_Write (0x54); // 'T'
            LCD_Write (0x3A); // ':'

            counter = 0;

            while (counter < 2) {
              os_wait (K_SIG, 0, 0);
              if (KeypadGetKey() < 10) {
                  if (minmax == 1 && counter == 0)
                    maxTemp += KeypadGetKey()*10;
                    else if (minmax == 0 &&
                        counter == 0)
                    minTemp =+ KeypadGetKey()*10;
                    else if (minmax == 1 &&
                        counter == 1)
                    maxTemp += KeypadGetKey();
```

```
                            else if (minmax == 0 &&
                                counter == 1)
                            minTemp += KeypadGetKey ();
                                counter++;
                            LCD_Write (convertKey
                                (KeypadGetKey ()));
                        }
                    }
                os_create_task (LCD);
            }
        }
}
void Timer3ISR () interrupt 14 {
    if (KeypadISR ()) {
            os_send_signal (KEYPAD);
        }
}
```


lcd.h:
```
//----------------------------------------------------//
//      LCD.H: LCD Function definitions               //
//----------------------------------------------------//


#ifndef _LCD_H
#define _LCD_H

//----------------------------------------------------//
//      Function Declarations                         //
//----------------------------------------------------//
void LCD_Command (char phrase);
void LCD_Write (char phrase);
void LCD_Init ();
void LCD_Clear ();
void LCD_Move (int row, int column);

char convertKey (int phrase);
void writeTemp (float temp);
void writeCelsius ();
void writeMinFail ();
void writeMaxFail ();
void writeNoFail ();

#endif
```

lcd.c:

```c
//------------------------------------------------------//
//        LCD.C: Functions to control the LCD        //
//------------------------------------------------------//
#include <c8051f000.h>      // SFR definitions
#include <rtx51tny.h>       // RTX51-Tiny function
#include "lcd.h"            // LCD functions


//------------------------------------------------------//
//        Global Constants                           //
//------------------------------------------------------//
#define LCD_DATA        P0  // definitions for LCD

sbit RS = P1^2;
sbit EN = P1^3;

void LCD_Command (char phrase) {
    RS = 0;                 // write instruction
    LCD_DATA = phrase;
    EN = 1;                 // pulse enable signal
    os_wait (K_TMO, 1, 0);
    EN = 0;
    os_wait (K_TMO, 1, 0);  // wait for instruction
                            // to complete
}
void LCD_Write (char phrase) {
    RS = 1;
    LCD_DATA = phrase;
    EN = 1;
    os_wait (K_TMO, 1, 0);
    EN = 0;
    os_wait (K_TMO, 1, 0);
}

void LCD_Init () {
    LCD_Command (0x0F);     // activate display,
                            // activate cursor,
    LCD_Command (0x01);     // blink cursor, clear
                            // display area, set
    LCD_Command (0x38);     // 8-bit data length,
                            // 2 lines
}

void LCD_Clear () {
    LCD_Command (0x01);
```

```
  }

  void LCD_Move (int row, int column) {
      LCD_Command (0x80 + (row << 6) + column);
  }

  char convertKey (int phrase)
  {
      switch (phrase)
      {
              // Keypad conversion
              case 0:
                      return 0x30;
              case 1:
                      return 0x31;
              case 2:
                      return 0x32;
              case 3:
                      return 0x33;
              case 4:
                      return 0x34;
              case 5:
                      return 0x35;
              case 6:
                      return 0x36;
              case 7:
                      return 0x37;
              case 8:
                      return 0x38;
              case 9:
                      return 0x39;
              case 10:
                      return 0x2A;
              case 11:
                      return 0x23;
      }
      return 0xFF;
  }

  void writeTemp (float temp) {
      int quotient;

      quotient = temp/10;
      LCD_Write (convertKey (quotient));
      temp = temp-quotient*10;
```

```
        quotient = temp;
        LCD_Write (convertKey (quotient));
        temp = 10*(temp-quotient);
        LCD_Write (0x2E);                 // decimal point
        quotient = temp;
        LCD_Write (convertKey (quotient));
    }

    void writeCelsius () {
        LCD_Write (0x20);
        LCD_Write (0xDF);                 // degree symbol
        LCD_Write (0x43);                 // 'C'
    }

    void writeMinFail () {
        LCD_Write (0x54);                 // 'T'
        LCD_Write (0x65);                 // 'e'
        LCD_Write (0x6D);                 // 'm'
        LCD_Write (0x70);                 // 'p'
        LCD_Write (0x3C);                 // '<'
        LCD_Write (0x4D);                 // 'M'
        LCD_Write (0x69);                 // 'i'
        LCD_Write (0x6E);                 // 'n'
    }

    void writeMaxFail () {
        LCD_Write (0x54);                 // 'T'
        LCD_Write (0x65);                 // 'e'
        LCD_Write (0x6D);                 // 'm'
        LCD_Write (0x70);                 // 'p'
        LCD_Write (0x3E);                 // '>'
        LCD_Write (0x4D);                 // 'M'
        LCD_Write (0x61);                 // 'a'
        LCD_Write (0x78);                 // 'x'
    }

    void writeNoFail () {
        LCD_Write (0x54);                 // 'T'
        LCD_Write (0x65);                 // 'e'
        LCD_Write (0x6D);                 // 'm'
        LCD_Write (0x70);                 // 'p'
        LCD_Write (0x20);                 // ' '
        LCD_Write (0x20);                 // ' '
        LCD_Write (0x4F);                 // 'O'
        LCD_Write (0x4B);                 // 'K'
```

```
}

keypad.h:
//-----------------------------------------------------//
//           KEYPAD.H: Keypad Function definitions  //
//-----------------------------------------------------//

#ifndef _KEYPAD_H
#define _KEYPAD_H

int KeypadGetKey();
bit KeypadISR();

#endif

keypad.c:
//-----------------------------------------------------//
//           KEYPAD.C:      Keypad functions        //
//-----------------------------------------------------//

#include <c8051f000.h>
#include "keypad.h"

sbit K0 = P3^0;                    // definitions for keypad
sbit K1 = P3^1;
sbit K2 = P3^2;
sbit K3 = P3^3;
sbit K4 = P3^4;
sbit K5 = P3^5;
sbit K6 = P3^6;
sbit K7 = P3^7;
sbit K8 = P1^7;
sbit K9 = P1^6;
sbit KS = P1^4;
sbit KP = P1^5;

int iCurrentKey;                   // holds input key
int iPressedKey;                   // holds detected key
int iDebounce = 0;                 // debounce counter
int iStatus = 0;

int KeypadGetKey() {
    return iCurrentKey;
}
bit KeypadISR()
```

```
{
    iPressedKey = -1;
    // assuming only one key is pressed at a time,
    // gets the pressed key
    if (K0 == 0) iPressedKey = 0;
    if (K1 == 0) iPressedKey = 1;
    if (K2 == 0) iPressedKey = 2;
    if (K3 == 0) iPressedKey = 3;
    if (K4 == 0) iPressedKey = 4;
    if (K5 == 0) iPressedKey = 5;
    if (K6 == 0) iPressedKey = 6;
    if (K7 == 0) iPressedKey = 7;
    if (K8 == 0) iPressedKey = 8;
    if (K9 == 0) iPressedKey = 9;
    if (KS == 0) iPressedKey = 10;
    if (KP == 0) iPressedKey = 11;

    // if iStatus=0 then looking for valid key press
    // if 1, then looking for valid key release
    if (!iStatus && (iPressedKey != -1)) {
        if (iDebounce == 0) {
                iCurrentKey = iPressedKey;
                iDebounce++;
        }
        else if (iDebounce <= 5) {
                if (iCurrentKey == iPressedKey)
                iDebounce++;
            else
                // input still bouncing, reset
                iDebounce = 0;
        }
        // assume only positive values for
        // iDebounce. If key held for 6ms, consider
        // debounced, change status
        else {
                iStatus = 1;
                iDebounce = 0;
                return 1;
        }
    }
    else if (iStatus == 1) {
        if (iPressedKey == -1) // no key pressed
            iDebounce++;
        else
        // still bouncing, reset
```

```
                    iDebounce = 0;
        if (iDebounce > 5) {
                // no key held for 6ms
                iStatus = 0;
                iDebounce = 0;
        }
    }
    return 0;
}
```

5.7 Summary

This chapter took a very in-depth look at programming using a multitasking RTOS, in this case the RTX51 from Keil. We saw that declaring tasks and having them run in round-robin scheduling was very easy. The standardized system calls allowed us to effortlessly control execution order in a cooperative multitasking setup. Pre-emptive priority multitasking made sure that time-critical tasks would get to run and finish before their deadline. Inter-task communication could be carried out by using signals or the larger messages in conjunction with mailboxes. Smaller projects might choose to forgo an RTOS for slimmer code or better efficiency. Large projects generally require the modularity and manageability afforded by an RTOS implementation.

5.8 Review Questions

1. A real-time embedded software must be implemented using an RTOS.

   a. T
   b. F

2. There may be multiple tasks in the RUNNING state.

   a. T
   b. F

3. In RTX51, Task 0 is always started running before other tasks.

   a. T
   b. F

4. RTX programs must have a main() function.

   a. T
   b. F

5. All concurrent tasks are isolated from each other.

   a. T
   b. F

6. Any two tasks in RTX51-Full must have different priorities

   a. T
   b. F

7. Using an RTOS helps code readability, modularity, and debugging

   a. T
   b. F

8. Tasks can use these methods to synchronize and communicate with each other EXCEPT

   a. Signals
   b. Messages
   c. Interrupts
   d. Semaphores

9. We can prevent memory conflicts between tasks by using

   a. Signals
   b. Messages
   c. Interrupts
   d. Semaphores

10. How many priority levels exist in RTX51-Full?

    a. 1
    b. 2
    c. 3
    d. 4
    e. 5

11. How many tasks can you attach a single hardware interrupt to?

    a. 0
    b. 1
    c. 2
    d. 3
    e. 4

12. Os_wait() moves the running task to

    a. RUNNING
    b. READY
    c. BLOCKED
    d. SLEEPING

13. When wait time is over, the task state is moved to

    a. RUNNING
    b. READY
    c. BLOCKED
    d. SLEEPING

14. Which state is the running state moved to when interrupted?

    a. RUNNING
    b. READY
    c. BLOCKED
    d. SLEEPING

15. At the start of an RTX51-Tiny program, every task except Task 0 is in which state?

    a. RUNNING
    b. READY
    c. BLOCKED
    d. SLEEPING

Answers:
1. B   2. B   3. A   4. B   5. B   6. B   7. A   8. C   9. D   10. D   11. B
12. C   13. B   14. B   15. D

5.9 Exercises

This exercise is intended to familiarize you with using the μVision IDE for debugging RTOS systems. It uses the RTX51-Tiny example that comes with the μVision evaluation software.

1. Start Keil μVision3 and open the **RTX_EX2** using **Project -> Open Project**, and selecting ~ **C51\RtxTiny2\Examples\Ex2\RTX_EX2.Uv2**.
2. The example is already compiled and linked for you. Do not try to recompile!
3. Enter the debug mode by going to **Debug -> Start/Stop Debug Session**.
4. Watch the status of your tasks in the tasklist window by going to **Peripherals -> Rtx-Tiny Tasklist**.

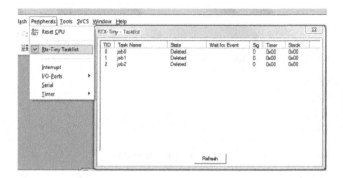

5. We can also look at how much processor time each of the tasks uses with the performance analyzer. Open the performance analyzer window by going to **View -> Performance Analyzer Window**.

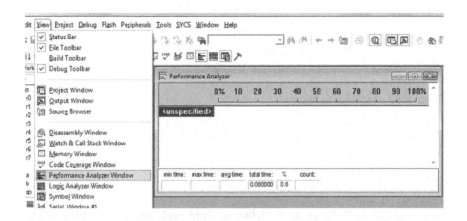

6. Add tasks to keep tabs on using the performance analyzer. Right-click in the Performance Analyzer window and select **Setup PA**.

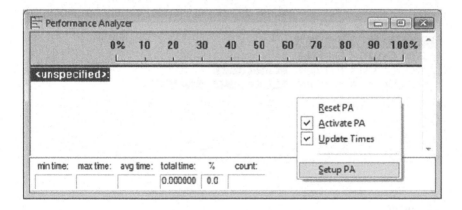

7. Add all three tasks by double-clicking on **job0, job1, job2**, and then **Define** each one.

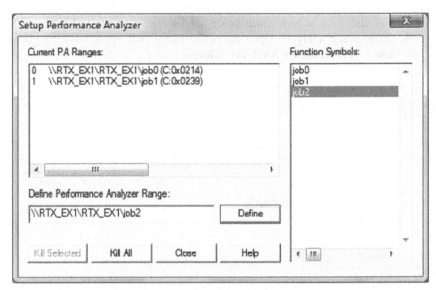

8. Run the program by going to **Debug -> Run**, and stop it at any time and go to the Performance Analyzer window. The Performance Analyzer now shows the percentage time each task has control of the processor and the total time of execution.

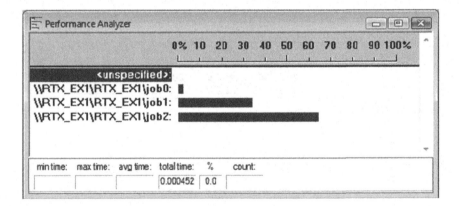

References

1. T. W. Schultz, C and the 8051, Pagefree Publishing, 2004
2. D. Kalinsky, Basic concepts of real-time operating systems, 2003
3. RTX51 User's Guide, Keil Electronik GmbH, 2002
4. 8051 Demo Kit User's Guide, Keil Electronik GmbH, 1998

Chapter 6
Serial Communications

Objectives

- Introduce the RS232 standard and position it within the crowded field of serial communications standards.
- Configure the 8051 serial port.
- Read and write to the serial port.
- Introduce software and hardware handshaking.

This chapter is a fast-paced introduction to RS232 serial communications. Unlike other books that start with a history lesson, this one will present material as it is needed and dispense as much as possible with needless baggage from the past.

6.1 Introduction

There are many types of serial communications. Here are a few worth noting:

- RS232.[1] Peer-to-peer (i.e. communications between two devices)
- RS485.[2] Multi-point (i.e. communications between two or more devices)
- USB (Universal Serial Bus).[3] Replaced RS232 on desktop computers.
- CAN (Controller Area Network).[4] Multi-point. Popular in the automotive industry.
- SPI (Serial Peripheral Interface).[5] Developed by Motorola. Synchronous master/slave communications.
- I²C (Inter-Integrated Circuit).[6] Developed by Philips. Multi-master communications.

---

[1] http://en.wikipedia.org/wiki/RS232

[2] http://en.wikipedia.org/wiki/RS485

[3] http://en.wikipedia.org/wiki/USB

[4] http://en.wikipedia.org/wiki/CAN_bus

[5] http://en.wikipedia.org/wiki/Serial_Peripheral_Interface

[6] http://en.wikipedia.org/wiki/I2C

K. Qian et al., *Embedded Software Development with C*,
DOI 10.1007/978-1-4419-0606-9_6, © Springer Science+Business Media, LLC 2009

The Silicon Laboratories 8051 development kit used in this book supports RS232, SPI and I^{2}C communications. This chapter, though, is about RS232 (Recommended Standard 232), the oldest method of serial communications that is still in widespread use. An RS232 serial port is included on most 8051 microcontrollers. It is usually listed on the datasheet as UART.

RS232 is also known by other more formal names: EIA RS-232C, V.24 and V.28. There are also updates to the standard: RS-232D, EIA/TIA-232E and TIA-232F. It is beyond the scope of this chapter to discuss the long history and slow evolution of this standard. For the modern programmer, it is only of historical interest.

6.1.1 Serial vs. Parallel

When we talk about serial communications, what do we really mean? How is the data transmitted? Serial data is transmitted between devices one bit at a time using agreed upon electrical signals. This is in contrast to parallel communications where data is transmitted between devices multiple bits at a time. See Figure 6.1. Note that each bit requires its own electrical path (i.e. line). Serial communications requires fewer electrical lines. In the old PC days that's why parallel printer cables were bulkier than serial modem cables. Parallel cables may be bigger, but they also transfer data faster given the same bit transfer rate. In the Figure 6.1 example, the parallel transfer is about eight times faster.

Another advantage of serial communications, though, is cable length. A serial cable can be much longer than a parallel cable and still provide reliable communications. For example, the parallel printer cable mentioned above can only be about 15 feet long. A serial cable can be as long as 1216 feet depending on the transmission speed. See Table 6.2.

6.1.2 Simplex and Duplex

The terms simplex and duplex will also come up when discussing serial communications. Simplex transmission is just data transmission in one direction. Duplex

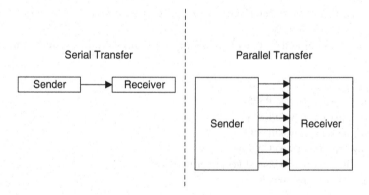

Fig. 6.1 Serial vs. Parallel Data Transfer

Fig. 6.2 Simplex vs. Duplex
Transmission

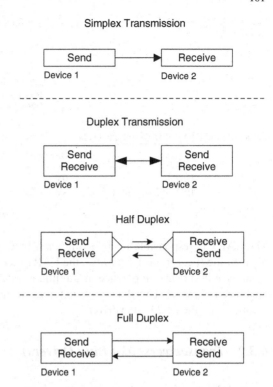

transmission is data transmission in both directions (i.e. send and receive). See Figure 6.2.

There are two forms of duplex transmission – half and full. Half duplex means that data can be transmitted in only one direction at a time. Full duplex means that data can be transmitted in both directions at the same time. For example, one-wire serial can only be half duplex. There is no other choice. Two-wire serial can be either half or full duplex. See Figure 6.3.

Serial communications is all about moving data one bit at a time. In our C programs, though, we read and write bytes to the serial port – not bits. To accomplish the necessary translation between bytes and bits, another piece of hardware is required – the UART.

6.2 UARTs and Transceivers

6.2.1 UART

UART (pronounced "You Art") is an industry acronym that stands for Universal Asynchronous Receiver Transmitter. It is the interface circuitry between the microprocessor and the serial port. This circuitry is built in to the 8051 microcontroller.

Fig. 6.4 UART to UART
data transfer

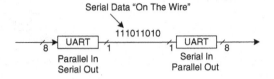

The UART is responsible for breaking apart bytes of data and transmitting it one bit at a time (i.e. serially). Likewise, the UART receives serialized bits and converts them back into bytes. In practice, it's a little more complicated, but that's the basic idea. See Figure 6.4. This diagram is not quite accurate. There is actually a missing component – the RS232 line driver.

Table 6.1 UART vs. RS232 voltage levels

Device	Binary 0	Binary 1
UART	0V	5V
RS232 Transceiver	3V to 25V	−3V to −25V

6.2.2 Transceivers (aka Line Drivers)

The UART doesn't operate at the line voltages required by the RS232 standard. The UART operates at TTL voltage levels (i.e. 0 to 5V). For noise immunity and transmission length, the RS232 standard dictates the transmission of bits at a higher voltage range and different polarities (i.e. typically −9V to +9V). See Table 6.1. To solve this problem, an external transceiver chip is needed. This chip may also be referred to as a line driver. Its main job is to convert the voltage levels from TTL to RS232 and vice-versa. The one discussed in this chapter is the DS275 chip from Dallas Semiconductor. It was chosen for its simplicity in interfacing to the microcontroller – no additional components like capacitors are needed. See Figure 6.5 for a schematic diagram showing the connection between the 8051 microcontroller and the DS275 transceiver. The datasheet for this chip is on the http://embeddedbook.x85.com/ website.

6.2.3 Asynchronous vs. Synchronous

UART communications is asynchronous (i.e. not synchronous). This means that there is no master clock used for timing data transfer between devices. The synchronous method also transfers data in blocks of bytes instead of one byte at a time. See Figure 6.6.

There are chips available for synchronous serial communications called USARTs (Universal Synchronous Asynchronous Receiver Transmitter), but they are not

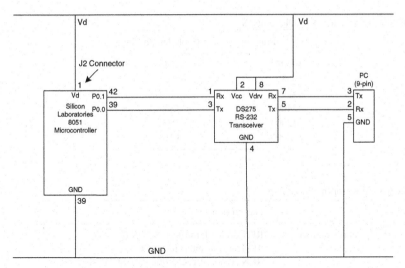

Fig. 6.5 8051 and DS275 RS-232 Transceiver

Fig. 6.6 Async and Sync
Data Streams

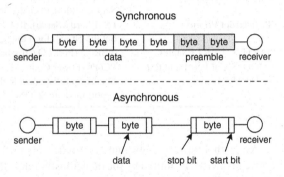

detailed in this chapter and are generally not built-in to the 8051. See Chapter 7
for a survey of microcontrollers that do feature the USART.

6.2.4 Data Transfer Rate

The UART is also responsible for baud rate generation. The baud rate is defined
as the number of signal changes per second. Another measure of speed is the data
rate which is the number of bits transferred per second (or bps). There is a subtle
difference between these two measurements. For example, if three bits (110) are
transmitted in one second, then the data rate is 3 bps, but the baud rate is only 1 baud
because the signal level changed just once. This is a source of great confusion in the
industry. Most people use baud and bps interchangeably.

Table 6.2 Data Rates vs. Cable Lengths

Data Rate (bps)	Cable length (feet)
19200	45
9600	76
4800	152
2400	304
1200	608
600	1216

Table 6.3 SFRs for the Serial Port

SFR	Description
SCON (Serial Port Control)	RI (Receive Interrupt). SCON.0
	TI (Transmit Interrupt). SCON.1
	REN (UART Receive Enable). SCON.4
	SM0 and SM1 (UART Operation Mode). SCON.6, SCON.7
SBUF (Serial Data Buffer)	This is a one-byte buffer for both receive and transmit.
IE (Interrupt Enable)	ES (Enable Serial). IE.4
	Set the bit to 1 to enable receive and transmit interrupts.
IP (Interrupt Priority)	PS (Priority Serial). IP.4
	Set the bit to 0 for a low priority or 1 for a high priority.
UARTEN (UART Enable)	XBR0.2 (Port I/O Crossbar Register 0, Bit 2)
SMOD (Serial Port Baud Rate Doubler Enable)	PCON (Power Control Register). PCON.7
	Set the bit to 1 to double the baud rate defined by serial port mode in SCON.

As of this writing, data rates can reach up to 230,400 bps. The cable length between devices is limited by the data transfer rate – the higher the speed, the shorter the cable. The RS-232C standard only permits transmission speeds up to 19200 bps with a cable length of 45 feet. With modern UARTs, 230,400 bps can be achieved with a short cable length of a few feet.[7] See Table 6.2 for a list of RS232C data rates versus cable lengths.

6.3 Configuring the Serial Port

The 8051 serial port is configured and accessed using a group of SFRs (Special Function Registers). See Table 6.3.

The UART has four operational modes. See Table 6.4. In this chapter, we will focus on mode 1. You will notice in the table that there is a column for start and

---

[7] http://www.acumeninstruments.com/Support/documentation/SerialPortBasics/index_pg2.shtml

Table 6.4 UART Modes[8]

Mode	Synchronization	Baud Clock	Data Bits	Start/Stop Bits
0	Synchronous	SYSCLK/12	8	None
1	Asynchronous	T1 or T2 Overflow	8	1 Start/1 Stop
2	Asynchronous	SYSCLK/32 SYSCLK/64	9	1 Start/1 Stop
3	Asynchronous	T1 or T2 Overflow	9	1 Start/1 Stop

Fig. 6.7 Serial Data Frame

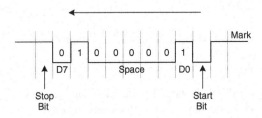

Data Frame for the ASCII Character "A"

stop bits. Another job of the UART is to frame the byte of data that is serialized and transmitted. See Figure 6.7. For the 8051 UART, there is always one start bit (set to 0) and one stop bit (set to 1). Looking at it another way, for every byte of data, 10 bits are transmitted. Serial communications configured this way has a 20 percent overhead. Two bits out of ten are not the data. The effective data transfer rate is therefore lower than the actual bps speed.

Figure 6.7 shows the framed 8-bit ASCII character "A" with one start bit and one stop bit. This is the most common scenario for 8051 asynchronous communications as implied by the options listed in Table 6.4. For completeness, however, there are some other ways that data can be framed under the RS232 standard:

- The data can be 7 or 8 bits.
- There can be either 1 or 2 stop bits.
- There can also be a parity bit before the stop bit(s). The parity bit is used to check the correctness of the data. If used, it is set to odd or even.

6.4 Setting the Baud Rate

Before we can finish our discussion about serial port configuration, we need to talk about the baud rate. You may have noticed that there are no bits in any of the registers discussed so far to set the baud rate. That's because the baud rate is a combination of factors:

---

[8] C8051F0xx datasheet

- UART mode.
- The crystal frequency.
- The number of instruction executed by the 8051 every clock cycle. This varies from 1 to 12. For the 8051 microcontroller used in this book, the value is 1.
- The setting of the SMOD bit (i.e. normal or double baud rate).
- The reload value for the Timer.

RS232 works in a restricted range of baud rates: 75, 110, 300, 1200, 2400, 4800, 9600, 14400, 19200, 28800, 33600, 56000, 115200 and 230400. With the UART operating in mode 1, the baud rate will be generated based on a formula using the factors listed above[9]:

$$\text{Baud rate}_{(\text{Mode1})} = (2^{\text{SMOD}^*}\text{Frequency}_{\text{osc}})/(32^*\text{Instructions}_{\text{cycle}}^*(256 - \text{TRV}))$$

Where:

- SMOD is the normal/double baud rate bit.
- $\text{Frequency}_{\text{osc}}$ is the clock rate in hertz.
- $\text{Instructions}_{\text{cycle}}$ is the machine instruction executed each clock cycle. It is one for the 8051 microcontroller used in this book. For comparison, the original 8051 by Intel used 12 clock cycles for each instruction.
- TRV is the reload value for the timer.

For example, to set the baud rate to 9600, we need to solve for TRV and plug in our known values. We choose an oscillator frequency of 11.0592MHz for reasons discussed shortly. The result is a value of 220, a nice even integer.

Choosing a different frequency may result in a TRV with a fractional value. When this happens, the number is rounded to the nearest integer which results in a slightly different baud rate. In practice, you can only have an error of $+/- 2.5\%$ in the baud rate. See question #1 in the Exercises section.

When designing and testing the labs, the author actually found out that the internal frequency of the Silicon Labs 8051 chip was off by several percent and had to experiment with the TRV to find a value that worked reliably. This is noted in the source code comments for the two serial labs.

So now we have a TRV value, but what do we do with it? The timer reload value must be plugged into an SFR for either timer 0 or timer 1. A few other parameters also need to be set to configure the timer's mode and get it running to create periodic signals for the UART. See Table 6.5 for a list of timer SFRs.

For example 1 in this chapter, we set timer 1 to the following values:

1. TMOD $= 0\times20$. (Timer 1, Mode 2, 8-bit auto reload)
2. TH1 $= 221$. (The TRV value for 1200 baud at 16MHz for a generic 8051)
3. TR1 $= 1$. (Start the timer which will allow the UART to generate the baud rate timing signals.)

---

[9] Embedded C, Michael J Pont, Addison-Wesley Professional, 2002

Table 6.5 Timer SFRs and control bits

SFR	Description
TMOD	Timer Mode
TCON	Timer Control
TR0	Timer 0 run bit (TCON bit 4)
TR1	Timer 1 run bit (TCON bit 6)
TL0	Timer 0 low byte
TL1	Timer 1 low byte
TH0	Timer 0 high byte
TH1	Timer 1 high byte

To summarize, use the following checklist for configuring the 8051 serial port:

1. Set the UART operational mode to 1. (SCON.6 = 1, SCON.7 = 0)
2. Set the REN bit to enable UART receive. (SCON.4 = 1)
3. Set the UART enable bit (UARTEN) in the XBR0 register. (XBR0.2 = 1)
4. Set the bit for normal or double baud rate (SMOD) in the PCON register. (PCON.7 = 1 for double)
5. Determine the TRV (Timer Reload Value) based on crystal frequency and desired baud rate.
6. Configure and run the timer.

To see this checklist put into practice, look at the examples in section 6.7 and the two serial labs in chapter 9.

6.5 Reading and Writing

After all that we went through to configure the port, reading and writing bytes is easy. We simply read from and write to the SBUF register. For example:

```
inByte = SBUF; // Read a character from the UART

SBUF = outByte; // Write a character to the UART
```

The register SBUF is used for both reading and writing bytes. Internally, there are two separate registers. They are both represented as SBUF for the convenience of the programmer.

That is simple enough, but there is a problem. The SBUF register (both transmit and receive) can only hold one byte. How do you know when the byte that you wrote to the port has been transmitted? Conversely, how do you know when a byte is available? There are ways to handle this using time delays and polling. If your application is simple enough, you may be able to get away with it. The best solution to the problem, however, is to use interrupts.

The two interrupts we are interested in were introduced in Table 6.3 but not discussed. They are TI (Transmit Interrupt) and RI (Receive Interrupt). The transmit interrupt flag is set by the UART when a byte in SBUF has been successfully transmitted. The receive interrupt flag is set by the UART when a byte has been received. If ES (Enable Serial) is set then a special function called an interrupt handler is automatically called when either TI or RI are set. It is up to the program to handle the interrupt and reset the flags. See example 2 in section 6.7.

6.6 Handshaking

The 8051 only has a one-byte buffer – SBUF. In contrast, a typical PC serial port with a 16550 UART has a 16-byte buffer. If SBUF is not serviced "quickly" enough, an incoming byte may overwrite a byte that has not yet been read and processed. Using a control technique called handshaking, it is possible to get the transmitting device to stop sending bytes until the 8051 is ready. Likewise, the 8051 can be signaled by the receiving device to stop transmitting. There are two forms of handshaking – software and hardware.

6.6.1 Software Handshaking

Software handshaking (also called XON/XOFF) uses control characters in the byte stream to signal the halting and resuming of data transmission. Control-S (ASCII 19) signals the other device to stop sending data. Control-Q (ASCII 17) signals the other device to resume sending data. The disadvantage with this approach is that the response time is slower and two characters in the ASCII character set must be reserved for handshaking use.

6.6.2 Hardware Handshaking

Hardware handshaking uses additional I/O lines. The most common form of hardware handshaking is to use two additional control wires called RTS (Ready to Send) and CTS (Clear to Send). One line is controlled by each device. The line (either RTS or CTS) is asserted when bytes can be received and unasserted otherwise. These two handshaking lines are used to prevent buffer overruns.

There are two other less commonly used lines – DTS (Data Terminal Ready) and DSR (Data Set Ready). These lines are typically used by devices signaling to each other that they are powered up and ready to communicate.

To summarize, RTS/CTS are used for buffer control and DTS/DSR are used for device present and working indicators. In practice, serial communication with no handshaking uses 3 wires (TX, RX and GND). Serial communications with basic hardware handshaking uses 5 wires (TX, RX, RTS, CTS and GND).

You may have noticed in the previous paragraphs that I didn't specify which device uses a given line. For example, does the 8051 use the RTS or CTS line? The answer to that question is "it depends". It depends on the device's function in the overall system and it brings us to an inescapable part of RS232 history.

We can't end this chapter without talking about DTE (Data Terminal Equipment) and DCE (Data Communications Equipment). In the beginning, it was pretty straightforward. RS232 is a point-to-point protocol meant to connect two devices together – terminals and modems. The terminal was the DTE and the modem was the DCE. Later, the PC became the DTE while the modem remained the DCE. But what about other types of devices like barcode scanners and weigh scales that connect to a PC. With respect to the PC, they are all DCE devices. If you take the PC out of the picture, however, that may change. If you are developing an 8051 application that logs data from a weigh scale, your 8051 device will become the DTE. Knowing whether your device is DTE or DCE is important because it will determine which handshaking line to control. The DTE controls the RTS and DTR lines. In this case, point of reference is very important. See Figure 6.8 and Table 6.6 for a diagram and pin-out, respectively, of the DB9 RS232 serial port found on a PC. Typically, the connector is "male" for DTE equipment and "female" for DCE equipment.

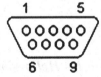

Fig. 6.8 RS232 DB9 pin
D-SUB male connector

Table 6.6 RS232 DB9 Pinout

Pin	Signal Name	Direction (DTE ← DCE)
1	CD (Carrier Detect)	←
2	RXD (Receive Data)	←
3	TXD (Transmit Data)	→
4	DTR (Data Terminal Ready)	→
5	GND (System Ground)	
6	DSR (Data Set Ready)	←
7	RTS (Request To Send)	→
8	CTS (Clear To Send)	←
9	RI (Ring Indicator)	←

Fig. 6.9 Hello World screenshot using STDIO

6.7 Examples

6.7.1 Example 1 – Hello World (Using STDIO)

The first example will transmit the string "Hello, World" out of the serial port using the *printf( )* function. It uses the Keil hardware simulator and a "generic" 8051. Note that using the *printf( )* function is an easy way to send data to the serial port, but it is also wasteful of the 8051's limited memory because it is a general purpose function.

To run this example, follow the steps below:

1. Start the Keil uVision3 IDE and open the project called **HelloWorld.** Select *Project → Open Project* on the menu bar.
2. Run the program. Select *Debug → Start/Stop Debug Session.* Then select *Debug → Run.*
3. View the output of the program. Select *View → Serial Window → UART #1.* The string "Hello, World!" should be displayed in this window. See Figure 6.9 for a screenshot.

Listing 6.1 – Hello World (using STDIO)

```c
/*-------------------------------------------------------------------
//-------------------------------------------------------------------
// Chapter 6, Example 1 - Hello World (using STDIO)
// Uses Keil hardware simulator
// Target - Generic 8051 (Keil hardware simulator)
//
// This program transmits the string "Hello, World!" to the UART.
// When running in the Keil hardware simulator, open the
// serial peripheral.
//
// It is adapted from one of the standard Keil examples
//-------------------------------------------------------------------

//-------------------------------------------------------------------
// Includes
//-------------------------------------------------------------------
*/

#include <REG52.H> /* special function register declarations  */
/* for the intended 8051 derivative          */

#include <stdio.h> /* prototype declarations for I/O functions */

/*-----------------------------------------------
The main C function.  Program execution starts
here after stack initialization.
-----------------------------------------------*/
void main( void )
    {

    /*-----------------------------------------------
    Setup the serial port for 1200 baud at 16MHz.
    -----------------------------------------------*/
    SCON = 0x50;   /* SCON: mode 1, 8-bit UART, enable rcvr    */
    TMOD |= 0x20;  /* TMOD: timer 1, mode 2, 8-bit reload      */
    TH1 = 221;     /* TH1:  reload value for 1200 baud @ 16MHz */
    TR1 = 1;       /* TR1:  timer 1 run                        */
    TI = 1;        /* TI:   set TI to send first char of UART  */

    /*-----------------------------------------------
    Note that an embedded program never exits (because
    there is no operating system to return to).  It
    must loop and execute forever.
    -----------------------------------------------*/
    while (1)
        {
        printf("Hello World\n"); /* Print "Hello World" */
        }
    }
```

Fig. 6.10 Hello World #2 Screenshot

6.7.2 Example 2 – Hello World (Beyond the Serial Port)

The second example will transmit the string "Hello, World" out of the serial port without using the *printf()* function. It will demonstrate Timer and UART configuration and will use the Keil hardware simulator configured for the Silicon Laboratories C8051F005 development kit. As a result, the code is a little more complicated than if we chose a "Generic" 8051 or 8052.

Since it is meant to be a simple example, there is no factoring of the code into separate modules. For larger projects (especially with more than one developer) this is important. For now, it isn't necessary.

To run this example, follow the steps below:

1. Start the Keil uVision3 IDE and open the project called **HelloWorld2.** Select *Project → Open Project* on the menu bar.
2. Run the program. Select *Debug → Start/Stop Debug Session*. Then select *Debug → Run*.
3. View the output of the program. Select *View → Serial Window → UART #1*. The string "Hello, World!" should be displayed in this window. See Figure 6.10 for a screenshot.

Listing 6.2 – Hello World (beyond the serial port)

```
//-----------------------------------------------------------------
// Chapter 6, Example 2 - Hello World (beyond the serial port)
// Uses Keil hardware simulator
// Target - Silicon Laboratories C8051F005
//
// This program transmits the string "Hello, World!" to the UART.
// When running in the Keil hardware simulator, open the
// serial peripheral.
//-----------------------------------------------------------------

//-----------------------------------------------------------------
// Includes
//-----------------------------------------------------------------
#include <C8051F000.h> // SFR declarations

//-----------------------------------------------------------------
// Global Constants
//-----------------------------------------------------------------
#define BAUDRATE 115200  // Baud rate of UART in bps
#define SYSCLK 22118400L // SYSCLK in Hz

//-----------------------------------------------------------------
// Global Variables
//-----------------------------------------------------------------
unsigned char Message[14] = "Hello, World!";
unsigned char Message_Ptr = 0;
unsigned char TX_Ready = 0;
static char Byte;
bit finished = 0; // "Hello, World!" sent to UART

//-----------------------------------------------------------------
// Function Prototypes
//-----------------------------------------------------------------
void OSCILLATOR_Init( void );
void PORT_Init( void );
void UART0_Init( void );

//-----------------------------------------------------------------
// main() Routine
//-----------------------------------------------------------------
void main( void )
    {
    WDTCN = 0xDE;       // Disable watchdog timer
    WDTCN = 0xAD;

    OSCILLATOR_Init(); // Initialize oscillator
    PORT_Init();       // Initialize crossbar and GPIO

    UART0_Init();      // Initialize UART0

    EA = 1;
```

```
    while (1)              // Super Loop
        {
        if ((TX_Ready == 1) && (finished == 0))
            {
            TX_Ready = 0; // Set the flag to zero
            TI = 1;       // Set transmit flag to 1
            }
        }
    }

//-----------------------------------------------------------------
// OSCILLATOR_Init
//-----------------------------------------------------------------
//
// Return Value : None
// Parameters   : None
//
// This function initializes the system clock to use an external
// 22.1184MHz crystal.
//
//-----------------------------------------------------------------
void OSCILLATOR_Init( void )
    {
    int i;           // Software timer

    OSCICN |= 0x80; // Enable the missing clock detector

    // Initialize external crystal oscillator to use
    // 22.1184 MHz crys-tal
    OSCXCN = 0x67;                 // Enable external crystal osc.
    for ( i = 0; i < 256; i++ );  // Wait at least 1 ms
    while (!(OSCXCN & 0x80));      // Wait for crystal osc to settle
    OSCICN |= 0x08;               // Select external clock source
    OSCICN &= ~0x04;              // Disable the internal osc.
    }

//-----------------------------------------------------------------
// PORT_Init
//-----------------------------------------------------------------
//
// Return Value : None
// Parameters   : None
//
// This function configures the crossbar and GPIO ports.
//
// Pinout:
//
// P0.0   digital   push-pull    UART TX
// P0.1   digital   open-drain   UART RX
//-----------------------------------------------------------------
void PORT_Init( void )
    {
    XBR0 = 0x04;    // Enable UART0
    XBR1 = 0x00;
```

```
   XBR2 = 0x40;      // Enable crossbar and weak pull-up

   PRT0CF |= 0x01; // Set TX pin to push-pull
   }

//-------------------------------------------------------------------
// UART0_Init    Variable baud rate, Timer 2, 8-N-1
//-------------------------------------------------------------------
//
// Return Value : None
// Parameters   : None
//
// Configure UART0 for operation at <baudrate> 8-N-1 using Timer2
// as baud rate source.
//
//-------------------------------------------------------------------
void UART0_Init( void )
   {
   CKCON = 0x20; // Timer2 uses the system clock
   T2CON = 0x34; // Timer2 used for TX and RX, enabled
   RCAP2L = -((long)(SYSCLK / BAUDRATE) / 32);
   TL2 = RCAP2L;
   TR2 = 1;       // Start Timer2

   SCON = 0x50;  // 8-bit variable baud rate;
   // 9th bit ignored; RX enabled
   // clear all flags
   TX_Ready = 1; // Flag showing that UART can transmit
   ES = 1;
   }

//-------------------------------------------------------------------
// UART0_Interrupt
//-------------------------------------------------------------------
//
// This routine is invoked whenever a character sent to
// the UART.
//
//-------------------------------------------------------------------

void UART0_Interrupt (void) interrupt 4
   {
   if ((SCON & 0x02) == 0x02) // Check if transmit flag is set
      {
      SCON = (SCON & 0xFD);  // Clear transmit flag

      if (finished == 0)
         {
         // Store a character in the variable byte
         Byte = Message[Message_Ptr];

         if (Byte != 0)
            {
            SBUF = Byte;
```

```
                    Message_Ptr++; // Update counter
                    }
            else
                    {
                    finished = 1; // Reached end of message
                    Message_Ptr = 0;
                    TX_Ready = 1;
                    }
            }
        }
    }
```

6.7.3   Example 3 – Interactive Console Using the Serial Port

The third example demonstrates the use of the serial port as an interactive console. It builds directly on the code of Example 2. The program will allow the user to toggle a port bit from the console. One menu choice will turn the bit on. The other menu choice will turn the bit off. It is a simple example that can be used as a foundation for the exercises in Section 6.10.

To run this example, follow the steps below:

1. Start the Keil uVision3 IDE and open the project called **Console**. Select *Project → Open Project* on the menu bar.

Fig. 6.11 Simple Console Screenshot

2. Run the program. Select *Debug → Start/Stop Debug Session*. Then select *Debug → Run*.
3. View the output of the program. Select *View → Serial Window → UART #1*. The menu should be displayed in this window.
4. Select *Peripherals → I/O-Ports → Port 1* to see the Port 1 bit that will be toggled by your menu selections.
5. See Figure 6.11 for a screenshot of the console menu.

Listing 6.3 – Simple Console Application

```
//----------------------------------------------------------------
// Chapter 6, Example 3 - Interactive Console
// Uses Keil hardware simulator
// Target - Silicon Laboratories C8051F005
//
// This program demonstrates a simple console to control a port bit
// There are two menu choices:
// The first choice will turn P1^0 on
// The second choice will turn P1^0 off
//----------------------------------------------------------------

//----------------------------------------------------------------
// Includes
//----------------------------------------------------------------
#include <C8051F000.h> // SFR declarations

//----------------------------------------------------------------
// 16-bit SFR Definitions for F005
//----------------------------------------------------------------
sfr16 RCAP2 = 0xCA; // Timer2 capture/reload
sfr16 TMR2 = 0xCC;  // Timer2

//----------------------------------------------------------------
// Global Constants
//----------------------------------------------------------------
#define BAUDRATE 115200   // Baud rate of UART in bps
#define SYSCLK 22118400L // SYSCLK in Hz

//----------------------------------------------------------------
// Global Variables
//----------------------------------------------------------------

unsigned char Menu[64] = "\nToggle P1^0\n 1)
Turn Bit On\n 2) Turn Bit Off\n ?";
unsigned char Menu_Ptr = 0;
unsigned char TX_Ready = 0;
static char Byte;
sbit Port_Bit = P1 ^ 0; // Port bit to control
bit Show_Menu = 1;       // Flag to display the menu

//----------------------------------------------------------------
// Function Prototypes
//----------------------------------------------------------------
void OSCILLATOR_Init( void );
void PORT_Init( void );
void UART0_Init( void );
```

```
//-------------------------------------------------------------------
// main() Routine
//-------------------------------------------------------------------
void main( void )
    {
    WDTCN = 0xDE;        // Disable watchdog timer
    WDTCN = 0xAD;

    OSCILLATOR_Init(); // Initialize oscillator
    PORT_Init();        // Initialize crossbar and GPIO

    UART0_Init();        // Initialize UART0

    EA = 1;

    while (1)            // Super Loop
        {
        if (TX_Ready && Show_Menu)
            {
            TX_Ready = 0; // Clear flag
            TI = 1;        // Set transmit flag (trigger interrupt)
            }
        }
    }

//-------------------------------------------------------------------
// OSCILLATOR_Init
//-------------------------------------------------------------------
//
// Return Value : None
// Parameters   : None
//
// This function initializes the system clock to use an external
// 22.1184MHz crystal.
//
//-------------------------------------------------------------------
void OSCILLATOR_Init( void )
    {
    int i;              // Software timer

    OSCICN |= 0x80; // Enable the missing clock detector

    // Initialize external crystal oscillator to use
    // 22.1184 MHz crys-tal
    OSCXCN = 0x67;                  // Enable external crystal osc.
    for ( i = 0; i < 256; i++ ); // Wait at least 1 ms
    while (!(OSCXCN & 0x80));     // Wait for crystal osc to settle
    OSCICN |= 0x08;                 // Select external clock source
    OSCICN &= ~0x04;                // Disable the internal osc.
    }

//-------------------------------------------------------------------
// PORT_Init
//-------------------------------------------------------------------
//
// Return Value : None
// Parameters   : None
//
// This function configures the crossbar and GPIO ports.
//
```

```
// Pinout:
//
// P0.0   digital   push-pull     UART TX
// P0.1   digital   open-drain    UART RX
//-----------------------------------------------------------------
void PORT_Init( void )
    {
    XBR0 = 0x04;    // Enable UART0
    XBR1 = 0x00;
    XBR2 = 0x40;    // Enable crossbar and weak pull-up

    PRT0CF |= 0x01; // Set TX pin to push-pull
    }

//-----------------------------------------------------------------
// UART0_Init   Variable baud rate, Timer 2, 8-N-1
//-----------------------------------------------------------------
//
// Return Value : None
// Parameters   : None
//
// Configure UART0 for operation at <baudrate> 8-N-1 using Timer2
// as baud rate source.
//
//-----------------------------------------------------------------
void UART0_Init( void )
    {
    CKCON = 0x20; // Timer2 uses the system clock
    T2CON = 0x34; // Timer2 used for TX and RX, enabled
    RCAP2 = -((long)(SYSCLK / BAUDRATE) / 32);
    TMR2 = RCAP2;
    TR2 = 1;      // Start Timer2

    SCON = 0x50;  // 8-bit variable baud rate;
    // 9th bit ignored; RX enabled
    // clear all flags
    TX_Ready = 1; // Flag showing that UART can transmit
    ES = 1;
    }

//-----------------------------------------------------------------
// UART0_Interrupt
//-----------------------------------------------------------------
//
// This routine is invoked whenever a character sent to
// the UART.
//
//-----------------------------------------------------------------

void UART0_Interrupt (void) interrupt 4
    {
    if ((SCON & 0x01) == 0x01) // Check if receive flag is set
        {
        SCON = (SCON & 0xFE);   // Clear receive flag
        Byte = SBUF;            // Read a character from the terminal

        switch( Byte )
            {
            case '1':
                {
```

```
                    Port_Bit = 1; // set P1^0
                    Show_Menu = 1;
                    break;
                    }

            case '2':
                    {
                    Port_Bit = 0; // clear P1^0
                    Show_Menu = 1;
                    break;
                    }
                }                          // end switch
        }

    if ((SCON & 0x02) == 0x02) // Check if transmit flag is set
        {
        SCON = (SCON & 0xFD);  // Clear transmit flag

        if (Show_Menu)
            {
            // Store a character in the variable byte
            Byte = Menu[Menu_Ptr];

            if (Byte != 0)
                {
                SBUF = Byte;
                Menu_Ptr++; // Update counter
                }
            else
                {
                Show_Menu = 0; // Finished displaying menu
                Menu_Ptr = 0;
                TX_Ready = 1;
                }
            }
        }
    }
```

6.8 Summary

This chapter introduced the RS232 serial communications standard and placed it in context with newer forms of serial communications. It also discussed the role of the UART and external transceiver circuits necessary to transmit bits of data at the proper voltage.

On the software side, this chapter discussed how to configure the serial port using the special function registers and also discussed issues pertaining to baud rate generation. Finally, reading and writing to the serial port was addressed and both software and hardware handshaking concepts were introduced.

Three simple examples were provided. For practical work on this subject, there are two serial communications labs in chapter 9.

6.9 Review Questions

1. What is the difference between peer-to-peer and multi-point communications?
2. What is the difference between simplex and duplex transmission?
3. What is the difference between half duplex and full duplex?
4. How many RS232 serial ports does the Silicon Laboratories C8051F005 support?
5. How many serial ports does the Silicon Laboratories C8051F005 support? List them.
6. What does the acronym UART stand for?
7. In the RS232 standard, what are the voltage levels for binary 0 and 1?
8. With a data rate of 19200bps, what is the maximum cable length between two devices?
9. What is the name of the SFR (Special Function Register) for serial port control?
10. What is the name of the SFR for the one-byte serial port buffer?
11. Which bit must be set to enable the UART?
12. What are two techniques for handshaking?
13. What are the two control characters for software handshaking?
14. Which set of hardware handshaking I/O lines are used for preventing buffer overruns?
15. What is the gender for the DB9 connector of a DTE (i.e. PC) serial port?
16. In Example #2 and Example #3, how did we know to use Interrupt 4 for the UART ISR?
17. In Example #2 and Example #3, which timer is used by the UART to generate the baud rate?

6.9.1 Key to the Review Questions:

1. Peer-to-peer communications is between two devices. Multi-point communications is between two or more devices. For multi-point, the maximum number of addressable devices depends on the communications standard.
2. Simplex refers to data transmission in one direction. Duplex refers to data transmission in both directions.
3. Half duplex limits data transmission to only one direction at a time. Full duplex allows data transmission in both directions at the same time.
4. One RS232 serial port. It is listed in the datasheet as UART.
5. Three serial ports – SMBus^{TM}, SPI^{TM} and UART.
6. Universal Asynchronous Receiver Transmitter.
7. Binary 0 is represented as a voltage between 3V and 25V. Binary 1 is between $-3V$ and $-25V$.
8. 46 feet.
9. SCON (Serial Port Control).
10. SBUF (Serial Data Buffer).

11. UARTEN (UART Enable). XBR0.2 (Port I/O Crossbar, bit 2)
12. Hardware and software handshaking.
13. Control-S (ASCII 19) to stop sending data. Control-Q (ASCII 17) to start sending data.
14. CTS (Clear to Send)/RTS (Ready to Send).
15. Male. Look on the back of an older PC to verify. Newer PCs don't have an RS232 serial port. In that case, look at the DB9 connector on a USB-Serial adapter cable.
16. Use the 8051 datasheet to determine interrupt setting.
17. Timer 2.

6.10 Exercises

1. Using an oscillator frequency of 12Mhz and a desired baud rate of 9600, calculate the resulting TRV. Now round to the nearest integer and calculate the actual baud rate that will be generated by the UART. What is the percent error? Will this choice of frequency work for an application that uses the serial port?
2. Modify Example 1 to prompt the user for his/her name and then print a greeting using the person's name (e.g. Hello, David"). **Hint:** Look at Example 2 for code that reads data from the serial port.
3. Modify Example 2 to toggle a port bit periodically. Prompt the user to enter a toggle rate (in seconds) between 0 – 9 (i.e. validate for ASCII characters 0–9). A single key press should change the toggle rate. A carriage return is not necessary. **Hint:** Use a separate timer and ISR to toggle the port bit. Do not implement the delay as a "busy loop".
4. Write a temperature conversion program that prompts the user for a temperature (in Fahrenheit) and then displays the temperature in Celsius to the nearest degree. On Port 2, display a running count of user queries.
5. Modify the program in Exercise #4. Add two menu choices that will allow the user to choose between F→C or C→F conversions. On Port 2, display a running count of F→C conversions. On Port 3, display a running count of C→F conversions. Finally, add a third menu choice to reset the counters.

Chapter 7
Survey of Popular Microcontrollers

Overview

1. Establish and discuss baseline features for comparison.
2. Review the range of hardware within the 8051 Family.
3. Compare the 8051 family with other microcontrollers including the PIC, Rabbit, AVR, ARM, ColdFire and the hybrid BASIC Stamp.

7.1 Introduction

In this chapter we will review (not exhaustively) the range of hardware within the 8051 family. We will also compare the 8051 with other microcontroller families. This is a dense chapter with many tables and should be treated as a reference or starting point for further research.

This book is about embedded programming in C. It is not an 8051 book. The 8051 is featured in this book because it is a common (and thriving) family of microcontrollers and has been in the marketplace for nearly 30 years.

It is important to understand the choices available in the marketplace to make good design decisions for a project or for your company's future direction. There is more to hardware selection then features. It's easy to get lost in the features. Other considerations include:

1. **Performance.** Is the MCU powerful enough to do the job?
2. **Hardware cost.** Is your product low volume or high volume?
3. **Number of vendors in the marketplace.** Will you be able to purchase parts in five years? That also brings up the issue of your product's life cycle. If it is only a few years, then the need to purchase parts five or more years down the road may not be that important.
4. **In-house engineering experience with a given microcontroller.** If you or your team has no experience with the MCU, you will need an extended development period to climb the learning curve.

K. Qian et al., *Embedded Software Development with C*,
DOI 10.1007/978-1-4419-0606-9_7, © Springer Science+Business Media, LLC 2009

5. **Quality of development tools.** Problems with tools can completely stall a project.
6. **Price of development tools.** A startup company may choose an MCU based on the initial cost of the tools. For example, Rabbit Semiconductor recently made almost all of their tools and libraries free of cost. The CodeWarrior tools (i.e. full version) for Freescale's ColdFire MCU, on the other hand, are very expensive.
7. **Time to market.** Usually an overriding factor.

This chapter will help put the hardware choices in perspective. Comparing MCUs is usually an apples-to-oranges comparison, but it still must be done. Some vendors have online tools to help in the selection process, but of course these tools only feature their devices. Ultimately, MCU selection becomes an exercise in risk management.

7.2   Features for Comparison

It is easy to insert prejudice or a marketing slant into feature comparisons. We will try to be as neutral as possible. Table 7.1 lists the features that will be shown in our comparison. Some of them are hard numbers while others are a little more subjective. Many features have been excluded for clarity.

Table 7.1 MCU Features

#	Feature	Description
1.	Company	MCU Manufacturer
2.	Family	MCU Family Type (e.g. 8051, PIC, etc)
3.	Model	MCU Model
4.	Package	MCU package type and pin count (e.g. 40-pin PDIP)
5.	MIPS	Million Instructions Per Second. Relative performance measurement.
6.	Frequency	MCU clock frequency. An alternative speed measure used when MIPS are not available
7.	Flash	Nonvolatile memory for the program. Measured in kilobytes. Could also be ROM, EPROM or EEPROM.
8.	RAM	Volatile memory for program data. Usually SRAM. Measured in bytes or kilobytes.
9.	Digital I/O	Number of digital I/O lines
10.	Timers	Number of timers
11.	PCA	Number of Programmable Counter Arrays
12.	ADC	Number of Analog to Digital Converters and resolution (e.g. 12-bit)
13.	DAC	Number of Digital to Analog Converters and resolution
14.	Comms	List of integrated serial and Ethernet communications.
15.	Price	Price for a given quantity

7.2.1 Packages

Chip packaging is important and roughly falls into two categories – through-hole and surface mount. Through-hole technology mounts chips by inserting the chip's pins into holes drilled into a printed circuit board. This technique was predominant until the late 1980s when surface mount started to become popular. Surface mount technology involves mounting the chip directly onto the surface of the board. Surface Mount Devices (SMDs) are typically smaller than their through-hole counterparts because the leads (i.e. pins) are smaller or there are no pins at all. See the photos in Table 7.2.

Table 7.2 Common Chip Packages

Package	Photograph
DIP (Dual Inline Package) • Through-Hole • Various pin counts (e.g. 8,16,20, 40) • CDIP (Ceramic DIP) • PDIP (Plastic DIP)	
SOIC (Small Outline Integrated Circuit) • Surface Mount • Dual Inline • Smaller surface area and thickness than DIP package • Typically the same pinouts as DIP counterparts.	
LQFP (Low Profile Quad Flat Pack) • Surface Mount • Quad Inline • Variant: TQFP (Thin), many others.	
PLCC (Plastic Leaded Chip Carrier) • Surface Mount or Socket • Quad Inline • Socket may be surface mount or through-hole	
BGA (Ball Grid Array) • Surface mount • Grid Array	

7.3   The Large 8051 Family

Intel developed the original 8051 in 1980 and sold them until the 1990s. Today, Intel does not sell them at all but there are about twenty manufacturers making enhanced 8051-compatible devices. This section will show in table form a selected range of devices for easy comparison. There is a separate table for each manufacturer.

This feature list is not complete. Showing all of the features would make it difficult to compare chips. One important way that this list was narrowed was the use of Flash memory to store the program. In fact, there are other forms of storage including ROM, EPROM and EEPROM memory chips. Flash memory, however, is a good narrowing choice because of its wide range of storage capacities and dropping prices. There are a few exceptions and they are noted in the tables.

7.3.1   8051 Development Tools

The 8051 family has both commercial and open source development tools. The most widely regarded commercial C compiler, C51, is from Keil – the one featured in this book. The most popular open source compiler is called SDCC (Small Device C Compiler). There is an advanced exercise in Chapter 8 that challenges the reader to integrate SDCC into the Silicon Labs IDE. With this accomplished, the reader doesn't have to work within the functional and memory limitations of the Keil evaluation version.

See Table 7.3 for a list of popular 8051 development tools. This is a C book, but Assembler and BASIC compilers were also included in the table for comparison.

Table 7.3 8051 Development Tools

Company/ Project	Description	URL
Keil	C Compiler (C51) Assembler (A51) IDE (uVision3)	http://keil.com
Silicon Labs	IDE MCU Configuration Wizard TCP/IP Configuration Wizard	http://silabs.com
SDCC	Open Source C Compiler	http://sdcc.sourceforge.net/
HI-TECH	C compiler for Silicon Labs 8051 MCUs	http://www.htsoft.com/
MCS Electronics	BASIC Compiler (BASCOM)	http://www.mcselec.com

Table 7.4 Silicon Labs 8051 Family Comparison

Model	C8051F305-GS	C8051F015-GQ	C8051F500-IQ	C8051F122-GQ
Package	14-pin SOIC	64-pin TQFP	48-pin QFP	100-pin TQFP
MIPS or Freq	25MIPS	25MIPS	50MIPS	100MIPS
Flash	2K	32K	64K	128K
RAM	256	2304	4352	8448
I/O	8	32	40	64
Timers	3	4	4	5
PCA	3	5	6	6
ADC	No	8 channels	32 channels	16 channels
DAC	No	2 channels	No	2 channels
Communications	UART, I2C	UART, I2C, SPI	CAN 2.0, LIN 2.0, SPI, UART, I2C	2 UARTs, I2C, SPI
Price	$1.74@100	$9.58@100	$4.91@100	$15.39@100

7.3.2 Silicon Laboratories Family[1]

Table 7.4 shows four Silicon Labs chips chosen from a product list of 184 chips. The complete spreadsheet, *SiLabs MCU List*, can be found on the http://embeddedbook. x85.com/ website. Silicon Labs acquired an 8051 product line when they purchased Cygnal. This company specializes in mixed signal MCUs and high performance. Their chips are the most costly, but no other manufacturer can get close to them in performance or number of ADC channels.

7.3.3 Atmel Family[2]

Table 7.5 shows four Atmel chips chosen from a product list of 59 chips. The complete spreadsheet, *Atmel MCU List*, can be found on the http://embeddedbook.x85. com/ website.

7.3.4 Maxim (i.e. Dallas) Family[3]

Table 7.6 shows four Maxim chips from a product list of 30 chips. The complete spreadsheet, *Maxim 8051 MCU List*, can be found on the http://embeddedbook.x85. com/ website. This company acquired an 8051 product line when they purchased Dallas Semiconductor.

---

[1] http://www.silabs.com

[2] http://atmel.com/

[3] http://www.maxim-ic.com/

Table 7.5 Atmel 8051 Family Comparison

Model	AT89C2051	AT89C51AC2	AT89C51RD2	AT89C51RE2
Package	PDIP 20	LQFP 44 PLCC 44 LQFP 44	VQFP 64	LQFP 44
MIPS or Freq	24MHz	40MHz	60MHz	60MHz
Flash	2K	32K + 2K EEPROM	64K	128K
RAM	128	1280	2048	8448
I/O	15	34	48	34
Timers	2	3	3	3
PCA	0	5	1	1
ADC	No	8 Ch (multiplexed)	No	No
DAC	No	No	No	No
Communications	UART	UART	UART, SPI	2 UARTS, SPI
Price	$0.853@100	$7.20@100	$7.91@100	$7.80@100

Table 7.6 Maxim 8051 Family Comparison

Model	DS80C320	DS89C450	DS80C411	DS2251T (Secure)
Package	MQFP/44, PDIP/32, PDIP/40, PLCC/44, TQFP/44	PDIP/40, PLCC/44, TQFP/44	LQFP/100	LQFP/100
MIPS or Freq	33MHz	33MIPS @33MHz	75MHz	16MHz
Flash	External Only	64kB	64kB	Up to 128kB (non-volatile SRAM)
RAM	256 + External	1280 Bytes	64kB	Up to 128kB (non-volatile SRAM), 128 bytes scratchpad RAM
I/O	32	32	64	32
Timers	3	3	4	2
PCA	0	0	0	0
ADC	No	No	No	No
DAC	No	No	No	No
Communications	2 UARTS	2 UARTS	3 UARTS, 1-wire, Ethernet	UART
Price	$6.00 @1k	$7.78 @1k	$8.00 @1k	$68.67 @1k

The DS2251T is a secure MCU with tamperproof features designed to prevent hacking of the program and data. This model uses up to 128kB of non-volatile SRAM for both program and data storage. The memory will last up to 10 years if no power is applied. It is a very expensive chip.

The DS80C411 has integrated Ethernet (10BaseT) – a rare feature for an 8051.

7.4 PIC Microcontrollers

The PIC is a family of 8-bit, 16-bit and 32-bit microcontrollers from Microchip Technology, Inc. See Figure 7.1 for a high-level view of the PIC family. The original PIC1640 was developed by General Instruments in the 1970s. The acronym PIC initially stood for **Programmable Interface Controller**, but it was later changed to **Programmable Intelligent Computer**. Both of these acronyms are only of historical interest, much like the acronym BASIC (**Beginners All purpose Symbolic Instruction Code**) is for all of the dialects of the BASIC computer language. In fact, Microchip Technology does not use PIC as an acronym. Unlike the 8051, the only major supplier of PIC chips is Microchip Technology. There are companies that make PIC clones, but for the most part it is a single-source family of chips. Despite this single-source limitation, the PIC is still an excellent MCU choice. Microchip claims to have sold over 6 billion PIC chips and 600,000 development systems between 1990 and early 2008[4].

Like the 8051, the PIC has a Harvard architecture meaning that there are separate areas of memory for program and data storage. There are also separate address and data lines to these memory areas so the PIC can access program and data memory simultaneously. The Harvard architecture makes it practical to use nonvolatile Flash or ROM memory for the program and volatile SRAM for the data.

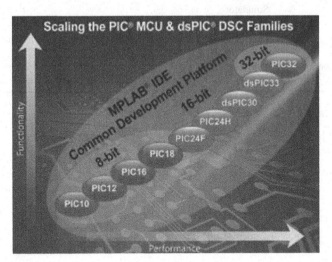

Fig. 7.1 PIC MCU Models[5]

---

[4] http://www.microchip.com/stellent/idcplg?IdcService=SS_GET_PAGE&nodeId=2018& mcparam=en534302

[5] Source: http://www.microchip.com

7.4.1 PIC Development Tools

PIC microcontrollers have a minimalist architecture and traditionally were not very powerful. The architecture and limited memory resources made it difficult to implement a C compiler that could generate efficient code. For many years, if you wanted to use a PIC, it was best to learn Assembler. With the introduction of more powerful models and the increased popularity of this device family, C compilers are now available from several sources including Microchip. See Table 7.7.

Microchip has a freeware IDE called MPLAB that includes an assembler, debugger and simulator. See Figure 7.2 for a screenshot of the IDE. Their C compiler as well as other third-party compilers integrate into the IDE. Microchip's C compiler,

Table 7.7 PIC Development Tools

Company/ Project	Description	URL
Microchip	IDE (MPLAB)	http://microchip.com
	C (PIC18, PIC24, dsPIC and PIC32 only)	
	Assembler	
	Debugger	
	Simulator	
HI-TECH	C compiler for all PICs	http://www.htsoft.com/
SDCC	Open Source C compiler for PIC16 and PIC18	http://sdcc.sourceforge.net/
Micro Engineering Labs, Inc.	BASIC compiler	http://www.microengineeringlabs.com

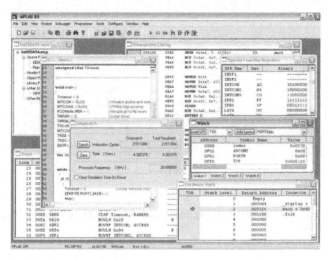

Fig. 7.2 Microchip's free MPLAB IDE

Table 7.8 PIC Family (8, 16 and 32-bit)

Model	PIC10F200 (8-bit)	PIC18F2610 (8-bit)	PIC24FJ256GA106 (16-bit)	PIC32MX 360F512L (32-bit)
Package	6/SOT-23 8/DFN 8/PDIP	28/PDIP 300mil 28/SOIC 300mil	100-Pin TQFP	100-Pin TQFP
MIPS or Freq	4MHz	10 MIPS	16 MIPS	80MHz
Flash	256 words	64K	256kB	512kB
RAM	16 bytes	3968 bytes	16384 bytes	32kB
I/O	4	25	53	85
Timers	1 (8-bit)	4	5	5
PCA	No	No	No	Yes
ADC	No	10 channels (10-bit)	1 channel (10-bit)	16 channels (10-bit)
DAC	No	No	No	No
Comms	None	EUSART, SPI, I2C	4UART, 3SPI, 3I2C	2UART, 2SPI, 2I2C
Price	$0.53@1K	$4.25@1K	$4.18@1K	$6.35@1K

unfortunately, is only for the PIC18, PIC24, dsPIC and PIC32 chips. MPLAB can be used for all PIC devices.

7.5 Rabbit Microprocessors

The Rabbit family is a direct descendant of the 8-bit Z80 / Z180 architecture. There are four chip generations:

1. Rabbit 2000 (Introduced in 1999)
2. Rabbit 3000 (Introduced in 2002)
3. Rabbit 4000 (Introduced in 2006)
4. Rabbit 5000 (Introduced in 2008)

Each generation builds on the capabilities of the previous generation. All Rabbit models are much more powerful than the original Z80 / Z180 chips and their efficient architecture rivals the performance of most 16-bit chips and some 32-bit chips. Rabbit Semiconductor markets the Rabbit as a microprocessor instead of a microcontroller. Most Rabbits have little or no on-chip memory. The Rabbit does not have a Harvard architecture like the 8051 or PIC.

In addition to selling the microprocessors, Rabbit Semiconductor also designs and sells feature-rich RCMs (Rabbit Core Modules) – daughter boards with memory and other peripherals – that plug into the customer's main board. This approach facilitates rapid prototyping of an embedded design. The strategy is to use the RCM for new, low-volume products. As volume increases, the product can be

Table 7.9 Rabbit MCU Family

Model	2000 (8-bit)	3000 (8-bit)	4000 (8-bit)	5000 (16-bit internal)
Package	100-pin PQFP	128-pin LQFP 128-ball TFBGA	128-pin LQFP 128-ball TFBGA	289-ball BGA
MIPS or Freq	30MHz	55MHz	60MHz	100MHz
Flash	External	External	External	External
RAM	External	External	External	128kB (16-bit)
I/O	40	56	40	48
Timers	1 8-bit, 1 10-bit	10 8-bit, 1 10-bit	10 8-bit, 1 10-bit, 1 16-bit	10 8-bit, 1 10-bit, 1 16-bit
PCA	None	2	2	2
ADC	None	None	None	3 10-bit channels
DAC	None	None	None	2 10-bit channels
Comms	4 UARTs, SPI	6 UART, SPI	6 UARTs, SPI Ethernet (10baseT)	6 UARTs, SPI Ethernet (10/100baseT), Wi-Fi
Price	$8.75@1K	$9.50@1K	$9.50@1K	Not yet listed on website

reengineered with all RCM components on the main circuit board. Table 7.9 features each generation of Rabbit microprocessor. See Figure 7.3 for a view of an RCM module with a Rabbit 5000, wireless Ethernet, 1MB Flash and 1MB of SRAM. For more information on Rabbit RCM modules, visit the company's website.[6]

7.5.1 Rabbit Development Tools

For the C developer, Rabbit is an excellent choice. The company has its own IDE, compiler (Dynamic C) and a large number of libraries. As of 2008, all of the tools are free except for the AES/SSL encryption library.

The Dynamic C language has been extended from ANSI C to include the following new language constructs:

1. **Costatements** – To simplify the implementation of state machines.
2. **Cofunctions** – To implement cooperative multitasking without an RTOS.
3. **Slice** – To implement preemptive multitasking without an RTOS.

These new language features can be combined in your program. Special libraries for Dynamic C include the following:

1. TCP/IP library
2. FAT File System

---

[6] http://www.rabbit.com

Fig. 7.3 Rabbit RCM5450W
(wireless, 1MB Flash, 1MB
SRAM)

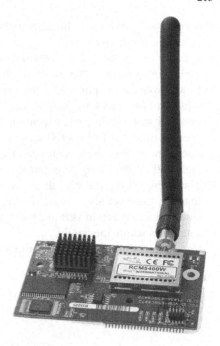

3. Point-to-Point Protocol (PPP)
4. RabbitWeb (web server)
5. Simple Network Management Protocol (SNMP)
6. Modbus TCP (for industrial automation communications)
7. uC/OS-II real-time kernel

There is also a utility to let the customer encrypt their own custom library modules.
This opens the door for a third-party Rabbit library market.

7.6 Atmel AVR Microcontrollers

Atmel has two distinct architectures for their AVR line of microcontrollers: 8-bit
and 32-bit. The first 8-bit AVR was released in 1997.

7.6.1 AVR 8-bit MCU[7]

The 8-bit architecture has the following features:

1. Harvard architecture (like the 8051 and PIC)
2. RISC (Reduced Instruction Set Computer) architecture.

---

[7] http://atmel.com/products/avr/default.asp

3. Single-cycle execution. In other words, a single clock cycle will execute a processor instruction.
4. Because of single-cycle execution, you get the easy to calculate One-MIP-Per-MHz. For example, a 20MHz clock speed yields about 20MIP performance.
5. Low power consumption with good performance. Generally speaking, the AVR runs at a lower clock frequency than other MCUs. This lowers power consumption, but with single-cycle execution, performance is maintained. The chip can operate from 1.8 to 5.5VDC so you can run battery-operated systems down. There are flexible sleep modes and the operating frequency is software controllable. All of these things translate to lower power consumption.
6. Many chips. Like the PIC, there are many choices in the AVR family. Unfortunately, there is only a single source. Packages range from 8 pins to 100 pins. Code sizes range from 1kB to 256kB. See Figure 7.4 for a high-level view of the categories within the family.
7. Code compatibility across the entire 8-bit family.

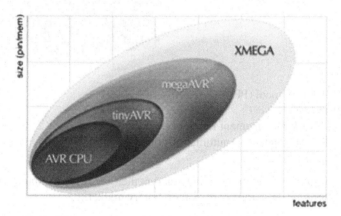

Fig. 7.4 Atmel 8-bit AVR Product Line

Table 7.10 AVR 8-bit Development Tools

Company/ Project	Description	URL
Atmel	AVR Studio IDE	http://www.atmel.com
HP InfoTech	CodeVision AVR C Compiler	http://www.hpinfotech.ro/
GCC	Open source C compiler	http://www.avrfreaks.net/AVRGCC/
FastAVR	Basic compiler	http://www.fastavr.com/
Forth, Inc.	Forth compiler	http://www.forth.com/
IAR Systems	IDE and C compiler	http://www.iar.com/

Table 7.11   Atmel 8-bit AVR Family

Model	ATtiny13A (tinyAVR)	ATtiny861 (tinyAVR)	ATmega1284P (megaAVR)	ATxmega384A1 (XMEGA)
Package	8-pin PDIP 8-pin SOIC	20-pin PDIP 20-pin SOIC	40-pin PDIP 44-pin TQFP 44-pin VQFN	100-pin TQFP 100-pin CBGA
MIPS or Freq	20MHz / 20MIPS	20MHz / 20MIPS	20MHz / 20MIPS	32MHz / 32MIPS
Flash	1kB 64 Byte EEPROM	8kB 512 Byte EEPROM	128kB 4kB EEPROM	384kB 4kB EEPROM 4kB Boot Code
RAM	64 Bytes 32 registers	512 Bytes	16kB	32kB
I/O	6	16	32	78
Timers	1, 8-bit	1, 16-bit 2, 8-bit	2, 16-bit 2, 8-bit	8, 16-bit
PCA	None	None	None	None
ADC	4, 10-bit channels	11, 10-bit channels	8, 10-bit channels (44-pin VQFN)	16, 12-bit Channels
DAC	None	None	None	4, 12-bit Channels
Comms	None	SPI	2UARTs, SPI	8USART, 4SPI
Price	$0.843@500	$1.83@500	Not Available	Not Available

7.6.2   AVR 8-bit Development Tools

Atmel provides a free IDE called AVR Studio that is used for the entire family. It includes an assembler and simulator. A C compiler must be purchased from a third-party vendor. See Table 7.10.

7.6.3   AVR 32-bit MCU[8]

The 32-bit architecture has the following features:

1. Harvard architecture.
2. DSP (Digital Signal Processing) instructions.
3. Embedded Ethernet and USB.
4. Two subfamilies: UC3 (Flash Microcontrollers) and AP7 (Application Processors).
5. For UC3, up to 83 DMIPS @ 66 MHz.
6. For UC3, power consumption is as low as 1.3mW / MHz.
7. For AP7, up to 210 DMIPS @ 150 MHz.
8. The AP7 family can run Linux.

The 32-bit family is a good choice for signal processing or multimedia applications.

---

[8] http://atmel.com/products/avr32/default.asp

7.6.4 AVR 32-bit Development Tools

Atmel provides a free IDE called AVR32 Studio that is used for the entire family.
There is a version for Windows and Linux. Atmel uses a customized version of the
open source GNU C compiler.

This is a newer architecture, so third part products are limited. See Table 7.12.

Table 7.13 shows chip models from both the UC3 and AP7 sub-families. Notice
that the UC3 is more like a "traditional" microcontroller, while the AP7 has features
that make it more like a microprocessor.

This is also an extreme case where the table doesn't do the microcontroller jus-
tice. There are many unique features that aren't shown in the table such as a pixel
co-processor, LCD interface and an image sensor interface – advanced features for
consumer products.

Table 7.12 AVR 32-bit Development Tools

Company/ Project	Description	URL
Atmel	AVR32 Studio IDE	http://www.atmel.com
	Atmel GCC C compiler	
	AVR32 UC3 Software Framework	
	AVR32 AP7 Software Framework	
IAR Systems	IDE, Assembler and C compiler	http://www.iar.com/

Table 7.13 Atmel 32-bit AVR Family

Model	AT32UC3B164 (UC3)	AT32UC3A0512 (UC3)	AT32AP7002 (AP7)	AT32AP7000 (AP7)
Package	48-pin TQFP 48-pin VQFN	144-pin LQFP	196-pin TFBGA	256-pin TFBGA
MIPS or Freq	60MHz / 72DMIPS	66MHz / 80DMIPS	150MHz / 210DMIPS	150MHz / 210DMIPS
Flash	64kB	512kB	None	None
RAM	16kB	64kB	32kB 16kB/16kb Inst/data cache	32kB 16kB/16kb Inst/data cache
I/O	28	109	85	160
Timers	3, 16-bit	3, 16-bit	3	3
PCA	None	None	3	3
ADC	10-bit, 8 channel	10-bit, 8 channel	12-bit channel for image sensor	12-bit channel for image sensor
DAC	None	16-bit stereo audio	16-bit stereo audio	None
Comms	2UARTs, USB2.0 Full Speed	4UARTs, USB2.0 Full Speed, Ethernet(10/100)	4UARTS, USB2.0 High Speed	4UARTS, USB2.0 High Speed, 2ETHERNET (10/100)
Price	$6.30@100	$11.985@800	$11.14@100	$14.413@100

7.7 ARM Microprocessors

The ARM microprocessor has a long and storied history that dates back to 1983 at Acorn Computers Limited in England. The acronym originally stood for Acorn RISC Machine and then later the Advanced RISC Machine. Today it is just called ARM. It is a 32-bit RISC processor by ARM, Limited that is used widely in embedded products like cell phones. For example, the ARM11 is used in the Apple iPod. The ARM architecture has power saving features which have made it very popular in the mobile market.

ARM currently has a majority market share in the 32-bit RISC microprocessor market. ARM, Limited licenses the ARM IP (Intellectual Property) core to partners who manufacture and sell the chips. As of January 2008, ARM and its partners have shipped more than 10 billion processors since 1990[9].

Despite its widespread use in mobile embedded devices and features such as low power consumption, it is really more of a traditional microprocessor and does not fit well into this chapter's survey. Compared to earlier products reviewed, the ARM operates are much higher clock speeds and requires external memory.

There are a number of IP cores to choose from and excellent development tools including ARM's RealView Development Suite. For more information, visit ARM's web page[10].

7.8 ColdFire Microprocessors (and Microcontrollers)

ColdFire is a 15-year old product line based architecturally on the Motorola 68000 microprocessor. It has a 32-bit "Variable Length RISC" architecture that is "assembly source" compatible, but not object code compatible with the 68K.

The ColdFire product line is owned by Freescale Semiconductor (formally the semiconductor arm of Motorola). Recently Freescale decided to license the ColdFire as an IP core to partners – no doubt to compete with ARM.

The ColdFire family has models that target both traditional microprocessor and microcontroller applications. There are four ColdFire cores – V1 to V4. The Flexis models in particular bridge the gap between their 8-bit MCUs and ColdFire. The Flexis line uses a V1 core. See Figure 7.5.

Although we are focusing on the 32-bit ColdFire in this section, Freescale also has both 8-bit (S08) and 16-bit (HCS12) product lines. In fact the HCS12 is instruction-set compatible with the well-known but legacy 68HC11 microcontroller.

---

[9] http://www.arm.com/news/19720.html

[10] http://www.arm.com

Fig. 7.5 Freescale ColdFire
Models[11]

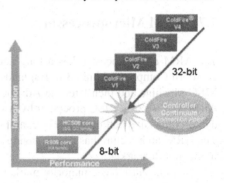

Table 7.14 Freescale 32-bit ColdFire Family

Model	MCF51QE32 (Flexis / V1 Core)	MCF51AC256 (Flexis / V1 Core)	MCF5213 (V2 Core)	MCF5282 (V2 Core)
Package	64-pin LQFP	80-pin LQFP 64-pin LQFP 64-in QFP	100-pin LQFP 81-pin MAPBGA	256-pin MAPBGA
MIPS or Freq	50MHz / 46MIPS	50MHz / 46MIPS	80MHz / 76MIPS	80MHz / 76MIPS
Flash	32kB	256kB	256kB	512kB
RAM	8kB	32kB	32kB	64kB
I/O	54	70	56	150
Timers	12, 16-bit	2, 16-bit	4, 32-bit 4, 16-bit	4, 32-bit 8, 16-bit
PCA	None	None	None	None
ADC	12-bit, 20 channels	12-bit, 24 channels	12-bit, 8 channels	10-bit, 8 channels
DAC	None	None	None	None
Comms	2SPI, 2I^{2}C	2SPI, 2I^{2}C,CAN	3UARTS, I^{2}C, CAN, QSPI	3UARTS, I^{2}C, CAN, QSPI, Ethernet (10/100)
Price	$1.94@10K	$3.81@10K	$7.59@10K	$17.45@10K

Visit the Freescale Semiconductor website for more information on these two product lines[12].

7.8.1 ColdFire Development Tools

CodeWarrior is the primary development environment for all Freescale MCUs. This tool is not free; however, they do offer free TCP/IP and USB protocol stacks.

See Table 7.14 for an overview of selected ColdFire chips.

---

[11] Source: http://www.freeescale.com

[12] http://www.freescale.com/

7.9 Basic Stamp

This chapter will end with a short discussion of the hybrid Basic stamp[13]. This is a book about embedded C development, but this chapter is a survey of "popular" microcontrollers, so it must be included.

The Basic stamp is not a microcontroller chip, but a small "daughterboard" that mounts onto the customer's main circuit board. It has the form factor of a DIP, but it is actually a PCB (Printed Circuit Board). See Figure 7.6. In this respect, it is much like the Rabbit RCM (Rabbit Control Module) discussed earlier in the chapter. What is different about the Stamp is that it has a Basic interpreter called

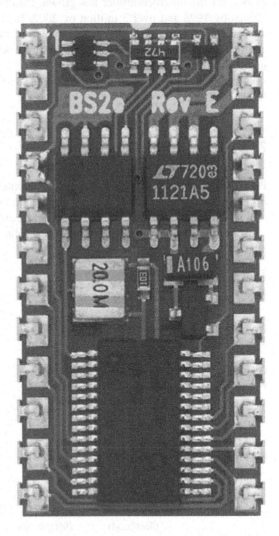

Fig. 7.6 Basic Stamp 2e

---

[13] http://www.parallax.com/

PBASIC in ROM. Application development is fast and easy which makes it popular for hobbyists and companies who need to develop and deploy projects quickly. On the downside, performance is relatively low because the Stamp uses an interpreter that executes a tokenized program.

The question for the hobbyist or developer is whether the Basic stamp is "fast enough" for the application. This question rings true for any of the MCUs discussed in this chapter. Additionally, because of its higher unit cost, the Stamp is only suitable for hobbyists or low volume applications where profit margins are higher.

The Basic stamp is distributed by Parallax, Inc. who released the first model in 1992. The first model used the PIC microcontroller. To get a sense of how the market for this microcontroller has grown, Parallax claims to have sold 125,000 stamps by 1998 and over 3 million by 2002. In recent years they have expanded their product line to include the 8-bit SX microcontroller and the Propeller which is a custom, single chip MCU with 8, 32-bit processors or "cogs" with performance up to 160MIPS (20MIPS/cog).

There is also a version of the Stamp called Javelin that is programmed in Java instead of Basic.

7.9.1 Basic Stamp Development Tools

Parallax has a free IDE for Basic Stamp development. The IDE tokenizes the PBA-SIC source code and downloads it to the Stamp using a serial cable. The Javelin (i.e. Java) Stamp requires a different (but still free) IDE.

Because of the uniqueness of this product, Table 7.15 has a modified feature set.

Table 7.15 Parallax Basic Stamp Family

Model	BS2-IC	BS2p40-IC	BS2px-IC	Javelin Stamp
Package	24-pin DIP	40-pin DIP	24-pin DIP	24-pin DIP
Microcontroller	Microchip PIC16C57c	Ubicom SX48AC	Ubicom SX48AC	Ubicom SX48AC
Language	PBASIC	PBASIC	PBASIC	Java
Frequency	20MHz	20MHz	32MHz	25MHz
Program Execution Speed	4000 inst/sec	12000 inst/sec	19000 inst/sec	8500 inst/sec
EEPROM	2kB	16kB	16kB	32kB
RAM	32 Bytes	38 Bytes	38 Bytes	32kB
Scratchpad RAM	None	128 Bytes	128 Bytes	None
I/O	18	34	18	16
Comms	UART (9600baud)	UART (9600 baud)	UART (19200 baud)	UART (28800 baud)
Price	$39.20@100	$71.20@100	$49.99@1	$80.99@10

7.10   Review Questions

You may need Internet access or other reference material to answer some of these questions.

1. What does the acronym ROM stand for?
2. What does the acronym EPROM stand for?
3. What does the acronym EEPROM stand for?
4. What is the difference between Flash, ROM, EPROM and EEPROM?
5. Which chip packages are listed in the MCU tables but were not discussed in section 7.3? Only include uniquely different packages – not variation on a package type.
6. What is the difference between MIPS and DMIPS?

7.11   Exercises

1. The Ubicom is a microcontroller used in the newer BASIC Stamps and the Javelin Stamp. This MCU was not reviewed in the chapter. Research the Ubicom product line and write a few paragraphs with an accompanying table similar to the format used in this chapter.
2. Using the answer in review question #1, describe each new package and provide a photo.

Chapter 8
Ethernet Applications and the Future of the Microcontroller

8.1 Objectives

1. Introduction to the TCP/IP protocol and related protocols necessary to build a web server.
2. Review an advanced networking project freely available on the Circuit Cellar® website that details how to build an 8051 web server.[1] This project uses a midrange 8051 and custom, partially implemented protocol stack.
3. Review the Silicon Labs Ethernet Development kit. This kit uses a high-end 8051, SI's TCP/IP Configuration Wizard and a third-part protocol stack.
4. Demonstrate the use of AJAX technology to dynamically update data in a web page.
5. Consider the future of the microcontroller.

This chapter introduces the TCP/IP protocol and then presents two networked applications for the 8051. One project is a "from scratch" hobbyist design and the other is a "rapid prototype" design that uses more expensive hardware and third-party software. This chapter concludes with a look forward to the future of the microcontroller and embedded software development.

8.2 Introduction

In the last chapter we surveyed the microcontroller landscape from an 8051 vantage point. We discovered a diverse range of silicon from 8-bit to 32-bit microcontrollers manufactured by a variety of companies. We also reviewed the large range of choices within the 8051 family itself.

Traditionally, microcontrollers work in isolation or at best are connected to a serial network like RS232, RS485 or CAN Bus. Increasingly, however, there is a need to connect devices to the Ethernet especially when they need to communicate

---

[1] http://www.circuitcellar.com/library/print/0902/brady/index.htm

K. Qian et al., *Embedded Software Development with C,*
DOI 10.1007/978-1-4419-0606-9_8, © Springer Science+Business Media, LLC 2009

back to a server, for example, over long distances. Many of the microcontrollers surveyed in Chapter 7 can be easily connected. Even the 8-bit Rabbit family has a range of RCMs (Rabbit Control Modules) with Ethernet along with the free Dynamic C compiler, IDE, TCP/IP stack and HTTP server. In the embedded world, though, manufacturing cost and power consumption are usually the overriding factors and unlike desktop computing, a microcontroller should only be powerful enough to accomplish its task. With that in mind, part of the 8051 family is at the low-end of the cost scale, but is it powerful enough to run a web server or even process TCP/IP packets for that matter?

The answer to both questions is a qualified "Yes". The 8051 family typically has a small memory, so some models don't have enough code memory for the TCP/IP stack and HTTP server or enough data memory to hold and process an Ethernet packet. Silicon Laboratories has an Ethernet Development Kit (ETHERNET-DK)[2] for one of their MCUs (C8051F120) that uses SI's own CP2200 Ethernet controller. This kit features the CMX-MicroNet protocol stack. There is nothing wrong with this MCU or Ethernet controller choice, but it does use a high-end 8051. If you want to use a cheaper model – the C8051F005 used in the book, for example – what options do you have?

That's where the Circuit Cellar® project comes in. In September, 2002 (Issue 146) this venerable magazine published a project by Jim Brady – Build Your Own 8051 Web Server. For this project, Jim used a Cygnal C8051F005. Does this part number look familiar? It's the same 8051 model used in this book. Silicon Laboratories acquired Cygnal in 2003[3]. This chapter presents the Circuit Cellar® project as a case study of an advanced 8051 application. For more detail, browse over to the Circuit Cellar® website and read the full article. It is also available as a PDF and a ZIP file with full C source code[4].

8.3 Introduction to TCP/IP

A comprehensive study of TCP/IP is beyond the scope of this book, but a brief introduction will be provided before examining the case study. TCP/IP is an industry acronym that stands for Transmission Control Protocol / Internet Protocol. It is a suite of communications protocols that is used by the Internet and Local Area Networks (LANs) as described by RFC 1122[5]. TCP and IP were the first two protocols developed, but there are many more in the suite. TCP/IP was originally developed in the 1970s by DARPA (Defense Advanced Research Projects Agency), a United States government agency. The TCP/IP protocol was ultimately used for

---

[2] https://www.silabs.com/products/mcu/Pages/EmbeddedEthernetDK.aspx

[3] http://www.8052.com/news.phtml?NEWSID=33

[4] http://www.circuitcellar.com/library/print/0902/brady/6.htm

[5] http://tools.ietf.org/html/rfc1122

the ARPANET, the world's first Wide Area Network (WAN) which slowly evolved into the Internet.

The TCP/IP suite (or Internet Protocol Suite) has four layers (listed from lowest to highest):

1. Link Layer (closest to the wire)
2. Internet Layer
3. Transport Layer
4. Application Layer (closest to the user)

Each layer encapsulates one or more protocols and provides services to the layer above it. The lowest layer deals directly with the hardware as we'll see in the case study.

This four-layer model should not be confused with the seven-layer OSI model. Many academics and practitioners have mapped TCP/IP into the OSI model, but it is not part of the standard. The IETF (Internet Engineering Task Force) maintains the standard and states that TCP/IP is not OSI compliant.

8.3.1 Link Layer

The link layer encapsulates the protocols defined by the IETF that are necessary at the lowest layer of the stack. This layer is closest to the hardware. The protocols at this level handle the links between network nodes. The protocols include:

1. MAC (Media Access Control). This is the low level driver for the physical network which could be Ethernet, FDDI, ISDN, DSL or any other type of network.
2. ARP (Address Resolution Protocol)
3. RARP (Reverse Address Resolution Protocol)

These are the protocols for IPv4. The newer IPv6 includes protocols which won't be discussed here. For the case study, Jim Brady implemented ARP which is needed to serve a web page. The web server must be able to send and receive ARP requests. The MAC driver is for the Ethernet network and includes the interface to the Cirrus Logic Ethernet controller discussed in section 8.4.

8.3.2 Internet Layer

The internet layer encapsulates the protocols needed for transmitting packets across network boundaries from the originating host to the destination host. This routing is accomplished using an IP (Internet Protocol) address. Individual networks are connected together using gateways. The most important protocol in this layer is the IP protocol. There are two versions of the IP protocol – IPv4 and IPv6. Jim Brady implemented the IPv4 protocol for the 8051 web server.

The internet layer has three functions regardless of the protocol:

1. Send incoming packets from the link layer up to the appropriate protocol in the transport layer.
2. Send outgoing packets from the transport layer to the appropriate protocol in the link layer after selecting the destination for the packet.
3. Detect errors.

The internet layer is not responsible for the reliable transmission of packets. That is the job of the transport layer. The IP protocol is responsible for creating packets using data from the transport layer and transmitting packets from the source host to the destination using an IP address. It is also responsible for receiving packets and using a checksum to detect corruption (in IPv4 at least).

8.3.3   Transport Layer

The transport layer is responsible for sending and receiving application data as packets over the network. The first transport layer protocol was TCP (Transmission Control Protocol). This is a connection-oriented protocol designed for the reliable communication of packets. A simpler protocol, UDP (User Datagram Protocol) is connectionless and not as reliable. In other words, packets could be lost. It is up to the protocol in the Application Layer to ensure reliable transmission of UDP packets. This is not necessary if using the TCP protocol which provides error detection and requests for retransmission of packets using ARQ (Automatic Repeat Request). Jim Brady partially implemented the TCP and UDP protocols.

8.3.4   Application Layer

The application layer consists of all the high level protocols used by an application. For example, a web server will use HTTP (Hypertext Transfer Protocol) to server up HTML web pages. To serve up a secure page, the web server would also use SSL (Secure Sockets Layer). A mail server will use SMTP (Simple Mail Transfer Protocol) to send email messages. An email client will use POP3 (Post Office Protocol) or IMAP (Internet Message Access Protocol). A web service may use SOAP (Simple Object Access Protocol). There are many more. See Figure 8.1 for a view of UDP data as it moves from the application layer to the link layer. Additionally, see Table 8.1 for a diagram showing which protocols are in each layer.

On traditional operating systems like Microsoft Windows or UNIX, these protocols are in the application programs and are not part of the TCP/IP service. This may not be true for embedded applications. Jim Brady's code, for example, integrates the TCP/IP code with the rest of the application code. The source is modular, but there is no distinct API (Application Program Interface). On the other hand, embedded applications may use a third-party protocol stack such as CMX-MicroNet. In this

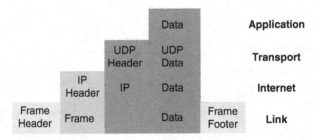

Fig. 8.1 Data traveling through the stack

Table 8.1 Typical protocols found in each layer

Application	HTTP	FTP	SMTP	DHCP	DNS	SOAP
Transport		TCP			UDP	
Internet	IPv4		IPv6		ICMP	
Link	MAC		ARP		RARP	

case, there may still be a single application, but the programmer would use the library much like the Winsock API in Windows. It is not necessary for the programmer to understand all of the details – just use the library functions. Both approaches are examined in this chapter. We will start with Jim Brady's custom implementation and then move to Silicon Labs third-party library approach.

8.4 Circuit Cellar® Project

Jim Brady's web server hardware consists of three chips, but only two are really necessary (See Figure 8.2):

1. Silicon Labs 8051 MCU (C8051F005). The development kit was used, so the 3.3VDC power supply is not shown.
2. Cirrus Logic (CS8900A) Ethernet controller.
3. Maxim RS232 line driver/receiver (MAX232). This chip was intended for troubleshooting, but it was not needed because of the JTAG interface which facilitates in-circuit debugging from the Keil or Silicon Labs IDE.

8.4.1 The Role of the Ethernet Controller

The Cirrus Logic Ethernet controller is the physical interface to the Ethernet network. Its job is to send and receive frames. As you can see from the circuit diagram, the 8051 reads a 16-bit word from the Ethernet controller using ports P2 and P3. The 8051 polls the Ethernet controller for new frames instead of waiting for an interrupt

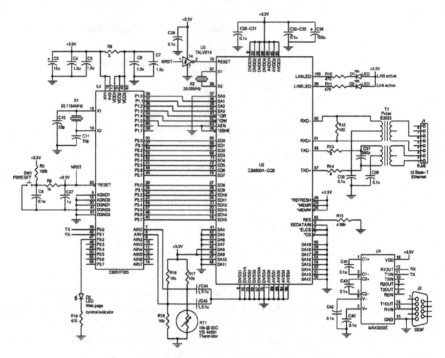

Fig. 8.2 Circuit Cellar® 8051 Web Server Diagram

because the Ethernet controller has a larger memory than the 8051 and it may not be possible to transfer the entire buffer to the 8051 as recommended by the Cirrus Logic datasheet. Additionally, the Ethernet Controller is configured to receive frames that are either broadcast or directed to the controller's MAC address. If the 8051 attempted to process every packet on a busy network, it may become overwhelmed. The Cirrus Logic Ethernet controller acts as both a memory buffer and filter for the 8051 MCU.

8.4.2 The Role of the 8051

The 8051 has 32K of FLASH memory for code and 2.4K of RAM for data. That is a small memory footprint for handling complicated networking protocols, but Jim was able to fit it in. The code space was also used for unchanging data – like a web page with an image. See Table 8.2.

To conserve memory, Jim only partially implemented the TCP/IP protocols, and left many more out that you would find in a desktop or server operating system. For example, Jim had to implement the basic functionality of ARP, TCP, IP and HTTP. The TCP protocol, however, has many optional features that help improve performance and reliability. Jim opted not to implement features for congestion avoidance and best time-out estimation. Another way he conserved memory was to

Table 8.2 Code Memory Usage

Description	Code Space
TCP/IP (partial implementation)	9.5KB
Web page with image	7.0KB
HTTP Server	3.8KB
ARP Protocol	2.5KB
C Library	2.9KB
UDP Protocol	1.4KB
CS8900 I/O	1.0KB
RS-232	0.5KB
Analog	0.3KB
Priority Task Switcher	0.3KB
Total	**29.2KB**

Fig. 8.3 Circuit Cellar®
project web page

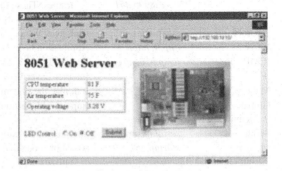

use dynamic memory allocation for storing frame data with the C library functions *malloc()* and *free()*.

The web page itself displays the CPU temperature, ambient air temperature and operating voltage. To demonstrate HTML form submission and the server's CGI (Common Gateway Interface) capabilities, there are controls to turn the 8051 development kit's LED on and off. See Figure 8.3 for a screenshot of the web page.

8.4.3 Code Organization

The source code is very modular[6]. The list of files roughly outlines the architecture of the application.

This example has shown a hobbyist approach to building an 8051-based web server. Modest hardware was used and the software was written from scratch. The next example shows an approach that an engineering company may take – the use of third-party software libraries and development kits. Additionally, a more powerful

---

[6] http://www.circuitcellar.com/library/print/0902/brady/6.htm

Table 8.3 Circuit Cellar® Project Code Organization

Module Name	Source Files	Description
Analog	*analog.h, analog.c*	Reads analog inputs for this application including an external temperature sensor, the on-chip temperature sensor and operating voltage.
ARP	*arp.h, arp.c*	Address Resolution Protocol. This link layer protocol translates IP addresses to hardware (i.e. MAC) addresses.
8051 Header	*c8051.h*	Standard definitions for the 8051 MCU.
Cirrus	*cirrus.h, cirrus.c*	Interface to Cirrus Logic Ethernet controller. Calls assembler routines included in *cs8900.h*.
Checksum	*cksum.h, cksum.a51*	Computes internet checksum. This is an assembler routine that can be called as a function by the C program.
CS8900	*cs8900.h, cs8900.a51*	Low level functions to read and write both words and frames. These functions are assembler routines that can be called as functions by the C program.
Ethernet	*eth.h, eth.c*	Link layer protocol (i.e. MAC driver for Ethernet).
HTTP	*http.h, http.c*	Application layer HTTP protocol (i.e. the web server).
ICMP	*icmp.h, icmp.c*	Internet Layer ICMP protocol (i.e. ping).
IP	*ip.h, ip.c*	Internet Layer IPv4 protocol.
Main	*main.c*	Initialize the system and start the main program loop.
Global definitions	*net.h*	Important definitions and structures for the application.
Serial	*serial.h, serial.c*	Serial communications module.
Memory Initialization	*startup.a51*	Assembly code that runs once during processor initialization to clear the memory and set the stack pointers.
TCP	*tcp.h, tcp.c*	TCP protocol.
Timers	*timers.h, timers.c*	8051 timer initialization and interrupt handling.
UDP	*udp.h, udp.c*	UDP protocol.
Web Page	*webdoc.c*	Web page, image and HTTP headers are hard-coded in this file.

8051 is used in the development kit, presumably because more powerful hardware is needed for Ethernet communications. Jim Brady has shown, however, that is not always the case.

8.5 Silicon Labs Ethernet Development Kit

The Silicon Labs Ethernet Development Kit (ETHERNETDK) is featured in this section. As of this writing, it cost $119 – definitely more expensive than the development kit used throughout this book.

This section will verify the operation of the hardware and then take the reader step-by-step through one of the example applications included with the kit. It will go one step further and demonstrate the use of AJAX (Asynchronous JavaScript And XML) technology to dynamically update data in the web page.

8.5.1 Stage 1: Setup the Hardware

The Silicon Labs Ethernet Development kit comes with the following:

1. C8051F120 Target Board and power supply
2. AB4 Ethernet Development Board
3. USB Debug Adapter and cables
4. Cat 5 patch cable
5. Two CDs with development software, documentation and other third-party tools
6. Quick start guides

Setup is simple. Plug the Ethernet board into the MCU target board and plug in the power supply. The red power light should illuminate. Plug the Ethernet cable into your local switch or use a cross-over cable to connect the board directly to your PC. Finally, plug the USB Debug adapter into the MCU target board and the PC USB port. See Figure 8.4 for an overhead view of the two boards connected together.

8.5.2 Stage 2: Setup the Software and Checkout the Hardware

Follow the quick start guide, *C8051FxxxDK Development Kit Quick-Start Guide for Kits Featuring the USB Debug Adapter*. It shows you step-by-step and pictorially how to install the development software and run the sample *"Blinky"* project. This is a good test for the MCU target board; however it doesn't test the Ethernet development board.

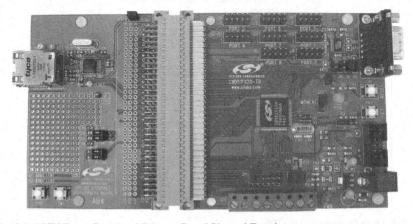

Fig. 8.4 MCU Target Board and Ethernet Board Plugged Together

To check the operation of the Ethernet development board, we will run a simple web server project that displays a static HTML page. In fact, this code can also be generated using the TCP/IP Configuration Wizard which will be introduced in the next section. To download and run the simple web server project, follow the directions below:

1. Open the Silicon Laboratories IDE.
2. Open the following project in the Examples folder by selecting **Project→Open Project** from the menu bar:
   C:\Silabs\MCU\Examples\C8051F12x_F13x\Ethernet\HTTP\web-server-1\web_server_1.wsp
3. In the IDE File View window, double-click on the *mn_userconst.h* file. The header file should display in the main source code window.
4. Change the constant *IP_SRC_ADDR* to the desired IP address. You should choose an unused address that can be seen (i.e. pinged) by your PC. For example, my PC is connected to a wireless switch. Its address was automatically assigned using DHCP to 15.15.15.104. I chose an unused address, 15.15.15.25, for the MCU address. You can check for an unused address by first "pinging"

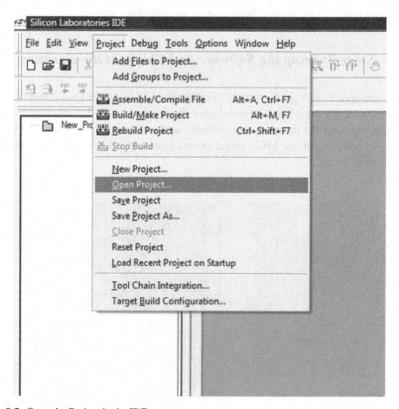

Fig. 8.5 Open the Project in the IDE

that address. To ping an address, open a command (i.e. black box) window and type "ping 15.15.15.25". If the address is already used, you will see reply messages.

5. Build the project by selecting **Project→Rebuild Project** from the menu bar. After this step, you should have zero errors and warnings shown in the lower build window.

6. Connect to the MCU by selecting **Debug→Connect** from the menu bar.

7. Download the object file to the MCU by clicking the **Download Code** button on the toolbar.

8. Start the program by clicking the Green **Go** button on the toolbar.

9. At this point, the web server is running. You should be able to ping the address you selected.

10. Test the web server by opening your web browser and going to the IP address defined in step #4. In our example, we entered http://15.15.15.25. See the screenshot in Figure 8.8.

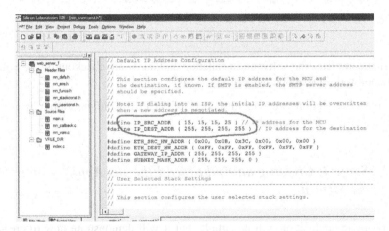

Fig. 8.6 Change the IP Address

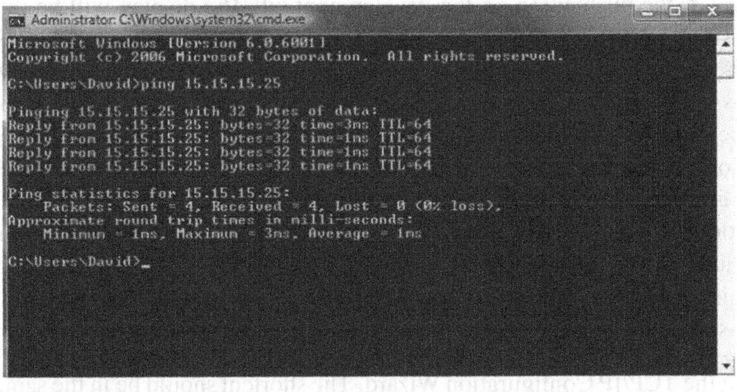

Fig. 8.7 Ping the 8051 Web Server

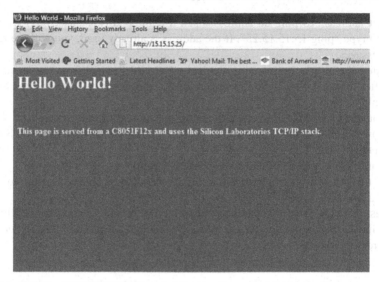

Fig. 8.8 Web Page from 8051 Web Server

11. This completes the software installation and hardware checkout of the Silicon
    Laboratories Development Kit.

In the next section, we will introduce the TCP/IP Configuration Wizard and
develop a project from scratch.

8.5.3 Stage 3: Creating an Embedded Ethernet Application using the Wizard

This example application will be simple, but it will demonstrate how to create a
basic project with a web server. The default web page will be modified to display
the status of the pushbutton on the development kit. The display will be dynamic
using a simple AJAX (Asynchronous JavaScript and XML) technique. Finally, a C
function will be written to return the status of the pushbutton. The function will be
called as a server-side CGI (Common Gateway Interface) routine by the web page.
If you've done web programming before, these terms are probably familiar to you.
If not, don't worry because they will be explained later as the example unfolds.

The first step in creating an Ethernet enabled application is to generate the
framework for your project using the TCP/IP Configuration Wizard. In Si-Labs
terminology this is referred to as generating the "firmware" for the application.
After this step, your application specific code can be added. The following is a
step-by-step procedure for generating an application using the wizard

1. Start the TCP/IP Configuration Wizard. The shortcut should be in the same Start
   menu folder as the IDE. You should see the window shown in Figure 8.9.

Fig. 8.9 TCP/IP Configuration Wizard

2. Select the communications adapter and MCU for your hardware configuration. In this case, they are already selected for the Silicon Lab kit – the CP220x and C8051F120x, respectively.
3. The next step is to determine which Application Layer protocols you need for your application. For this example, we will choose HTTP for a web server, and NetFinder to set the IP address manually over Ethernet. When you check these protocols, notice that needed Transport Layer protocols are automatically checked as well. For example, HTTP needs the TCP protocol and NetFinder needs the UDP protocol.
4. Try clicking on different protocols. Notice that there are different settings in the right-hand side of the Wizard's window. For example, if you click on the SMTP protocol, you can set the IP address of the mail server. When you generate the project, these settings will be included as constants in the C code.
   Notice that the different layer categories in the wizard match the four layers discussed earlier in the chapter.
5. Save this configuration by selecting **File→Save** on the menu bar.

Bug Note: As of this writing, the wizard doesn't save the configuration correctly. The NetFinder option is not saved and will be unchecked if you open the configuration file.

6. Generate the C code by selecting **File→Generate Project** on the menu bar. A *Browse for Folder* dialog will be displayed. Choose a folder or create a new one for the project. When finished a *Project Generated Successfully* dialog will be displayed.

7. Close the TCP/IP Configuration Wizard.

8. Open an Explorer window and look at the generated code. The project header and C files are in the folder. Source files with a prefix of "mn" are for the CMX MicroNet TCP/IP stack.

9. There is another folder inside the project folder, *VFILE_DIR*, which contains the default web page. The web page file, *index.html*, has two accompanying files, *index.h* and *index.c*. These two C files were generated by the HTML2C application also included in the folder. The application converts the HTML text file into a C byte array. The web page "array" is physically stored in 8051 code memory. See Figure 8.10. When you add your own web page or modify the default page, you must run the HTML2C utility to update the C source files.

10. Let's compile the project and download it to the 8051. Open the Silicon Labs IDE project file called *TCPIP_Project.wsp*. Examine the source tree in the left File View window. It is an organized view of the project folder.

11. Select **Project→Rebuild** Project from the menu bar. There should be no errors or warnings in the lower build window.

12. Select **Debug→Connect** from the menu bar.

13. Click the **Download Code** button on the toolbar or press **ALT-D** to download the code into the 8051. A dialog will display the progress of the download.

14. If everything went well, you should see the **Go** button on the toolbar light up green. Click this button or select **Debug→Go** from the menu bar to run the application.

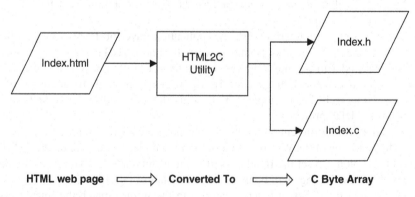

Fig. 8.10 HTML2C Conversion Utility

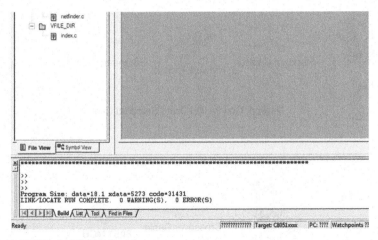

Fig. 8.11 IDE Build Window Results

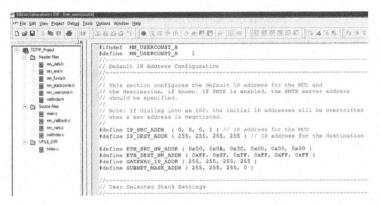

Fig. 8.12 Manually set the IP address in the C source code

15. Before we can view the web page, we must set the IP addresses. For this project, there are two ways to set the address. The first method is to manually set it in the source code, recompile the project and download it to the MCU again. To do this, open the source file, *mn_userconst.h*, and change the constant, *IP_SRC_ADDR*, to an unused address. See Figure 8.12.

This address completely depends on your network setup. If you have the MCU plugged into a network switch, the address should be in the same subnet as your PC's address. For example, if your PC has an address of 192.168.0.5, then a possible address for the MCU would be 192.168.0.25 – as long as it isn't in use by another device. If you connect your computer directly to the MCU, use a crossover cable. With this type of connection, virtually any address can be used as long as they are in the same subnet. For example, 192.168.0.1 and 192.168.0.2 are good choices. See Figure 8.13.

The other way to set the IP address is to use the NetFinder utility. That's why we included the protocol in our project. This utility transmits a multicast packet

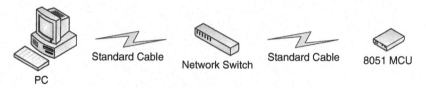

Network Connection Using Standard Cables

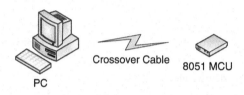

Network Connection Using Crossover Cable

Fig. 8.13 Network Cable Connections

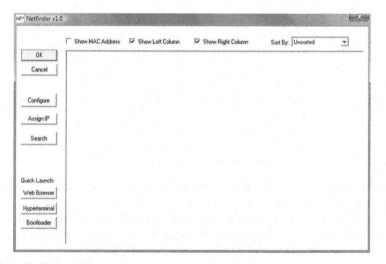

Fig. 8.14 NetFinder Utility

and waits for responses from devices on the network that support the NetFinder protocol. A multicast packet is one that is send to all possible addresses within a subnet. The MCU will respond back to the NetFinder utility with information about its IP address and a few other statistics. If the IP address is configured, the MCU will be green; otherwise it will be yellow.

To find devices on the network, click the **Search** button. See Figure 8.14.

To set the IP address, click on the **Assign IP** button.

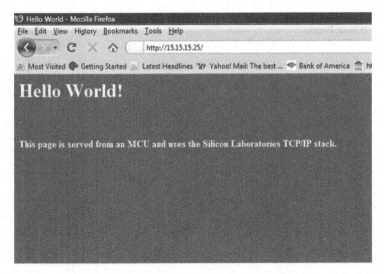

Fig. 8.15 Default web page for our project

Bug Note: As of this writing, the NetFinder utility does not work properly with Windows Vista.

Troubleshooting Tip: By default, the NetFinder utility uses port 3040 to send and receive UDP packets. If you have a firewall, this UDP port must be opened up or the utility will not find any devices on the network.

16. Once the IP address is assigned, open your web browser and navigate to the address. You should see the default web page which is the same as the one from the earlier example when we were testing the hardware and software. See Figure 8.15.

17. The next step is to modify the C code and add a function to return the state of the pushbutton on the kit. Before we add this simple function, though, let's take a look at the generated application's structure and see where the code should be placed.

Figure 8.16 shows the main processing loop for a TCP/IP wizard project. The *mn_server()* function handles all network functions including web browser requests, ping and the virtual file system. Application code can be added in three places:

Interrupt Service Routines: Application code that requires precise timing should be placed in an ISR. Interrupt sources include external pin, timer overflow and ADC end-of-conversion.

Callback Functions: Application code that does not require precise timing should be placed in a callback function. These callbacks are from the TCP/IP library. They are used to signal certain events to the application code that include "packet received" and "server idle".[7]

---

[7] See Silicon Laboratories Application Note 237 (AN237), the TCP/IP Library Programmers Guide, for a complete list of callback functions.

Fig. 8.16 Main Application
Loop for TCP/IP Project

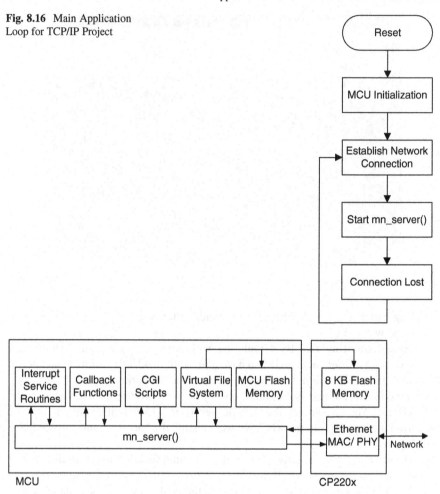

Fig. 8.17 Application Code Model for TCP/IP Project[8]

Common Gateway Interface (CGI) Scripts: CGI is a standard protocol for communications between a web browser and web server. This is where we will place our code. CGI functions can be called from a web browser. Data can be sent to a CGI function and the CGI function can dynamically create new web pages that are sent back to the web browser.

See Figure 8.17 for a graphical view of the TCP/IP Application Code Model.

18. We will add a new CGI function to the *main.c* source file. The function will be called *read_switch( )*. It will return a "1" if switch P3.7 on the development kit is pressed and "0" otherwise. We could return an entire web page with the result

---

[8] Silicon Laboratories Application Note (AN292).

embedded in it. In this case, though, we will return a minimal amount of data for performance reasons.

The web page will use an AJAX technique to call the function periodically and update the web page. The function will be called asynchronously (i.e. in the background) four times per second. A manual refresh of the web page will not be necessary.

Here is the code to include libraries needed by the CGI function:

```
#include "stdio.h"
#include "string.h"
```

Here is the function prototype that should be added to the Function Prototypes section:

```
void read_switch(PSOCKET_INFO socket_ptr);
```

The return data will be passed to the web server using the PSOCKET_INFO structure.

Here is the initialization code that should be placed above the *main()* function:

```
#define PRESSED 0
sbit SW1 = P3^7; // 0 = PRESSED
static byte html_buffer[32]; //used by read_switch()
```

Here is the function definition that can be added at the end of the *main.c* file:

```
void read_switch(PSOCKET_INFO socket_ptr)
{
   if (SW1 == PRESSED)\\
   {
     // Write the result to a buffer.
     sprintf(html_buffer, "%i", 1);
   }
   else
   {
     // Write the result to a buffer.
     sprintf(html_buffer, "%i", 0);
   }
   // Transfer result to socket
   socket_ptr->send_ptr = html_buffer;
   socket_ptr->send_len = strlen(html_buffer);
   // Return from the CGI script
   return;
}
```

To make this new function visible to a web browser, it must be added to the Virtual File System. This code should be added in the *main()* function before the call to the *mn_server()* function:

```
// Add CGI Script to Virtual File System
mn_pf_set_entry((byte*)"read_switch", read_switch);
```

The first parameter is the name that the web browser will use to call the function. The second parameter is a function pointer to the new CGI script.

19. The last step before compiling and downloading the project is to make sure that there are enough empty slots in the Virtual File System. Open the header file, *mn_userconst.h*, and check the *num_post_funcs* constant. Its value should be greater than or equal to the number of CGI scripts in the application. In our case, the value should be 1 or greater.

20. Compile the project, download the code and run it in the IDE.

    Tip: The Keil compiler is an evaluation edition with limits on the size of your program. If your application won't compile due to this limitation, rerun the TCP/IP Configuration Wizard and leave out the NetFinder protocol to save memory.

21. Verify that the web server is working by using your browser. The default web page should be displayed.

22. Before we modify the default web page to display the switch state, let's check the CGI function manually. Open your web browser and enter the following URL (adjust the IP address for your setup): **http://15.15.15.25/read_switch?/**

    Bug Note: You may be wondering why the trailing backslash is necessary. The Silicon Labs AN292 document states that the URL should be "http://15.15.15. 25/read_switch?". The server's response to this, however, is the error message "Bad Request". If you put **any** character after the question mark, it will work correctly.

    The web page displayed should show a "0" or a "1" depending on whether the pushbutton is pressed. To see changes in state, you will have to manually refresh the browser window. See Figure 8.18.

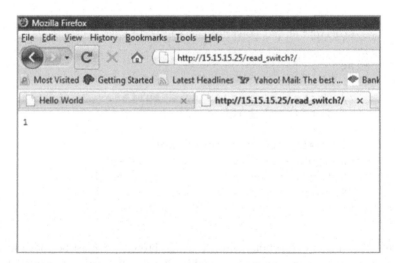

Fig. 8.18 read_switch() return result – the pushbutton is pressed

23. The next step is to modify the default web page to display the state of the push-button. Here is the HTML (HyperText Markup Language) code for the default web page:

```
<html>
<head><title>Hello World</title><head>

<body bgcolor="green" text="white" link="yellow" vlink="red"
alink="blue">
<h1>Hello World!</h1>    <br><br>
<B>This page is served from an MCU and uses the Silicon Laboratories
TCP/IP stack.</B>
</body>
</html>
```

24. The modified HTML code is shown below:

```
<html>
<head>
<title>Chapter 8 AJAX Demo</title>
<script language = "javascript">
var XMLHttpRequestObject = false;
if (window.XMLHttpRequest) {
XMLHttpRequestObject = new XMLHttpRequest();
} else if (window.ActiveXObject) {
XMLHttpRequestObject = new ActiveXObject("Microsoft.XMLHTTP");
}
function getData(dataSource, divID)
{
if (XMLHttpRequestObject) {
var obj = document.getElementById(divID);
XMLHttpRequestObject.open("GET", dataSource);
XMLHttpRequestObject.onreadystatechange = function()
{
if (XMLHttpRequestObject.readyState == 4 &&
XMLHttpRequestObject.status == 200) {
if (XMLHttpRequestObject.responseText == '1')
obj.innerHTML = "The pushbutton is PRESSED!"
else
obj.innerHTML = "The pushbutton is NOT PRESSED!"
}
}
XMLHttpRequestObject.send(null);
}
}
function readSwitch()
{
getData("http://15.15.15.25/read_switch?/", "SwitchState");
}
setInterval ( "readSwitch()", 250);
</script>
</head>
<body bgcolor="blue" text="white" link="yellow" vlink="red"
alink="blue">
<h1>AJAX Demo</h1>
<br>
<h2>Display state of Silicon Labs development kit pushbutton (P3.7)</h2>
<br>
```

```
<div id="SwitchState">  <h2>???</h2></div>
</body>
</html>
```

25. The new web page must first be converted to a C byte array as discussed earlier in the chapter. Open the VFILE_DIR folder and run the *Update* batch file. You can also run the *html2c* application and manually open *index.html* to do the conversion. See Figure 8.19.

26. Rebuild the project and download the code to the 8051. Run the project and browse to the web page. Try pressing the pushbutton. The text on the web page should change to indicate the status of the pushbutton. The web page update rate is set to 250ms (i.e. 4 updates per second). See Figure 8.20.

Fig. 8.19 HTML2C Conversion Utility

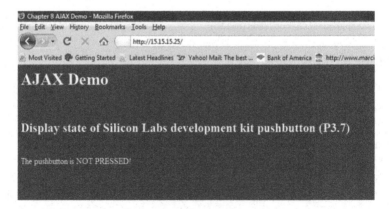

Fig. 8.20 Completed TCP/IP Project Web Page

8.5.4   Stage 4: The uWeb Embedded Web Server

We will wrap up the evaluation of the ETHERNETDK kit with a look at their main demonstration application – the uWeb server. This demo has multiple web pages, images, a Java temperature display applet and a CGI script to view and control the status of an LED. This example is too large to compile with the evaluation Keil compiler, so a pre-compiled HEX file is included instead. The source files are still included, though, for study and compilation using a fully licensed compiler.

Use the following procedure to download and run the demo:

1. Open the IDE and connect to the 8051 MCU.
2. Select **Debug→Download Object File** from the menu. A Download dialog will be displayed.
3. Click the **Browse** button. A File dialog will be displayed.
4. Navigate to the *SiLabs\MCU\Examples\C8051F12x_13x\Ethernet\HTTP\ uWeb* folder and select the *uweb_f120_3_1.hex* file.
5. Click the **Download** button. The pre-compiled hex file will be downloaded to the MCU.
6. Click the Run button on the IDE toolbar. The green LED on the MCU board will flash indicating that the IP address needs to be configured.
7. Notice that the link light on the network (i.e. RJ45) connector is not on. There is no way to configure the IP address using DHCP or NetFinder. For this application, the IP address must be configured using the serial port. The ETHERNETDK kit came with a serial cable. Connect this cable to your PC and the MCU.
8. Make sure that J6 and J9 have jumpers installed. They are installed by default from the factory. See Figure 8.21 for jumper locations.
9. Open HyperTerminal or another similar type of application and connect to the MCU using the following parameters: **9600, 8, N, 1**. Make sure that flow control is set to **none**.
   Vista Compatibility Note: HyperTerminal is not bundled with Windows Vista. A free version is still available from the original company – Hilgraeve, Inc.[9] Another option is to use a popular (and free) program called PuTTY which now has support for serial ports[10].
10. You should see a "Press any key to continue" message repeated over and over until you press a key.
11. Press any key and you will be prompted to enter and confirm an IP address. When finished you should see a screen similar to the one in Figure 8.22. The flashing LED will now remain on and the RJ45 link light will also come on.
12. Open your web browser and navigate to the 8051's IP address. You should see the web page shown in Figure 8.23. Try toggling the LED and click the link to display a second web page with a temperature chart Java applet.

---

[9] www.hilgraeve.com

[10] http://www.chiark.greenend.org.uk/~sgtatham/putty/

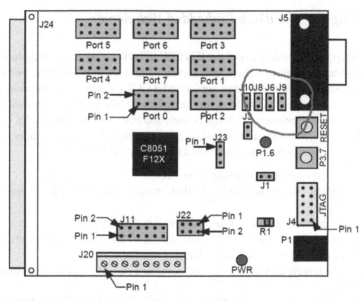

Fig. 8.21 8051 MCU Board Jumper Locations

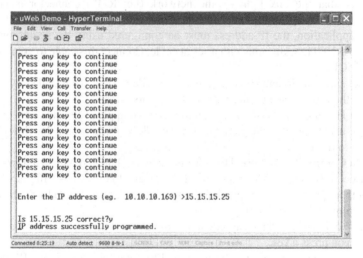

Fig. 8.22 Serial Port Configuration of uWeb

8.6   The Future of the Microcontroller

This chapter ends with a look at the future of the microcontroller. The chapter's focus has been on Ethernet networking of an MCU. There are many other types of networks prevalent in the embedded world, but Ethernet and the TCP/IP protocol

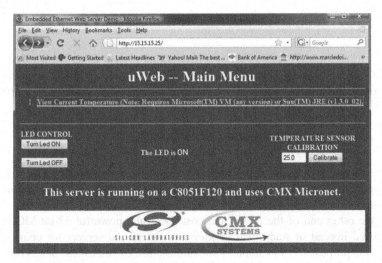

Fig. 8.23 uWeb Server Main Page

stack are the most ubiquitous. Trying to predict the future of something is fun to do, but is usually wrong.

8.6.1 Dominant Market Share

For the future of the microcontroller, we can look at statistics and trends. It is a fact that microcontrollers make up most of the microprocessor market share. This includes 8, 16 and 32-bit microcontrollers. Industry focus is currently on 32-bit microcontrollers and DSP (Digital Signal Processor) chips, but the volume is still with 8 and 16-bit MCUs.

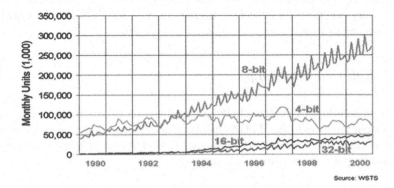

8.6.2 Networking, Networking, Networking

A major trend for MCU's of all types is networking such as Ethernet, wireless Ethernet, Zigbee mesh networks and CAN bus. As we have shown in this chapter, even a mid-range, 8-bit 8051 can run a web server. This networking trend will continue.

8.6.3 New Applications and Role Blurring

As cost drops, MCUs are also finding new applications in areas where discrete semiconductors and electromechanical devices have flourished. One such area is the "smart switch". This trend is still in its infancy.

On the other end of the power and cost spectrum, powerful 32-bit MCUs are being used instead of traditional desktop computers and servers for control and monitoring purposes. For example, some of these MCUs run Linux; others run Java Virtual Machines and Smalltalk Virtual Machines.

VMware announced recently that it will develop a tiny virtual machine for cell phones that will sit on top of a variety of microprocessors. The idea is to write your application for the VM without having to worry about constantly changing hardware. This is not a new idea, of course, and we also have to be careful about the distinction between a microprocessor and a microcontroller.

8.6.4 Better and Cheaper Development Tools

Another trend is the sophistication of compilers and integrated development environments. Ten years ago, the In-Circuit Emulator (ICE) was common and expensive. Today, they have been largely replaced by simulators and JTAG-based debuggers.

Open source projects provide tools for the hobbyist that would not have been available ten years ago. For example, there is an open-source C compiler called the Small Device C Compiler (SDCC) for the 8051, PIC and other platforms[11]. This trend is very beneficial for education. Barriers to entry for hardware and software are continuing to drop.

8.6.5 Roll your Own Chips

Another trend is to use FPGA (Field Programmable Gate Array) chips to create your own custom microcontroller. FPGAs can be programmed using a language called VHDL (VHSIC hardware description language). IP (Intellectual Property) cores are available for purchase or you can roll your own[12].

---

[11] http://sdcc.sourceforge.net/

[12] http://www.opencores.org/projects.cgi/web/8051/overview

With this flexibility, functions traditionally found only in software are making their way down into silicon. The TCP/IP protocol stack is a good example.

8.7 Review Questions

1. What does the acronym TCP/IP stand for?
2. What American government funded network evolved into the Internet?
3. Name the two RFC documents that describe the four communications layers of the TCP/IP stack.
4. Name the four communication layers as described in the RFC documents.
5. What relationship does this four-layer model have with the seven-layer OSI model?
6. Which layer does the MAC protocol reside in?
7. Which layer does the IP protocol reside in?
8. Which layer does the TCP protocol reside in?
9. Which layer do protocols like HTTP and FTP reside in?
10. What does the acronym UDP stand for?
11. Why is UDP considered a higher performance protocol than TCP?
12. Which Ethernet controller chip was used in the Circuit Cellar® project?
13. For the Circuit Cellar® project, is the data path between the 8051 and Ethernet controller 8 bits wide or 16 bits wide?
14. What does the acronym DHCP stand for?
15. What is DHCP used for?
16. What is the Silicon Labs NetFinder protocol used for?
17. After creating a project using the Silicon Labs TCP/IP Configuration Wizard, where are the three places that you can put your application code?
18. What is the name of the function used to add a CGI script to the Virtual File System?
19. After making a change to a web page, what utility must be run before recompiling the C project?

8.7.1 Key to the review questions:

1. Transmission Control Protocol / Internet Protocol.
2. ARPANET.
3. RFC1122 and RFC1123. If you ever have to implement a TCP/IP protocol stack, these two documents should be read completely.
4. From the wire to the user – Link, Internet, Transport and Application.
5. There is no official relationship according to the IETF, although TCP/IP has been mapped into the OSI model by academics and practitioners.
6. The Link layer.
7. The Internet layer.

8. The Transport layer.
9. The Application layer.
10. User Datagram Protocol.
11. It is higher performance because it is connectionless and doesn't have error checking. There is less overhead involved in packet transmission and reception.
12. Cirrus Logic (CS8900A) Ethernet controller.
13. 16 bits wide.
14. Dynamic Host Configuration Protocol.
15. Automatic assignment of an IP address.
16. Automatic discovery of MCUs on the network and manual assignment of IP addresses.
17. Interrupt Service Routines (ISRs), Callback Functions, CGI Scripts.
18. mn_pf_set_entry().
19. The HTML2C conversion utility must be run to convert the HTML text file to a C byte array which will be stored in Flash code memory.

8.8 Exercises

8.8.1 Note: The ETHERNETDK kit is needed for these exercises.

1. Connecting serial devices to the Ethernet is a common application in both commercial and manufacturing environments. Create a simple serial-to-Ethernet application that uses the 8051 UART and UDP protocol. **Hint:** Start with the UDP sample application. Hardcode all configuration setting.
2. The evaluation version of the Keil compiler is a problem for developing larger applications for the hobbyist or student. Study application note AN198 and integrate the SDCC into the Silicon Labs IDE. For this exercise, you must successfully compile, download and run the Blinky project discussed in the Application Note.
3. Using the SDCC compiler configured in Exercise #2, convert, compile, download and run the uWeb application included as an example in the kit. This is the application that included the pre-compiled HEX file because it was too large for the evaluation version of the Keil compiler.

Chapter 9
Hands-On Labs

Overview

This chapter includes eight labs using the Silicon Labs Microcontroller Development Kit (C8051F005):

- **Lab 1:** Getting Started with the 8051 (reading and writing ports).
- **Lab 2:** Intro to the 7-segment LED (direct driven and decoded).
- **Lab 3:** Intro to A/D conversion using a light sensor (start using ISRs).
- **Lab 4:** Intro to the keypad.
- **Lab 5:** Intro to D/A conversion using a speaker.
- **Lab 6:** RS232 serial communication.
- **Lab 7:** Intro to the LCD display.
- **Lab 8:** Advanced RS232 communications (software/hardware handshaking).

Up to this point you have been using the Keil IDE. It is an excellent environment with sophisticated tools like hardware simulation and performance profiling. For the labs, however, we will be using the Silicon Laboratories IDE that comes with the development kit. If you prefer to keep using the Keil IDE, feel free to do so.

If you find the first few labs difficult, refer to Appendix D. It offers a more detailed and gentle introduction to building the labs. This appendix showcases a variation of Lab 2.

K. Qian et al., *Embedded Software Development with C*,
DOI 10.1007/978-1-4419-0606-9_9, © Springer Science+Business Media, LLC 2009

9.1   Lab 1: Getting Started with The 8051 – Reading and Writing Ports

Purpose:

This lab has two main purposes:

1. Become familiar with the Silicon Laboratories 8051 development kit and IDE (Integrated Development Environment).
2. Understand the need to "debounce" a mechanical switch in software.

Assignment:

In this lab, you will do the following:

1. Setup the development kit for the first time.
2. Install the Silicon Laboratories IDE if you are using your own computer.
3. Write a simple C program that counts the number of times a button is pressed and displays it on an LED "bar graph".
4. Observe the effect of removing the switch debounce code from the program.

Equipment:

1. Si Labs 8051 development kit
2. (4) LED (2.1V, 25mA or similar)
3. (4) 100Ω resistor
4. (1) Momentary pushbutton

Schematic:

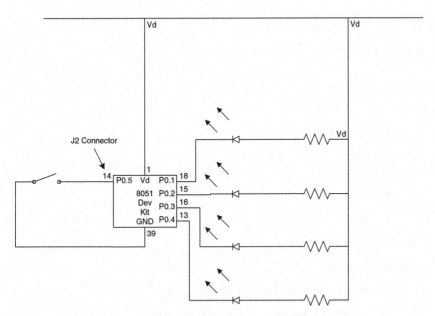

Fig. 9.1 8051 port driven LEDs with current limiting resistors

Program:

Program Listing for Lab 1

```
//------------------------------------------------------------------------------
// Lab1.c (Reading and Writing Ports)
//------------------------------------------------------------------------------
//
// This program uses 4 LEDs to create a "bar graph" and one momentary button
// for input.
// An LED will light up with each press of the button.
//
// This lab demonstrates reading and writing ports on the 8051. It also
// demonstrates the need for debouncing a mechanical switch. Try commenting
// out the debounce function call to see what I mean.
//
//
// Tool chain: KEIL Eval 'c'
//

//------------------------------------------------------------------------------
// Includes
//------------------------------------------------------------------------------
```

```c
#include "C8051F000.h"
#include <stdio.h>

//------------------------------------------------------------------------------
// Function PROTOTYPES
//------------------------------------------------------------------------------

void Debounce( const unsigned int ms );

//------------------------------------------------------------------------------
// Global CONSTANTS
//------------------------------------------------------------------------------
#define ON 0
#define OFF 1
#define PRESSED 0

sbit LED1 = P0 ^ 1;
sbit LED2 = P0 ^ 2;
sbit LED3 = P0 ^ 3;
sbit LED4 = P0 ^ 4;
sbit SW1 = P0 ^ 5; // 0 = PRESSED

//------------------------------------------------------------------------------
// MAIN Routine
//------------------------------------------------------------------------------
void main( void )
    {
    // by default the C8051005 runs at 2MHz (1 osc cycles)

    int count = 0; // number of times switch pressed

    XBR2 = 0x40;   // Enable crossbar and weak pull-ups
    PRT0CF = 0x1E; // Enable P0 outputs 1-4 as push-pull outputs

    WDTCN = 0xde;  // disable watchdog timer
    WDTCN = 0xad;

    while (1)
        {
        // read switch input
        if (SW1 == PRESSED)
            {
            Debounce(200); // wait for the mechanical switch to settle down

            while (SW1 == PRESSED); // loop until released

            count++;
            }

        // update LED display
        switch( count )
            {
            case 0:
                LED1 = OFF;
                LED2 = OFF;
                LED3 = OFF;
                LED4 = OFF;
                break;

            case 1:
```

```
                     LED1 = ON;
                     LED2 = OFF;
                     LED3 = OFF;
                     LED4 = OFF;
                     break;

             case 2:
                     LED1 = ON;
                     LED2 = ON;
                     LED3 = OFF;
                     LED4 = OFF;
                     break;

             case 3:
                     LED1 = ON;
                     LED2 = ON;
                     LED3 = ON;
                     LED4 = OFF;
                     break;

             case 4:
                     LED1 = ON;
                     LED2 = ON;
                     LED3 = ON;
                     LED4 = ON;
                     break;

             default: // button press number 5 or any invalid count value
                     count = 0;
                     LED1 = OFF;
                     LED2 = OFF;
                     LED3 = OFF;
                     LED4 = OFF;
             }
     }
  }

//-----------------------------------------------------------------------------
// Functions
//-----------------------------------------------------------------------------

//-----------------------------------------------------------------------------
// Debounce()
//-----------------------------------------------------------------------------
//
// Simple delay loop to "debounce" mechanical switch
//
// TODO: Inner loop is un-calibrated, but close. This is left for Exercise 1
// Default oscillator setpoint is 2MHz (1 osc cycles).
//
//
void Debounce( const unsigned int ms )
     {
     unsigned int x, y;

     for ( x = 0; x <= ms; x++ )
         {
         for ( y = 0; y <= 200; y++ );
         }
     }
```

Step-By-Step:

1. Setup your Si Labs development kit and install the IDE using the fold-out quick start guide included with the kit.
2. *Tip:* The poster includes steps to compile and download a test program. It also has debugging tips using the IDE. ˙
3. Wire up the circuit as shown in the schematic. See photo of completed project.
4. Open the IDE and close any open projects.
5. *Tip:* To close an open project, select *Project* → *Close Project* from the menu.
6. Your lab instructor should provide you with the source files for this lab. Open the project file **Lab1.c** by selecting *File* → *Open File* from the menu.
7. *Tip:* If you don't have the source files, create a new file and enter the source code provided in the Program section of this lab.
8. Compile and download the program using the following steps:

   - Select *Project* → *Rebuild Project* from the menu or use the toolbar button.
   - Select *Debug* → *Connect* from the menu or use the toolbar button.
   - Click the *Download Code* button on the toolbar.
   - If your code is correct and you have a good connection to your board, the program should compile, connect and download to the 8051.

9. Press the green *RUN* button on the toolbar to run your program.
10. Press the momentary pushbutton that you wired into your circuit. Each press of the button should light up one LED on the "bar graph". On the fifth button press, all four LEDs should turn off and the process will repeat.
11. Comment out the Debounce function call from the program. Recompile, download and test the program again. Answer lab question #1.
12. Uncomment the Debounce function call and incrementally lower the time delay until you observe the effect of mechanical bounce. Answer lab question #2.

Lab Wrap-up:

1. Demonstrate that your program works to the lab instructor.

Fig. 9.2 Photograph of Lab 1

Questions:

1. What happened when you removed the debounce function call from the program?
2. When lowering the debounce time delay, at what value did you start to observe the effect of the switch's mechanical bounce?

Additional Exercises (Optional):

1. Using the performance profile tool in the Keil IDE verify the accuracy of the Debounce function. If it is not correct, calculate the correct inner loop value or experiment to find the correct value.

9.2 Lab 2: Intro to the 7-segment LED (Direct Driven and Decoded)

Purpose:

This lab has three main purposes:

1. Become familiar with the BCD to 7-segment LED decoder/driver chip.
2. Examine different ways to solve a problem and determine the pros and cons of each approach.
3. Introduce a more advanced approach for creating time delays.

Assignment:

In this lab, you will do the following:

1. Wire up a directly driven 7-segment LED to the 8051 microcontroller.
2. Write a C program to make the LED count from 0–9.
3. Modify the circuit to use a BCD to 7-segment LED decoder/driver chip.
4. Modify the C program to work with the decoder chip.

Equipment:

1. Si Labs 8051 development kit
2. (1) 7-segment LEDs (**common cathode**)
3. (7) 100Ω resistor
4. (1) HEF4511B BCD to 7-segment LED decoder/driver chip
5. (1) 5VDC voltage regulator (7805)

The 7-segment LED is an integrated circuit package with seven Light Emitting Diodes (LEDs) in it. The diagram in Figure 9.3 shows the layout for each LED segment. Additionally, Figure 9.6 shows the wiring diagram for the LED.

The 5VDC voltage regulator is needed to power the decoder chip. The voltage that's available on the development kit board is only 3.3VDC. The input voltage to the regulator is the 9VDC on the P1 barrel connector.

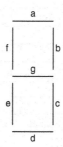

Fig. 9.3 LED Segments

Schematic:

The connection diagram for the 7-segment LED is shown in the table below:

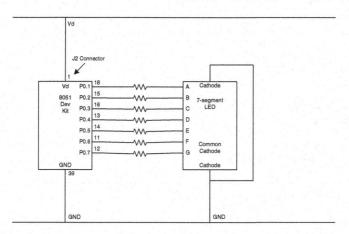

Fig. 9.4 Directly driven 7-segment LED

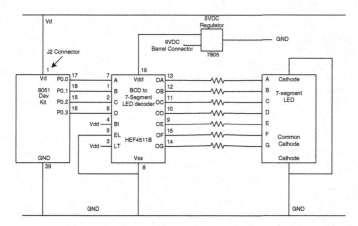

Fig. 9.5 7-segment LED driven by decoder chip

1 Anode F	Top	14 Anode A
2 Anode G		13 Anode B
3 No pin		12 Common
4 Common		11 No pin
5 No pin		10 No pin
6 Anode E		9 Anode RHDP
7 Anode D	Bottom	8 Anode C

Fig. 9.6 Wiring diagram for 7-segment LED

Program:

Program Listing for Lab 2 (direct driven)

```
//-----------------------------------------------------------------------
// Lab2.c (Intro 7-segment LEDs that are directly driven and decoded)
//-----------------------------------------------------------------------
//
// Tool chain: KEIL Eval 'c'
//

//-----------------------------------------------------------------------
// Includes
//-----------------------------------------------------------------------
#include "C8051F000.h"
#include <stdio.h>

//-----------------------------------------------------------------------
// 16-bit SFR Definitions for 'F00x
//-----------------------------------------------------------------------

sfr16 DP = 0x82;      // data pointer
sfr16 RCAP2 = 0xca;  // Timer2 capture/reload
sfr16 T2 = 0xcc;      // Timer2

//-----------------------------------------------------------------------
// Function PROTOTYPES
//-----------------------------------------------------------------------

void DisplayNumber( int number );
void OSCILLATOR_Init( void );
void PORT_Init( void );
void Wait_MS( unsigned int ms );

//-----------------------------------------------------------------------
// Global CONSTANTS
//-----------------------------------------------------------------------
#define ON 1
#define OFF 0

#define SYSCLK 16000000 // Internal crystal oscillator frequency
#define DELAY 1000       // 1 second delay
```

```
//-----------------------------------------------------------------------
// MAIN Routine
//-----------------------------------------------------------------------

void main( void )
    {
    int count = 0;

    // Initialize device
    WDTCN = 0xde;       // disable watchdog timer
    WDTCN = 0xad;

    OSCILLATOR_Init(); // Initialize oscillator
    PORT_Init();       // Initialize crossbar and GPIO

    while (1)
        {
        DisplayNumber(count);
        Wait_MS(DELAY); // Wait for 1 second
        count++;

        if (count == 10)
            count = 0;
        } // while
    }

//-----------------------------------------------------------------------
// Functions
//-----------------------------------------------------------------------
//-----------------------------------------------------------------------
// OSCILLATOR_Init
//-----------------------------------------------------------------------
//
// Return Value : None
// Parameters   : None
//
//
//-----------------------------------------------------------------------
void OSCILLATOR_Init( void )
    {
    OSCXCN = 0x00; // external oscillator off
    OSCICN = 0x07; // internal oscillator set to 16MHz
    }

//-----------------------------------------------------------------------
// PORT_Init
//-----------------------------------------------------------------------
//
// Return Value : None
// Parameters   : None
//
// This function configures the crossbar and GPIO ports.
//
//-----------------------------------------------------------------------

void PORT_Init( void )
```

```
    {
    XBR2 = 0x40;    // Enable crossbar and weak pull-ups
    PRT0CF = 0xFE; // Enable P0 outputs 1-7 as push-pull outputs
    P0 = 0x00;      // Turn off P0 outputs (init)
    }

//----------------------------------------------------------------------
// DisplayNumber()
//----------------------------------------------------------------------
//
// Display a number on the 7-segment LED
//
//
void DisplayNumber( int number )
    {
    switch( number )
        {
        case 0:
            P0 = 0x7E; // Segments A,B,C,D,E,F ON
            break;

        case 1:
            P0 = 0x0C;
            break;

        case 2:
            P0 = 0xB6;
            break;

        case 3:
            P0 = 0x9E;
            break;

        case 4:
            P0 = 0xCC;
            break;

        case 5:
            P0 = 0xDA;
            break;

        case 6:
            P0 = 0xF8;
            break;

        case 7:
            P0 = 0x0E;
            break;

        case 8:
            P0 = 0xFE;
            break;

        case 9:
            P0 = 0xCE;
            break;
```

```
        default:
            P0 = 0x00; // All segments OFF
        }
    }

//-------------------------------------------------------------------------
// Wait_MS
//-------------------------------------------------------------------------
//
// Return Value : None
// Parameters:
//   1) unsigned int ms - number of milliseconds of delay
//        range is full range of integer: 0 to 65335
//
// This routine inserts a delay of <ms> milliseconds.
//
//-------------------------------------------------------------------------
void Wait_MS( unsigned int ms )
    {

    CKCON &= ~0x20;                 // use SYSCLK/12 as timebase

    RCAP2 = -(SYSCLK / 1000 / 12); // Timer 2 overflows at 1 kHz
    T2 = RCAP2;

    ET2 = 0;                        // Disable Timer 2 interrupts

    TR2 = 1;                        // Start Timer 2

    while (ms)
        {
        TF2 = 0;       // Clear flag to initialize

        while (!TF2); // Wait until timer overflows

        ms--;          // Decrement ms
        }

    TR2 = 0;           // Stop Timer 2
    }
```

Step-By-Step:

1. Wire up the circuit for the directly driven 7-segment LED as shown in Figure 9.1.
2. Open the IDE and close any open projects.
3. Your lab instructor should provide you with the source files for this lab. Open the project file **Lab2.c** by selecting *File* → *Open File* from the menu.
4. Compile and download the program using the following steps:

   – Select *Project* → *Rebuild Project* from the menu or use the toolbar button.
   – Select *Debug* → *Connect* from the menu or use the toolbar button.
   – Click the *Download Code* button on the toolbar.

Fig. 9.7 Photo of Lab 2 (direct driven)

Fig. 9.8 Photo of Lab 2 (BCD decoder)

- If your code is correct and you have a good connection to your board, the program should compile, connect and download to the 8051.

5. Click the green **RUN** button on the toolbar to run your program.
6. The LED should count from 0–9 repeatedly.
7. Modify the circuit by adding the decoder chip as shown in Figure 9.2.
8. Modify the *DisplayNumber()* function to output a BCD number to 4 pins (P0.0 – P0.3) instead of the "7-segment" byte to 7 pins (P0.1–P0.7).

Lab Wrap-up:

1. Demonstrate that your program works to the lab instructor using the following steps:

   - Demonstrate that the program will count from 0-9 for the directly driven 7-segment LED.
   - Demonstrate that the program will count from 0-9 for the decoded 7-segment LED.

Questions:

1. What are the advantages and disadvantages of these two approaches for driving a 7-segment LED? Think about this question in terms of design requirements and the potential cost of manufacturing a product.
2. This lab used a different method for creating time delays than Lab 1. Describe the difference between the two approaches.
3. Do either of the two time delay methods use ISRs (Interrupt Service Routines)?
4. If you used a common anode 7-segment LED instead of a common cathode one, what change would you have to make in the wiring and the code?

Additional Exercises (Optional):

1. Create a "Lamp Test" feature. This feature will turn on all LEDs when the push button (P1.7) on the 8051 development board is pressed. First, modify the C program only to implement this feature. Second, use the LT input on the decoder chip to implement this feature. What are the pros and cons of these two approaches? Which approach is the most economical for a manufactured product?
2. Add a second decoder chip and 7-segment LED to the circuit. Modify the existing C program to count from 0–99.
3. Create a spreadsheet showing the bit pattern of the LED byte for the direct-driven LED. Show each byte for the numbers 0 through 9. Use the 7-segment LED diagram as a guide and verify the C code.

9.3   Lab 3: Intro to A/D Conversion Using a Light Sensor

Purpose:

This lab has three main purposes:

1. Become familiar with the A/D (Analog to Digital) capabilities of the 8051 microcontroller.
2. Learn the basics of using ISRs (Interrupt Service Routines) with the C language.
3. Learn how to write C functions to scale and calibrate the light sensor.

Assignment:

In this lab, you will do the following:

1. Wire up a light sensor to an analog input.
2. Wire up a 7-segment LED to display a value (0–9) based on the intensity of the light in the room.
3. Write a simple C program that reads the analog signal from the light sensor and displays an intensity value on the 7-segment LED.
4. Add a feature to put the program in "calibrate" mode to set the min and max light intensities.

Equipment:

1. Si Labs 8051 development kit
2. (1) 7-segment LED (**common cathode**, 1.7VDC, 20mA)
3. (7) 100Ω resistor
4. (1) Flashlight or other suitable light source
5. (1) Photo IC for brightness control (PNA4603H-ND)
6. (1) 5VDC voltage regulator (7805)

The 5VDC voltage regulator is needed to power the decoder chip. The voltage that's available on the development kit board is only 3.3VDC. The input voltage to the regulator is the 9VDC on the P1 barrel connector.

Schematic:

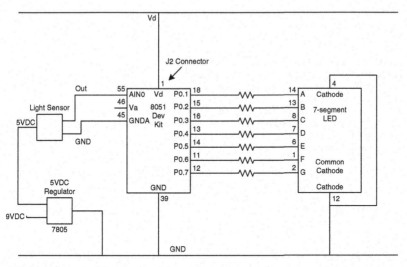

Fig. 9.9 Light Intensity Meter

Program:

Program Listing for Lab 3

```
//----------------------------------------------------------------------------
// Lab3.c (Intro to A/D Conversion Using a Light Sensor)
//----------------------------------------------------------------------------
// Copyright (C) 2008 David den Haring
//
// Tool chain: KEIL Eval 'c'
//

//----------------------------------------------------------------------------
// Includes
//----------------------------------------------------------------------------
#include "C8051F000.h"
#include <stdio.h>

//----------------------------------------------------------------------------
// Function PROTOTYPES
//----------------------------------------------------------------------------

void DisplayNumber( int number );
void OSCILLATOR_Init( void );
void PORT_Init( void );
void ADC0_Init( void );
void TIMER3_Init( int counts );
void ADC0_ISR( void );
void Wait_MS( unsigned int ms );
```

```
int Scale( long measurement );
void Calibrate();

//-----------------------------------------------------------------------------
// 16-bit SFR Definitions for 'F00x
//-----------------------------------------------------------------------------

sfr16 DP = 0x82;      // data pointer
sfr16 TMR3RL = 0x92; // Timer3 reload value
sfr16 TMR3 = 0x94;    // Timer3 counter
sfr16 ADC0 = 0xbe;    // ADC0 data
sfr16 ADC0GT = 0xc4; // ADC0 greater than window
sfr16 ADC0LT = 0xc6; // ADC0 less than window
sfr16 RCAP2 = 0xca;   // Timer2 capture/reload
sfr16 T2 = 0xcc;      // Timer2
sfr16 DAC0 = 0xd2;    // DAC0 data
sfr16 DAC1 = 0xd5;    // DAC1 data

//-----------------------------------------------------------------------------
// Global CONSTANTS
//-----------------------------------------------------------------------------
#define ON   1
#define OFF 0
#define PRESSED 1

#define SYSCLK       16000000 // Internal crystal oscillator frequency
#define SAMPLE_RATE  50000    // Sample frequency in Hz
#define INT_DEC      256      // Integrate and decimate ratio
#define SAR_CLK      2500000  // Desired SAR clock speed

#define SAMPLE_DELAY 50       // Delay in ms before taking sample

sbit SW1 = P1 ^ 7;            // 1 = PRESSED (Located on dev kit board.
                             // Calibration button)

//-----------------------------------------------------------------------------
// Global Variables
//-----------------------------------------------------------------------------

long Result; // ADC0 decimated value

//-----------------------------------------------------------------------------
// MAIN Routine
//-----------------------------------------------------------------------------
void main( void )
    {

    // calibrate state (0 = off, 1 = min value, 2 = max value)
    int calibrate_state = 0;
    long measurement; // Measured voltage in mV

    // Initialize device
    WDTCN = 0xde;                        // disable watchdog timer
    WDTCN = 0xad;

    OSCILLATOR_Init();                   // Initialize oscillator
    PORT_Init();                         // Initialize crossbar and GPIO
    // Initialize Timer3 to overflow at sample rate
```

```
    TIMER3_Init(SYSCLK / SAMPLE_RATE);
    DisplayNumber(0);

    ADC0_Init();                         // Init ADC

    ADCEN = 1;                           // Enable ADC

    EA = 1;                              // Enable global interrupts

    while (1)
        {
        EA = 0; // Disable interrupts

        // The 12-bit ADC value is averaged across INT_DEC measurements.
        // The result is then stored in Result, and is right-justified
        // The measured voltage applied to AIN 0.1 is then:
        //
        //                          Vref (mV)
        //    measurement (mV) =   --------------- * Result (bits)
        //                          (2^12)-1 (bits)
        //measurement =  Result * 2430 / 4095; // calculate mV

        measurement = Result;// just get raw value (0-4095)
        // scale measurement to 0-9 value on LED and display it
        DisplayNumber(Scale(measurement));

        if (calibrate_state > 0)
            Calibrate(); // handle min/max light intensity calibration

        EA = 1;// Re-enable interrupts

        Wait_MS(SAMPLE_DELAY);// Wait 50 milliseconds before taking another
        sample
        } // while
    }

//-----------------------------------------------------------------------------
// Functions
//-----------------------------------------------------------------------------
//-----------------------------------------------------------------------------
// OSCILLATOR_Init
//-----------------------------------------------------------------------------
//
// Return Value : None
// Parameters   : None
//
//
//-----------------------------------------------------------------------------
void OSCILLATOR_Init( void )
    {
    OSCXCN = 0x00; // external oscillator off
    OSCICN = 0x07; // internal oscillator set to 16MHz
    }

//-----------------------------------------------------------------------------
// PORT_Init
//-----------------------------------------------------------------------------
//
```

```
// Return Value : None
// Parameters   : None
//
// This function configures the crossbar and GPIO ports.
//
//-----------------------------------------------------------------------------

void PORT_Init( void )
    {
    XBR2 = 0x40;    // Enable crossbar and weak pull-ups
    PRT0CF = 0xFE;  // Enable P0 outputs 1-7 as push-pull outputs
    P1 |= 0xFF;     // Set P1 latches to '1' for use as inputs
    P0 = 0x00;      // Turn off P0 outputs (init)
    }

//-----------------------------------------------------------------------------
// DisplayNumber()
//-----------------------------------------------------------------------------
//
// Display a number on the 7-segment LED
//
//
void DisplayNumber( int number )
    {
    switch( number )
        {
        case 0:
            P0 = 0x7E; // Segments A,B,C,D,E,F ON
            break;

        case 1:
            P0 = 0x0C;
            break;

        case 2:
            P0 = 0xB6;
            break;

        case 3:
            P0 = 0x9E;
            break;

        case 4:
            P0 = 0xCC;
            break;

        case 5:
            P0 = 0xDA;
            break;

        case 6:
            P0 = 0xF8;
            break;

        case 7:
            P0 = 0x0E;
            break;
```

```
        case 8:
            P0 = 0xFE;
            break;

        case 9:
            P0 = 0xCE;
            break;

        default:
            P0 = 0x00; // All segments OFF
        }
    }

//-----------------------------------------------------------------------------
// TIMER3_Init
//-----------------------------------------------------------------------------
//
// Return Value : None
// Parameters   :
//   1)  int counts - calculated Timer overflow rate
//                        range is postive range of integer: 0 to 32767
//
// Configure Timer3 to auto-reload at interval specified by <counts> (no
// interrupt generated) using SYSCLK as its time base.
//
//-----------------------------------------------------------------------------

void Timer3_Init( int counts )
    {
    TMR3CN = 0x02; // Stop Timer3; Clear TF3;
    // use SYSCLK as timebase
    TMR3RL = -counts; // Init reload values
    TMR3 = 0xffff;    // set to reload immediately
    EIE2 &= ~0x01;    // disable Timer3 interrupts
    TMR3CN |= 0x04;   // start Timer3
    }

//-----------------------------------------------------------------------------
// ADC0_Init
//-----------------------------------------------------------------------------
//
// Configure ADC0 to use Timer3 overflows as conversion source, to
// generate an interrupt on conversion complete, and to use left-justified
// output mode.  Enables ADC end of conversion interrupt. Leaves ADC disabled.
//
//-----------------------------------------------------------------------------

void ADC0_Init( void )
    {
    ADC0CN = 0x04; // ADC0 disabled; normal tracking
    // mode; ADC0 conversions are initiated
    // on overflow of Timer3; ADC0 data is
    // right-justified
    REF0CN = 0x07; // enable temp sensor, on-chip VREF,
    // and VREF output buffer
    AMX0SL = 0x00;    // Select AIN0 as ADC mux output
    ADC0CF = 0x80;    // ADC conversion clock = SYSCLK/16
    ADC0CF &= ~0x07; // PGA gain = 1
```

```
    EIE2 |= 0x02;      // enable ADC interrupts
    }

//-----------------------------------------------------------------------------
// ADC0_ISR
//-----------------------------------------------------------------------------
//
// Here we take the ADC0 sample, add it to a running total <accumulator>, and
// decrement our local decimation counter <int_dec>.  When <int_dec> reaches
// zero, we post the decimated result in the global variable <Result>.
//
//-----------------------------------------------------------------------------
void
ADC0_ISR( void )
interrupt

15
    {
    static unsigned int_dec = INT_DEC; // Integrate/decimate counter
    // we post a new result when
    // int_dec = 0
    static long accumulator = 0L; // Here's where we integrate the
    // ADC samples

    ADCINT = 0; // clear ADC conversion complete
    // indicator

    accumulator += ADC0; // Read ADC value and add to running
    // total
    int_dec--;                 // Update decimation counter

    if (int_dec == 0)        // If zero, then post result
        {
        int_dec = INT_DEC; // Reset counter
        Result = accumulator >> 8;
        accumulator = 0L;  // Reset accumulator
        }
    }

//-----------------------------------------------------------------------------
// Wait_MS
//-----------------------------------------------------------------------------
//
// Return Value : None
// Parameters:
//   1) unsigned int ms - number of milliseconds of delay
//                         range is full range of integer: 0 to 65335
//
// This routine inserts a delay of <ms> milliseconds.
//
//-----------------------------------------------------------------------------
void Wait_MS( unsigned int ms )
    {

    CKCON &= ~0x20;                 // use SYSCLK/12 as timebase

    RCAP2 = -(SYSCLK / 1000 / 12); // Timer 2 overflows at 1 kHz
```

```
    T2 = RCAP2;

    ET2 = 0;                        // Disable Timer 2 interrupts

    TR2 = 1;                        // Start Timer 2

    while (ms)
        {
        TF2 = 0;        // Clear flag to initialize

        while (!TF2); // Wait until timer overflows

        ms--;           // Decrement ms
        }

    TR2 = 0;            // Stop Timer 2
    }

//------------------------------------------------------------------------------
// Scale()
//------------------------------------------------------------------------------
//
// Return Value : int
//
// This routine scales the mV measure to a 0-9 value to display on the LED
//
//------------------------------------------------------------------------------
int Scale( long measurement )
    {
    // scale raw value (0-4095) to scaled value (0-9)
    return measurement*9 / 4095;
    }

//------------------------------------------------------------------------------
// Calibrate()
//------------------------------------------------------------------------------
//
// Return Value : none
//
// This routine uses the LED display and pushbutton on the development kit
// to calibrate the min and max values for the light intensity.
//
//
//------------------------------------------------------------------------------
void Calibrate()
    {
    // TODO by student
    }
```

Step-By-Step:

1. Wire up the circuit as shown in the schematic. Remember that this lab uses a **common cathode** 7 segment LED.
2. Open the IDE and close any open projects.

3. Your lab instructor should provide you with the source files for this lab. Open the project file **Lab3.c** by selecting *File → Open File* from the menu.
4. Compile and download the program using the following steps:

   – Select *Project → Rebuild Project* from the menu or use the toolbar button.
   – Select *Debug → Connect* from the menu or use the toolbar button.
   – Click the *Download Code* button on the toolbar.
   – If your code is correct and you have a good connection to your board, the program should compile, connect and download to the 8051.

5. Click the green *RUN* button on the toolbar to run your program.
6. At this point, the Scale() and Calibrate() functions are not finished, but the program works well enough to measure values in the debugger.
7. Click the red *STOP* button on the toolbar.
8. Go to the line in the program where the variable *measurement* is calculated.
9. Right-click on the measurement variable and select *Add Measurement To Watch → Default → Default Type.*
10. Click the green *Run* button again and use the watch variable to determine the min and max variables for the light intensity. Try to obtain as great a range as possible between low light conditions and the maximum brightness of your light source.
11. Using the numbers obtained in step 10, finish writing the Scale() function to display the min and max light variables as 0 to 9 on the LED.

Lab Wrap-up:

1. Demonstrate that your program works to the lab instructor using the following steps:

   – Demonstrate that the program will display the min and max values on the LED.

Questions:

1. Describe how the ISR (Interrupt Service Routine) works in this program.
2. What is the advantage of using ISRs in embedded software?

Additional Exercises (Optional):

1. A simple framework for a calibration feature is already in the program. This includes the prototype function *Calibrate()*, the variable *calibrate_state* and

Fig. 9.10 Photo of Lab 3

the pushbutton SW1. Finish writing the *Calibrate()* function. Here is how the calibrate procedure should work:

– Press the pushbutton once to put the program into a calibrate mode for the minimum value.
– The function should turn on the bottom segment D to indicate MIN calibration.
– Adjust light intensity to the minimum value and press the button again. Light at this intensity should now display as a 0 on the LED when not in calibrate mode. A lower light intensity should still display a 0. Negative values will not be supported.
– The program will now turn on the top segment A to indicate MAX calibration.
– Adjust light intensity to the maximum value and press the button again. Light at this intensity should now display as a 9 on the LED when not in calibrate mode. A higher light intensity should still display a 9.
– The program will exit calibrate mode and display values in the newly calibrated range.

9.4   Lab 4: Intro to the Keypad

Purpose:

This lab has two main purposes:

1. Introduction to interfacing a keypad to an 8051 microcontroller.
2. Become familiar with using manufacturer datasheets to determine how to wire up a circuit. All datasheets can be found at the Digikey website.

Assignment:

In this lab, you will do the following:

1. Wire up an industry standard keypad to the 8051 microcontroller. This keypad was not intended for a breadboard, but it is an easy modification to make it fit.
2. Wire up an LED to the 8051 microcontroller to display the last key press.
3. Write a C program to display the last key press.

Equipment:

1. Si Labs 8051 development kit
2. (1) 12-key keypad (GH5008-ND)
3. (1) 7-segment LED
4. (7) 100 ohm or 220 ohm resistors

Fig. 9.11 The GrayHill keypad used for Lab 4

Schematic:

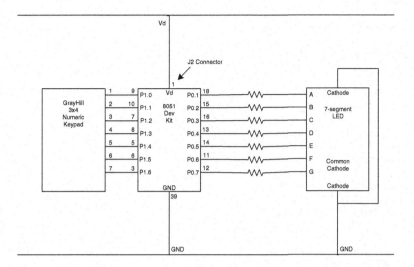

Program:

Program Listing for Lab 4

```
//--------------------------------------------------------------------
// Lab4.c (Intro to the Keypad)
//--------------------------------------------------------------------
// Copyright (C) 2008 David den Haring
//
// Tool chain: KEIL Eval 'c'
//

//--------------------------------------------------------------------
// Includes
//--------------------------------------------------------------------
#include "C8051F000.h"
#include <stdio.h>

//--------------------------------------------------------------------
// Function PROTOTYPES
//--------------------------------------------------------------------

unsigned char ReadKeypad( void );
void DisplayNumber( int number );
void OSCILLATOR_Init( void );
void PORT_Init( void );

//--------------------------------------------------------------------
// Global CONSTANTS
//--------------------------------------------------------------------
```

```
#define ON   1
#define OFF  0

#define SYSCLK       16000000 // Internal crystal oscillator
                              // frequency
#define DELAY   20            // 20ms delay

//-------------------------------------------------------------------
// Global Variables
//-------------------------------------------------------------------

sbit row1 = P1 ^ 0;
sbit row2 = P1 ^ 1;
sbit row3 = P1 ^ 2;
sbit row4 = P1 ^ 3;
sbit col1 = P1 ^ 4;
sbit col2 = P1 ^ 5;
sbit col3 = P1 ^ 6;


//-------------------------------------------------------------------
// MAIN Routine
//-------------------------------------------------------------------
void main( void )
    {
    unsigned char count = 0;

    // Initialize device
    WDTCN = 0xde;       // disable watchdog timer
    WDTCN = 0xad;

    OSCILLATOR_Init(); // Initialize oscillator
    PORT_Init();       // Initialize crossbar and GPIO

    while (1)
        {
        count = ReadKeypad();

        if (count != 255)
            DisplayNumber(count);
        } // while
    }

//-------------------------------------------------------------------
// Functions
//-------------------------------------------------------------------
//-------------------------------------------------------------------
// OSCILLATOR_Init
//-------------------------------------------------------------------
//
// Return Value : None
// Parameters   : None
//
//
```

```
//-------------------------------------------------------------------
void OSCILLATOR_Init( void )
    {
    OSCXCN = 0x00; // external oscillator off
    OSCICN = 0x07; // internal oscillator set to 16MHz
    }

//-------------------------------------------------------------------
// PORT_Init
//-------------------------------------------------------------------
//
// Return Value : None
// Parameters   : None
//
// This function configures the crossbar and GPIO ports.
//
//-------------------------------------------------------------------

void PORT_Init( void )
    {
    XBR2 = 0x40;   // Enable crossbar and weak pull-ups
    PRT0CF = 0xFE; // Enable P0 outputs 1-7 as push-pull outputs
    P0 = 0x00;     // Turn off P0 outputs (init)
    PRT1CF = 0x0F; // Enable P1 outputs 0-3 as push-pull outputs
    col1 = 1;      // Set for reading
    col2 = 1;
    col3 = 1;
    }

//-------------------------------------------------------------------
// DisplayNumber()
//-------------------------------------------------------------------
//
// Display a number on the 7-segment LED
//
//
void DisplayNumber( unsigned char number )
    {
    switch( number )
        {
        case 1:
            P0 = 0x0C;
            break;

        case 2:
            P0 = 0xB6;
            break;

        case 3:
            P0 = 0x9E;
            break;

        case 4:
            P0 = 0xCC;
```

```
                   break;

           case 5:
               P0 = 0xDA;
               break;

           case 6:
               P0 = 0xF8;
               break;

           case 7:
               P0 = 0x0E;
               break;

           case 8:
               P0 = 0xFE;
               break;

           case 9:
               P0 = 0xCE;
               break;

           case 11:        // digit 0 on keypad
               P0 = 0x7E; // Segments A,B,C,D,E,F ON
               break;

           default:
               P0 = 0x00; // Invalid number -- all segments OFF
           }
       }

   unsigned char ReadKeypad()
       {
       unsigned char i, k, key = 0;
       k = 1;
       P1 = 0xFF;        // all rows on, all columns set for input

       for ( i = 0; i < 4; i++ )
           {                //loop for 4 rows
           switch( i ) // scan next row by looking for OFF condition
               {
               case 0:
                   row1 = OFF;
                   break;

               case 1:
                   row1 = ON;
                   row2 = OFF;
                   break;

               case 2:
                   row2 = ON;
                   row3 = OFF;
                   break;
```

```
            case 3:
                row3 = ON;
                row4 = OFF;
                break;
        }

    if (!col1)
        {                   //check if key1 is pressed
        key = k + 0;    //set key number

        while (!col1); //wait for release

        return key;     //return key number
        }

    if (!col2)
        {                   //check if key2 is pressed
        key = k + 1;    //set key number

        while (!col2); //wait for release

        return key;     //return key number
        }

    if (!col3)
        {                   //check if key3 is pressed
        key = k + 2;    //set key number

        while (!col3); //wait for release

        return key;     //return key number
        }
    k += 3;             //next row key number
    }
return 255;             // no key pressed
}
```

Step-By-Step:

1. The keypad is wired internally as a matrix of switches. See the datasheet for the matrix configuration. Compare the datasheet configuration table with the *Read-Keypad()* function. This code works by turning off a row output and looking for a corresponding column input that is low. The rows are outputs and the columns are inputs.

2. Wire up the circuit as shown in the schematic. If you use the keypad suggested in this lab, you will also have to break off the top two mounting spacers so it will mount properly on the breadboard. The spacers are soft plastic so the modification is easily accomplished without tools. See the lab photo for a suggested mounting.
3. Open the IDE and close any open projects.
4. Your lab instructor should provide you with the source files for this lab. Open the project file **Lab4.c** by selecting *File → Open File* from the menu.
5. Compile and download the program using the following steps:

   - Select *Project → Rebuild Project* from the menu or use the toolbar button.
   - Select *Debug → Connect* from the menu or use the toolbar button.
   - Click the *Download Code* button on the toolbar.
   - If your code is correct and you have a good connection to your board, the program should compile, connect and download to the 8051.

6. Press the green *RUN* button on the toolbar to run your program.
7. The LED display should be blank.
8. Press and hold one of the buttons. The LED should still be blank.
9. Release the button. The LED should display the number pressed.

Fig. 9.12 Lab 4 Photo

10. Pressing the "*" or "#" keys should blank the display because they return numbers not recognized by the *DisplayNumber( )* function.
11. The buttons on the keypad are not debounced. This may produce erratic behavior once in a while. It is left as an exercise to add this code.

Lab Wrap-up:

1. Demonstrate that your program works to the lab instructor.

Questions:

1. There is a more succinct and elegant way to change the state of the row output. What is it? **Hint:** Operate on the P1 byte.
2. Suppose you want to add more digits to the design of this circuit. Using this approach, you will quickly run out of ports. What alternatives are available to add digits and conserve on the use of port pins?

Additional Exercises (Optional):

1. Draw the circuit showing the internal switch representation of the keypad.
2. Add debounce code to the *ReadKeypad( )* function.
3. Add a simple up/down counter function to the program. Press the "*" key to increment the currently displayed number. Press the "#" key to decrement the currently display number. Limit the range to 0–9. Pressing the number keys should still work as they did before.

9.5   Lab 5: Intro to D/A Conversion Using a Speaker

Purpose:

This lab has two main purposes:

1. Become familiar with generating tones using a port pin.
2. Become familiar with the D/A (Digital to Analog) capabilities of the 8051 microcontroller. Use the DAC to generate a "siren" sound.

Assignment:

In this lab, you will do the following:

1. Wire up a speaker to a power transistor. The power transistor will switch on and off via an 8051 port pin. The port pin will create a square wave with a variable frequency.
2. Download and run a C program that will produce a tone using a timer interrupt.
3. Wire up a speaker to an analog output on the 8051 microcontroller. The speaker will be driven directly by the DAC output. For simplicity, there will not be an audio amplifier.
4. Download and run a C program that will produce sine wave output. The frequency of the sine wave will be changed over time to produce a "siren" or "alarm" sound effect.

Equipment:

1. Si Labs 8051 development kit
2. (1) 8-ohm speaker (GF0571-ND)
3. (1) N-channel MOSFET transistor (IRF510)
4. Oscilloscope (optional)

Schematic:

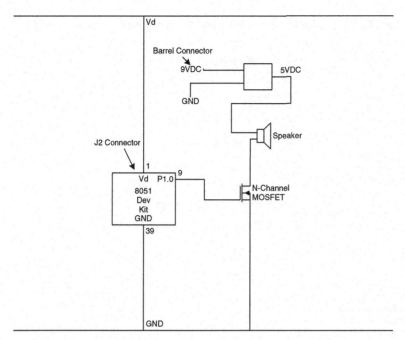

Fig. 9.13 Square wave sound using port pin

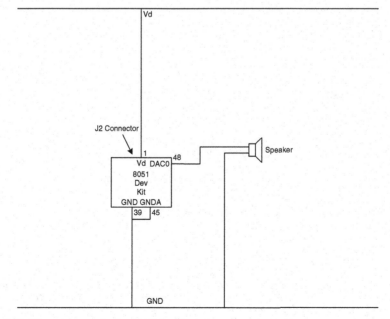

Fig. 9.14 Sine wave sound using DAC (no amp)

Program:

Program Listing for Lab 5 (Generate sound using a square wave on a port pin)

```c
//-------------------------------------------------------------------------
// Lab5_tone.c (Intro to D/A Conversion Using a Speaker)
//-------------------------------------------------------------------------
//
// Create a 1KHz square wave using port pin to drive a speaker
// Tool chain: KEIL Eval 'c'
// Adapted from SiLabs DAC example program

//-------------------------------------------------------------------------
// Includes
//-------------------------------------------------------------------------
#include "C8051F000.h"

//-------------------------------------------------------------------------
// Function PROTOTYPES
//-------------------------------------------------------------------------

void Timer1Init( void );

//-------------------------------------------------------------------------
// Global CONSTANTS
//-------------------------------------------------------------------------
#define ON 0
#define OFF 1
#define PRESSED 1

//-------------------------------------------------------------------------
// Global Variables
//-------------------------------------------------------------------------

sbit SPEAKER = P1 ^ 0;
sbit SW = P1 ^ 7; // 0 = PRESSED

int count;

//-------------------------------------------------------------------------
// MAIN Routine
//-------------------------------------------------------------------------
void main( void )
    {
    // by default the C8051005 runs at 2MHz (1 osc cycles)
    // 1 machine cycle is typically .5us

    XBR2 = 0x40;   // Enable crossbar and weak pull-ups
    PRT1CF = 0x01;

    WDTCN = 0xde; // disable watchdog timer
    WDTCN = 0xad;

    count = 0;
    SPEAKER = OFF;

    while (SW != PRESSED) { } // don't start until the button is pressed

    // initialize timer 1
```

```
    Timer1Init();

    while (1) { }  // super loop (speaker control is in the ISR)
    }
//-------------------------------------------------------------------------
// Timer 1 Init
//-------------------------------------------------------------------------
void Timer1Init( void )
    {
    ET1 = 1;      // Enable timer 1 interrupt
    TMOD = 0x20;  // Timer 1, Mode 2
    TH1 = 0x6;    // 250us count
    EA = 1;       // Enable interrupts
    TR1 = 1;      // Start timer 1
    }

//-------------------------------------------------------------------------
// Timer 1 Interrupt Service Routine (ISR)
//-------------------------------------------------------------------------
void Timer1(void) interrupt 3
    {
    count++;

    if (count == 2)
        {
        count = 0;
        SPEAKER = ~SPEAKER;
        }
    }
```

Program Listing for Lab 5 (Generate a "siren" sound using sine wave on DAC)

```
//-------------------------------------------------------------------------
// Lab5.c (Intro to D/A Conversion Using a Speaker)
//-------------------------------------------------------------------------
//
// Create a simple siren using a DAC output
//
// Target:       C8051F0xx
// Tool chain:   Keil EVAL C51


//-------------------------------------------------------------------------
// Includes
//-------------------------------------------------------------------------

#include <c8051f000.h>              // SFR declarations

//-------------------------------------------------------------------------
// 16-bit SFR Definitions for 'F02x
//-------------------------------------------------------------------------

sfr16 TMR3RL  = 0x92;               // Timer3 reload
sfr16 TMR3    = 0x94;               // Timer3
sfr16 DAC0    = 0xd2;               // DAC0 data
```

```
//---------------------------------------------------------------------------
// Global Constants
//---------------------------------------------------------------------------


#define USE_EXT_OSC      0                 // 0 = use internal oscillator
                                           // 1 = use external oscillator


#if(USE_EXT_OSC == 0)
 #define SYSCLK 16000000      // Internal oscillator frequency in Hz
#endif

#if(USE_EXT_OSC == 1)
 #define SYSCLK 22118400      // External oscillator frequency in Hz
#endif

#define SAMPLE_RATE_DAC 100000L      // DAC sampling rate in Hz
#define PHASE_PRECISION 65536        // range of phase accumulator

#define LO_FREQ 750 // low siren frequency
#define HI_FREQ 5000 // high siren frequency
#define FREQ_STEP 1 // frequency step increase for every Timer 3 ISR call
// number of Timer 3 ISR calls before frequency changes
#define FREQ_CHANGE_PRESET 5
// <PHASE_ADD> is the change in phase between DAC samples; It is used in
// the set_DACs routine.

unsigned int freq = LO_FREQ; // starting frequency
unsigned int PHASE_ADD = LO_FREQ * PHASE_PRECISION / SAMPLE_RATE_DAC;
unsigned int count = 0;

int code SINE_TABLE[256] = {

    0x0000, 0x0324, 0x0647, 0x096a, 0x0c8b, 0x0fab, 0x12c8, 0x15e2,
    0x18f8, 0x1c0b, 0x1f19, 0x2223, 0x2528, 0x2826, 0x2b1f, 0x2e11,
    0x30fb, 0x33de, 0x36ba, 0x398c, 0x3c56, 0x3f17, 0x41ce, 0x447a,
    0x471c, 0x49b4, 0x4c3f, 0x4ebf, 0x5133, 0x539b, 0x55f5, 0x5842,
    0x5a82, 0x5cb4, 0x5ed7, 0x60ec, 0x62f2, 0x64e8, 0x66cf, 0x68a6,
    0x6a6d, 0x6c24, 0x6dca, 0x6f5f, 0x70e2, 0x7255, 0x73b5, 0x7504,
    0x7641, 0x776c, 0x7884, 0x798a, 0x7a7d, 0x7b5d, 0x7c29, 0x7ce3,
    0x7d8a, 0x7e1d, 0x7e9d, 0x7f09, 0x7f62, 0x7fa7, 0x7fd8, 0x7ff6,
    0x7fff, 0x7ff6, 0x7fd8, 0x7fa7, 0x7f62, 0x7f09, 0x7e9d, 0x7e1d,
    0x7d8a, 0x7ce3, 0x7c29, 0x7b5d, 0x7a7d, 0x798a, 0x7884, 0x776c,
    0x7641, 0x7504, 0x73b5, 0x7255, 0x70e2, 0x6f5f, 0x6dca, 0x6c24,
    0x6a6d, 0x68a6, 0x66cf, 0x64e8, 0x62f2, 0x60ec, 0x5ed7, 0x5cb4,
    0x5a82, 0x5842, 0x55f5, 0x539b, 0x5133, 0x4ebf, 0x4c3f, 0x49b4,
    0x471c, 0x447a, 0x41ce, 0x3f17, 0x3c56, 0x398c, 0x36ba, 0x33de,
    0x30fb, 0x2e11, 0x2b1f, 0x2826, 0x2528, 0x2223, 0x1f19, 0x1c0b,
    0x18f8, 0x15e2, 0x12c8, 0x0fab, 0x0c8b, 0x096a, 0x0647, 0x0324,

    0x0000, 0xfcdc, 0xf9b9, 0xf696, 0xf375, 0xf055, 0xed38, 0xea1e,
    0xe708, 0xe3f5, 0xe0e7, 0xdddd, 0xdad8, 0xd7da, 0xd4e1, 0xd1ef,
    0xcf05, 0xcc22, 0xc946, 0xc674, 0xc3aa, 0xc0e9, 0xbe32, 0xbb86,
    0xb8e4, 0xb64c, 0xb3c1, 0xb141, 0xaecd, 0xac65, 0xaa0b, 0xa7be,
    0xa57e, 0xa34c, 0xa129, 0x9f14, 0x9d0e, 0x9b18, 0x9931, 0x975a,
    0x9593, 0x93dc, 0x9236, 0x90a1, 0x8f1e, 0x8dab, 0x8c4b, 0x8afc,
    0x89bf, 0x8894, 0x877c, 0x8676, 0x8583, 0x84a3, 0x83d7, 0x831d,
    0x8276, 0x81e3, 0x8163, 0x80f7, 0x809e, 0x8059, 0x8028, 0x800a,
    0x8000, 0x800a, 0x8028, 0x8059, 0x809e, 0x80f7, 0x8163, 0x81e3,
```

```
     0x8276, 0x831d, 0x83d7, 0x84a3, 0x8583, 0x8676, 0x877c, 0x8894,
     0x89bf, 0x8afc, 0x8c4b, 0x8dab, 0x8f1e, 0x90a1, 0x9236, 0x93dc,
     0x9593, 0x975a, 0x9931, 0x9b18, 0x9d0e, 0x9f14, 0xa129, 0xa34c,
     0xa57e, 0xa7be, 0xaa0b, 0xac65, 0xaecd, 0xb141, 0xb3c1, 0xb64c,
     0xb8e4, 0xbb86, 0xbe32, 0xc0e9, 0xc3aa, 0xc674, 0xc946, 0xcc22,
     0xcf05, 0xd1ef, 0xd4e1, 0xd7da, 0xdad8, 0xdddd, 0xe0e7, 0xe3f5,
     0xe708, 0xea1e, 0xed38, 0xf055, 0xf375, 0xf696, 0xf9b9, 0xfcdc,
};

//-------------------------------------------------------------------------
// Function Prototypes
//-------------------------------------------------------------------------

void main(void);
void OSCILLATOR_Init(void);
void DAC0_Init (void);
void TIMER3_Init(int counts);
void Set_DAC(void);

//-------------------------------------------------------------------------
// MAIN Routine
//-------------------------------------------------------------------------

void main (void)
{
    WDTCN = 0xde;                        // Disable watchdog timer
    WDTCN = 0xad;

    OSCILLATOR_Init ();                  // Initialize oscillator
    DAC0_Init ();                        // Initialize DAC0

    TIMER3_Init(SYSCLK/SAMPLE_RATE_DAC);// Initialize Timer3 to overflow
                                         // <SAMPLE_RATE_DAC> times per
                                         // second

    EA = 1;                              // Enable global interrupts

    while(1);
}

//-------------------------------------------------------------------------
// Interrupt Service Routines
//-------------------------------------------------------------------------

//-------------------------------------------------------------------------
// TIMER3_ISR -- Wave Generator
//-------------------------------------------------------------------------
//
// This ISR is called on Timer3 overflows. Timer3 is set to auto-reload mode
// and is used to schedule the DAC output sample rate in this example.
//
void TIMER3_ISR (void) interrupt 14
{
    static int count;
    TMR3CN &= ~0x80;                     // Clear Timer3 overflow flag

    Set_DAC();

    // frequency modification
    count++;
```

```
   if (count == FREQ_CHANGE_PRESET)
   {
    freq = freq + FREQ_STEP;
    if (freq == HI_FREQ) freq = LO_FREQ;
    PHASE_ADD = freq * PHASE_PRECISION / SAMPLE_RATE_DAC;
count = 0;
   }
}


//-----------------------------------------------------------------------------
// Initialization Routines
//-----------------------------------------------------------------------------

//-----------------------------------------------------------------------------
// OSCILLATOR_Init
//-----------------------------------------------------------------------------
//
// Return Value : None
// Parameters   : None
//
// This routine initializes the system clock to either the 16 Mhz or the
// external crystal oscillator depending on #define USB_EXT_OSC
//
//-----------------------------------------------------------------------------

void OSCILLATOR_Init (void)
{

#if(USE_EXT_OSC == 0)

   OSCICN = 0x07;                       // Set internal oscillator to 16 Mhz

#endif

#if (USE_EXT_OSC == 1)

   int i;                               // Delay counter

   OSCXCN = 0x67;                       // Start external oscillator with
                                        // 22.1184 MHz crystal

   for (i = 0; i < 256; i++);           // XTLVLD blanking interval (>1ms)

   while (!(OSCXCN & 0x80));            // Wait for crystal osc. to settle

   OSCICN = 0x88;                       // Select external oscillator as SYSCLK
                                        // source and enable missing clock
                                        // detector
#endif

}


//-----------------------------------------------------------------------------
// DAC0_Init
//-----------------------------------------------------------------------------
//
// Return Value : None
// Parameters   : None
```

```
//
// Enable the DAC and the VREF buffer.
//
//-----------------------------------------------------------------------------

void DAC0_Init(void)
{
   DAC0CN = 0x87;                    // Enable DAC0 in left-justified mode

   REF0CN |= 0x03;                   // Enable the internal VREF (2.4v) and
                                     // the Bias Generator

}


//-----------------------------------------------------------------------------
// TIMER3_Init
//-----------------------------------------------------------------------------
//
// Return Value : None
// Parameters   :
//    1)  int counts - calculated Timer overflow rate
//                     range is positive range of integer: 0 to 32767
//
// Configure Timer3 to auto-reload at interval specified by <counts> using
// SYSCLK as its time base.
//
//-----------------------------------------------------------------------------

void TIMER3_Init (int counts)
{
   TMR3CN  = 0;                      // STOP timer; set to auto-reload mode
   TMR3CN |= 0x02;                   // Timer3 counts SYSCLKs

   TMR3RL  = -counts;                // Set reload value
   TMR3    = TMR3RLL;                // Initialize Timer to reload value

   EIE2   |= 0x01;                   // Enable Timer3 interrupts
   TMR3CN |= 0x04;                   // Start Timer3

}

//-----------------------------------------------------------------------------
// Set_DAC
//-----------------------------------------------------------------------------
//
// Return Value : None
// Parameters   : None
//
// Calculates the update values for the two DACs using SINE_TABLE.
//
//-----------------------------------------------------------------------------

void Set_DAC(void)
{
   static unsigned phase_acc = 0;    // Holds phase accumulator

   int SIN_temp;            // Temporary 16-bit variables
   unsigned char index;             // Index into SINE table
```

```
    phase_acc += PHASE_ADD;                  // Increment phase accumulator
    index = phase_acc >> 8;

    SIN_temp = SINE_TABLE[index];            // Read the table value

    // Add a DC bias to change the the rails from a bipolar (-32768 to 32767)
    // to unipolar (0 to 65535)
    // Note: the XOR with 0x8000 translates the bipolar quantity into
    // a unipolar quantity.

    DAC0 = SIN_temp ^ 0x8000;                // Write to DAC0
}

//--------------------------------------------------------------------------
// End Of File
//--------------------------------------------------------------------------
```

Step-By-Step:

1. Wire up the circuit as shown in the Figure 9.13 schematic.
2. Open the IDE and close any open projects.
3. Your lab instructor should provide you with the source files for this lab. Open the project file **Lab5_tone.c** by selecting *File → Open File* from the menu.
4. Compile and download the program using the following steps:

   – Select *Project → Rebuild Project* from the menu or use the toolbar button.
   – Select *Debug → Connect* from the menu or use the toolbar button.
   – Click the *Download Code* button on the toolbar.
   – If your code is correct and you have a good connection to your board, the program should compile, connect and download to the 8051.

5. Press the green *RUN* button on the toolbar to run your program.
6. You should hear nothing.
7. Press the push button (i.e. P1.7) on the development board.
8. You should hear a 1 KHz tone produced by the square wave on pin P1.0.
9. Verify the frequency using an oscilloscope. The waveform should be a square wave.
10. Examine the code. Make sure you understand how it works before proceeding to the second part of this lab.
11. Wire up the circuit as shown in the Figure 9.14 schematic.
12. Your lab instructor should provide you with the source files for this lab. Open the project file **Lab5.c** by selecting *File → Open File* from the menu.
13. Compile and download the program using the following steps:

    – Select *Project → Rebuild Project* from the menu or use the toolbar button.
    – Select *Debug → Connect* from the menu or use the toolbar button.
    – Click the *Download Code* button on the toolbar.

    – If your code is correct and you have a good connection to your board, the program should compile, connect and download to the 8051.

14. Press the green **RUN** button on the toolbar to run your program.
15. You should hear a rapidly changing tone that sounds similar to a siren or alarm. This sound is a sine wave with a constantly changing frequency.
16. Observe the output using an oscilloscope. The waveform should be a sine wave.
17. Examine the code. Try changing the following constants to see how they affect the generated sound: *LO_FREQ, HI_FREQ, FREQ_STEP* and *FREQ_CHANGE_PRESET*.

Lab Wrap-up:

1. Demonstrate that both programs work to the lab instructor.

Fig. 9.15 Lab 5 Photo (DAC output)

Questions:

1. In part 1 of the lab, describe how the timer is used to create the square wave output on the port pin.
2. In part 1 of the lab, how do you change the frequency of the square wave?
3. In part 2 of the lab, describe how the timer is used to create a sine wave output at DAC0.
4. In part 2 of the lab, describe how the frequency is changed to produce the "siren" sound effect.
5. In part 2 of the lab, why is the sound weak? What can be done to increase the strength of the sound?

Additional Exercises (Optional):

1. In part 1 of the lab, modify the program to produce a "siren" sound.
2. In part 2 of the lab, modify the program so the "siren" sound goes from low-to-high and then from high-to-low. Right now it only goes from low-to-high.

9.6   Lab 6: 3-Wire RS232 Serial Communication

Purpose:

This lab has four main purposes:

1. Become familiar with the RS232 serial communication capabilities of the 8051 microcontroller.
2. Learn to use the Silicon Labs Configuration Wizard to set the serial communications parameters in the C program.
3. Learn to use a Timer as a baud rate generator.
4. Learn to use ISRs (Interrupt Service Routines) for serial communication.

Assignment:

In this lab, you will do the following:

1. Wire up a serial communications interface to communicate with a PC.
2. Use HyperTerminal to test serial communication.
3. The focus of this lab in on serial communication. The actual task for the 8051 to perform is simple case conversion. You will type a word or phrase in Hyper-Terminal and press ENTER. When the 8051 sees a carriage return character, the entered word or phrase will be converted to uppercase and sent back to HyperTerminal.

Equipment:

1. Si Labs 8051 development kit
2. (1) Line-Powered RS-232 Transceiver Chip (MAX233). This chip was chosen because it doesn't require external capacitors – an unusual feature for transceiver chips.
3. (1) 5VDC voltage regulator (7805)
4. Female DB9 connector with three wires for TxD, RxD and GND.
5. PC with HyperTerminal or equivalent. **NOTE:** HyperTerminal is not available in Windows Vista.

The 5VDC voltage regulator is needed to power the transceiver chip. The voltage that's available on the development kit board is only 3.3VDC. The input voltage to the regulator is the 9VDC on the P1 barrel connector.

For simplicity, the 8051's internal oscillator will be used and set to 16MHz. This is not the best frequency for generating baud rates, but it can produce a few good ones. We will use 9600bps for this lab.

Schematic:

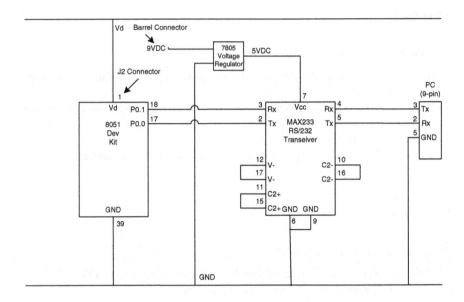

Program:

Program Listing for Lab 6

```
//--------------------------------------------------------------------------
// Lab6.c (3-wire serial communication)
//--------------------------------------------------------------------------
//
//
// Tool chain: KEIL Eval 'c'
//
//--------------------------------------------------------------------------
// Includes
//--------------------------------------------------------------------------

#include <C8051F000.h> // SFR declarations
#include <stdio.h>

//--------------------------------------------------------------------------
// Global Constants
//--------------------------------------------------------------------------


//--------------------------------------------------------------------------
// Function Prototypes
//--------------------------------------------------------------------------

void OSCILLATOR_Init( void );
void PORT_Init( void );
void UART0_Init( void );
```

```c
//-----------------------------------------------------------------------------
// Global Variables
//-----------------------------------------------------------------------------

#define UART_BUFFERSIZE 64

unsigned char UART_Buffer[UART_BUFFERSIZE];
unsigned char UART_Buffer_Size = 0;
unsigned char UART_Input_First = 0;
unsigned char UART_Output_First = 0;
unsigned char TX_Ready = 1;
static unsigned char Byte;

//-----------------------------------------------------------------------------
// main() Routine
//-----------------------------------------------------------------------------

void main( void )
    {
    WDTCN = 0xDE;        // Disable watchdog timer
    WDTCN = 0xAD;

    OSCILLATOR_Init(); // Initialize oscillator
    PORT_Init();        // Initialize crossbar and GPIO

    UART0_Init();       // Initialize UART0

    EA = 1;

    while (1)
        {
        // If the complete word has been entered via the hyperterminal followed
        // by carriage return
        if ((TX_Ready == 1) && (UART_Buffer_Size != 0) && (Byte == 13))
            {
            TX_Ready = 0; // Set the flag to zero
            TI = 1;       // Set transmit flag to 1
            }
        }
    }

//-----------------------------------------------------------------------------
// Initialization Subroutines
//-----------------------------------------------------------------------------

//-----------------------------------------------------------------------------
// OSCILLATOR_Init
//-----------------------------------------------------------------------------
//
// Return Value : None
// Parameters   : None
//
//
//-----------------------------------------------------------------------------
void OSCILLATOR_Init( void )
    {
    // If the line below is commented out, then the speed defaults to 2Mhz
    OSCICN = 0x07; // Internal oscillator -- 16Mhz
    }

//-----------------------------------------------------------------------------
// PORT_Init
```

```
//------------------------------------------------------------------------------
//
// Return Value : None
// Parameters   : None
//
// This function configures the crossbar and GPIO ports.
//
// Pinout:
//
// P0.0   digital   push-pull    UART TX
// P0.1   digital   open-drain   UART RX
//------------------------------------------------------------------------------
void PORT_Init( void )
    {
    XBR0 = 0x04;   // Enable UART0
    XBR2 = 0x40;   // Enable crossbar and weak pull-up

    PRT0CF = 0x01; // Set TX pin to push-pull
    IE = 0x10;
    }


//------------------------------------------------------------------------------
// UART0_Init   Variable baud rate, Timer 2, 8-N-1
//------------------------------------------------------------------------------
//
// Return Value : None
// Parameters   : None
//
// Configure UART0 for operation at <baudrate> 8-N-1 using Timer2 as
// baud rate source.
//
//------------------------------------------------------------------------------
void UART0_Init( void )
    {
    CKCON = 0x20;
    T2CON = 0x34;
// The two lines below are for a clock speed of 2Mhz
//RCAP2L = 0x2C; // 300bps (set to 294.81bps to compensate for oscillator drift)
//RCAP2H = 0xFF; // values are from Config2 tool
// The two lines below are for a clock speed of 16Mhz
//RCAP2L = 0x60; // 300bps (set to 294.81bps to compensate for oscillator drift)
//RCAP2H = 0xF9; // values from Config2 tool
// The two lines below are for a clock speed of 16Mhz
    RCAP2L = 0xCB; // 9600bps (set to 9433.96bps to compensate for oscillator drift)
    RCAP2H = 0xFF; // values from Config2 tool
    TL2 = RCAP2L;
    TH2 = RCAP2H;
    TR2 = 1;       // Start Timer2

    SCON = 0x50; // 8-bit variable baud rate;
    // 9th bit ignored; RX enabled
    // clear all flags
    TX_Ready = 1; // Flag showing that UART can transmit
    ES = 1;
    }


//------------------------------------------------------------------------------
// UART0_Interrupt
//------------------------------------------------------------------------------
//
// This routine is invoked whenever a character is entered or displayed on the
// Hyperterminal.
//
```

```
//--------------------------------------------------------------------------------

void UART0_Interrupt( void ) interrupt 4
    {
    if ((SCON & 0x01) == 0x01)
        {
        // Check if a new word is being entered
        if (UART_Buffer_Size == 0)
            {
            UART_Input_First = 0;
            }

        SCON = (SCON & 0xFE); //RI1 = 0;
        Byte = SBUF;            // Read a character from Hyperterminal

        if (UART_Buffer_Size < UART_BUFFERSIZE)
            {
            UART_Buffer[UART_Input_First] = Byte; // Store character

            UART_Buffer_Size++;                    // Update array's size

            UART_Input_First++;                    // Update counter
            }
        }

    if ((SCON & 0x02) == 0x02) // Check if transmit flag is set
        {
        SCON = (SCON & 0xFD);

        if (UART_Buffer_Size != 1) // If buffer not empty
            {

            // Check if a new word is being output
            if (UART_Buffer_Size == UART_Input_First)
                {
                UART_Output_First = 0;
                }

            // Store a character in the variable byte
            Byte = UART_Buffer[UART_Output_First];

            if ((Byte >= 0x61) && (Byte <= 0x7A))
                { // If lower case letter
                Byte -= 32;
                }

            SBUF = Byte;

            UART_Output_First++; // Update counter
            UART_Buffer_Size--;  // Decrease array size
            }
        else
            {
            UART_Buffer_Size = 0; // Set the array size to 0
            TX_Ready = 1;         // Indicate transmission complete
            }
        }
    }

//--------------------------------------------------------------------------------
// End Of File
//--------------------------------------------------------------------------------
```

Step-By-Step:

1. Wire up the circuit as shown in the schematic.
2. Connect the PC to the 8051 using the female DB9 serial connector.
3. Open the IDE and close any open projects.
4. Your lab instructor should provide you with the source files for this lab. Open the project file **Lab6.wsp** by selecting *Project* → *Open Project* from the menu.
5. Compile and download the program using the following steps:

   - Select *Project* → *Rebuild Project* from the menu or use the toolbar button.
   - Select *Debug* → *Connect* from the menu or use the toolbar button.
   - Click the *Download Code* button on the toolbar.
   - If your code is correct and you have a good connection to your board, the program should compile, connect and download to the 8051.

6. Use the SI Configuration Wizard to determine the serial communication, oscillator, port and timer variables. Compare the results of the wizard with the supplied C program. Save the results for later.
7. Click the green *RUN* button on the toolbar to run your program.
8. Open HyperTerminal and connect to the serial port. The HyperTerminal connection should be set for 9600,8,N,1.

Fig. 9.16 Lab 6 Photo

9. Type a word in lowercase and press the return key.
10. HyperTerminal should print out a response from the 8051. The returned word should be in uppercase.
11. **Tip:** If you receive some (or all) "garbage" characters back, it may be a problem with the baud rate. Check both HyperTerminal and C program settings. When designing and testing this lab, we found the internal oscillator to be inaccurate and had to experiment with the baud rate within $+/-$ 1%. This is reflected in the code comments.

Lab Wrap-up:

1. Demonstrate that your program works to the lab instructor using HyperTerminal or a similar program on your PC.
2. Show your lab instructor the results of the SI Configuration Wizard. They should match (or be close to) the values in the supplied C program.

Questions:

1. How many serial ports are available on the Silicon Labs 8051 microcontroller?
2. Which baud rates can be generated with the internal oscillator set to 16MHz with an error of less than two percent? **Hint:** There is a web page at the Keil website that will generate a table of these values.[1]
3. For serial communications, what is a good reason for running at 16MHz instead of a lower oscillator frequency?
4. For serial communications, what are the two best external crystal frequencies that can be used by the Silicon Labs development kit? **Hint:** One is a multiple of the other.
5. What is the maximum baud rate for the MAX233 transceiver?
6. What happens in the program if you send more then 64 characters before a carriage return?

Additional Exercises (Optional):

1. Modify the program to accept a simple command language to read and write bits on any of the ports. The case-sensitive command language should work as follows:

---

[1] http://www.keil.com/products/c51/baudrate.asp

- READ P1.7 (i.e. read the value in P1.7 and display it in HyperTerminal.)
- WRITE P1.6,1 (i.e. write the value 1 to P1.6).
- Use the built-in LED (P1.6) and switch (P1.7) for testing.
- This version is case-sensitive and doesn't tolerate extra spaces (e.g. WRITE P1.6, 1) for simplicity.
- Make sure to exclude P0.0 and P0.1 which are used for serial communications. Send back an error message for these two bits.

2. Using the program developed in exercise 1, add the following features:

- Make the language case-insensitive. For example "**WRITE P1.6,1**" should be parsed the same as "**write p1.6,1**".
- Allow extra spaces or no spaces. For example, "**WRITE P1.6, 1**" should be parsed the same as "**WRITEP1.6,1**".

3. Modify the READ and WRITE command for byte values as well as bit values. For example, READ P1 should return the byte value as a hex number and WRITE P1,0xFF should set the byte value.

9.7   Lab 7: Intro to the LCD Display

Purpose:

This lab has two main purposes:

1. Learn how to interface to a typical LCD display.
2. Learn how to use (and adapt) a third-party library of functions to communicate with the display.

Assignment:

In this lab, you will do the following:

1. Wire up a circuit that interfaces the 8051 microcontroller to an industry standard LCD display.
2. Run a simple test program (similar to Lab 2) to test the display and modified library functions.

Equipment:

1. Si Labs 8051 development kit
2. (1) LCD Display (67-1778-ND)

Schematic:

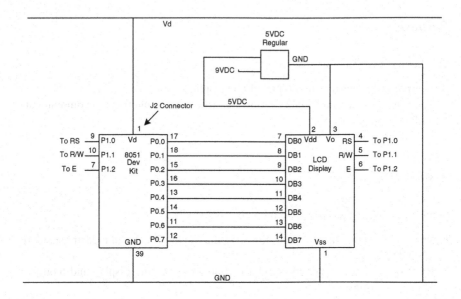

Program:

Program Listing for Lab 7 (main)

```
//----------------------------------------------------------------------
// Lab7.c (Intro to the LCD Display)
//----------------------------------------------------------------------
// Copyright (C) 2008 David den Haring
//
// Tool chain: KEIL Eval 'c'
//

//----------------------------------------------------------------------
// Includes
//----------------------------------------------------------------------
#include "lcd.h"
#include "C8051F000.h"
#include <stdio.h>
#include <limits.h>
#include <string.h>

//----------------------------------------------------------------------
// 16-bit SFR Definitions for 'F00x
//----------------------------------------------------------------------

sfr16 RCAP2 = 0xca; // Timer2 capture/reload
sfr16 T2 = 0xcc;    // Timer2

//----------------------------------------------------------------------
// Function PROTOTYPES
```

```
//---------------------------------------------------------------------------

void OSCILLATOR_Init( void );
void PORT_Init( void );
void Wait_MS( unsigned int ms );

//---------------------------------------------------------------------------
// Global CONSTANTS
//---------------------------------------------------------------------------
#define ON   1
#define OFF  0

#define SYSCLK  2000000 // Internal crystal oscillator frequency
#define DELAY   1000         // 1 second delay

//---------------------------------------------------------------------------
// MAIN Routine
//---------------------------------------------------------------------------

void main( void )
    {
    int count = 0;
    char num[16];
    num[0] = '\0'; // null terminated

    // Initialize device
    WDTCN = 0xde;       // disable watchdog timer
    WDTCN = 0xad;

    OSCILLATOR_Init(); // Initialize oscillator
    PORT_Init();       // Initialize crossbar and GPIO
    LcdInit();         // Initialize LCD display

    while (1)
        {
        sprintf(num, "%d", count); // convert count to a string
        LcdWriteString(&num);
        Wait_MS(DELAY);             // Wait for 1 second
        LcdClear();
        count++;

        if (count == INT_MAX)
            count = 0;
        } // while
    }

//---------------------------------------------------------------------------
// Functions
//---------------------------------------------------------------------------
//---------------------------------------------------------------------------
// OSCILLATOR_Init
//---------------------------------------------------------------------------
//
// Return Value : None
// Parameters   : None
//
//
//---------------------------------------------------------------------------
void OSCILLATOR_Init( void )
    {
```

```
    // Run the internal oscillator at 2MHz. This slow speed is an easy way
    // to avoid timing issues with the much slower LCD display device
    OSCXCN = 0x00; // external oscillator off
    }

//-----------------------------------------------------------------------
// PORT_Init
//-----------------------------------------------------------------------
//
// Return Value : None
// Parameters   : None
//
// This function configures the crossbar and GPIO ports.
//
//-----------------------------------------------------------------------

void PORT_Init( void )
    {
    XBR2 = 0x40;   // Enable crossbar and weak pull-ups
    PRT1CF = 0x07; // RS, R/W, E
    }


//-----------------------------------------------------------------------
// Wait_MS
//-----------------------------------------------------------------------
//
// Return Value : None
// Parameters:
//   1) unsigned int ms - number of milliseconds of delay
//                        range is full range of integer: 0 to 65335
//
// This routine inserts a delay of <ms> milliseconds.
//
//-----------------------------------------------------------------------
void Wait_MS( unsigned int ms )
    {

    CKCON &= ~0x20;                     // use SYSCLK/12 as timebase

    RCAP2 = -(SYSCLK / 1000 / 12); // Timer 2 overflows at 1 kHz
    T2 = RCAP2;

    ET2 = 0;                        // Disable Timer 2 interrupts

    TR2 = 1;                        // Start Timer 2

    while (ms)
        {
        TF2 = 0;      // Clear flag to initialize

        while (!TF2); // Wait until timer overflows

        ms--;         // Decrement ms
        }

    TR2 = 0;          // Stop Timer 2
    }
```

Program Listing for Lab 7 (LCD library – lcd.c)

```
/*****************************************************************************
 * LCD control functions.
 * lcd.c
 * Copyright (C) 2004,2006 ASP Digital.  All rights reserved.
 * Andy Peters, ASP Digital
 * devel@latke.net
 *
 * various functions to support the usual sort of LCD display.
 * Created: 19 Jul 2004
 * Modified:
 *   11 Dec 2006: Add LcdWriteCGRAM().
 *      08 Oct 2008: Modified for Embedded C book (David den Haring)
 *****************************************************************************/

#include "lcd.h"
#include "lcdcmd.h"
#include "C8051F000.h"

/*
 * Private prototypes:
 */

void LcdWriteCmd( unsigned char cmd );
bit isLcdBusy( void );
void waitUntilDone( void );

sbit LCD_E  = P1 ^ 2;
sbit LCD_RW = P1 ^ 1;
sbit LCD_RS = P1 ^ 0;

sbit LCD_BUSY = P0 ^ 7;

/*
 * Fetch LCD's busy flag.
 * Put P0 into read mode before attempting to read!
 */
bit isLcdBusy( void )
    {
    bit retbit;

    retbit = 0;

    PRT0CF = 0x00;
    LCD_RW = 1;
    LCD_RS = 0;
    LCD_E = 1;
    P0 = 0xFF;
    retbit = P0 ^ 7;
    LCD_E = 0;
    PRT0CF = 0xFF;
    LCD_RW = 0;
    return (retbit);
    } // isLcdBusy

void waitUntilDone( void )
    {
    bit retbit = 1;
    PRT0CF = 0x00;
    P0 = 0xFF;
```

```
    LCD_RW = 1;
    LCD_RS = 0;

    while (retbit == 1)
        {
        LCD_E = 1;
        retbit = LCD_BUSY;
        LCD_E = 0;
        } //while retbit == 1
    PRT0CF = 0xFF;
    LCD_RW = 0;
    } // waitUntilDone()

/*
 * Write a character to the display at the current cursor position.
 */
void LcdWriteChar( unsigned char dval )
    {
    LCD_RW = 0;
    LCD_RS = 1;
    LCD_E = 1;
    P0 = dval;
    LCD_E = 0;
    waitUntilDone();
    } // LcdWriteChar()

/*
 * Write a string to the display, starting at the current cursor position.
 */
void LcdWriteString( unsigned char* str )
    {
    while (*str != '\0')
        {
        LcdWriteChar(*str);
        ++str;
        }
    } // LcdWriteString

/*
 * Move the cursor to the specified row and column.
 */
void LcdMoveCursor( unsigned char row, unsigned char col )
    {
    LcdWriteCmd(LCD_MOVEDISPLAY | (row << 6) | col);
    } // LcdMoveCursor

/*
 * Write a command to the LCD.
 */
void LcdWriteCmd( unsigned char cmd )
    {
    LCD_RW = 0;
    LCD_RS = 0;
    LCD_E = 1;
    P0 = cmd;
    LCD_E = 0;
    waitUntilDone();
    } // LcdWriteCmd
```

```
/*
 * Initialize the LCD.
 */

void LcdInit( void )
    {
    P0 = 0xFF; // enable port 1 digital inputs, needed for LCD_BUSY.
    LCD_RW = 0;
    LCD_RS = 0;
    LCD_E = 0;

    LcdWriteCmd(0x30);
    LcdWriteCmd(0x30);
    LcdWriteCmd(0x30);
    LcdWriteCmd(LCD_SETIFLEN | LCD_SETIFLEN_N | LCD_SETIFLEN_DL);

    // should be initialized here.

    LcdWriteCmd(LCD_DISPEN); // display off, cursor off, no blink
    LcdWriteCmd(LCD_CLEAR);
    LcdWriteCmd(LCD_DISPEN | LCD_DISPEN_DISP); // | LCD_DISPEN_CURSOR);
    LcdWriteCmd(LCD_MOVEDIR | LCD_MOVEDIR_ID);
    }                                              // LcdInit

/*
 * Clear the LCD.
 */
void LcdClear( void )
    {
    LcdWriteCmd(LCD_CLEAR);
    } // LcdClear()

/*
 * Write the given pattern to the CGRAM at the given address.
 */
void LcdWriteCGRAM( unsigned char addr, unsigned char pattern )
    {
    // First, move the cursor into the CGRAM area:
    LcdWriteCmd(LCD_MOVERAM | addr);
    // Then write the pattern to that location:
    LcdWriteChar(pattern);
    } // LcdWriteCGRAM())
```

Program Listing for Lab 7 (LCD library – lcd.h)

```
/*
 * lcd.h: definitions and headers for LCD control.
 *
 * Copyright (C) 2004, 2006 ASP Digital.  All rights reserved.
 * Andy Peters, devel@latke.net
 * 11 Dec 2006: add LcdWriteCGRAM()
 */
#ifndef _LCD_H

#define _LCD_H

/*
 * LcdWriteChar()
 * Writes a character to the display at the current cursor location.
 * Parameters:
```

```
 *      unsigned char dval: the character to write to the display (see
 *          the Hitachi data sheet)
 * Returns: nothing
 */

void LcdWriteChar( unsigned char dval );

/*
 * LcdWriteString()
 * Writes a string to the display, starting at the current cursor location.
 * Parameters:
 *      unsigned char *str: pointer to the string to write to the display
 * Returns: nothing
 */
void LcdWriteString( unsigned char *str );

/*
 * LcdMoveCursor()
 * Moves the cursor to a specific row and column.
 * Parameters:
 *      unsigned char row: Put the cursor on this row.
 *      unsigned char col: Put the cursor in this column.
 * Returns: nothing
 * Note: No bounds checking is performed, so it's possible to set an illegal
 *          location.
 */
void LcdMoveCursor( unsigned char row, unsigned char col );

/*
 * LcdInit()
 * Prepare the LCD for use. This function should be called before attempting
 * to actually use the LCD.
 * Parameters: none.
 * Returns: nothing.
 */
void LcdInit( void );

/*
 * LcdClear()
 * Clear the display and return the cursor to the home position.
 * Parameters: none.
 * Returns: nothing
 */
void LcdClear( void );

/*
 * LcdWriteCGRAM()
 * Store a pattern in the CGRAM at the given address.
 * Parameters:
 *      unsigned char addr: where we store pattern
 *      unsigned char pattern: bit pattern to store at addr
 */
void LcdWriteCGRAM( unsigned char addr, unsigned char pattern );

#endif
```

Program Listing for Lab 7 (LCD library – lcdcmd.h)

```
/*
 * lcdcmd.h: Convenient constants used by the LCD controller interface, lcd.c
 *
 * Copyright (C) 2004 ASP Digital.  All rights reserved.
 * Andy Peters, devel@latke.net
 */
#ifndef _LCDCMD_H

#define _LCDCMD_H

/*
 * LCD commands.
 */
// Clear display:

const unsigned char LCD_CLEAR = (1 << 0);

// return cursor and LCD to home position:
const unsigned char LCD_HOME = (1 << 1);

// set cursor move direction:
const unsigned char LCD_MOVEDIR = (1 << 2);
// shift display when byte written to display
const unsigned char LCD_MOVEDIR_SHIFT = (1 << 0);
// increment the cursor after each byte written:
const unsigned char LCD_MOVEDIR_ID = (1 << 1);

// Enable display/cursor:
const unsigned char LCD_DISPEN = (1 << 3);
// turn cursor blink on:
const unsigned char LCD_DISPEN_BLINK = (1 << 0);
// turn cursor on:
const unsigned char LCD_DISPEN_CURSOR = (1 << 1);
// turn display on:
const unsigned char LCD_DISPEN_DISP = (1 << 2);

// move cursor/shift display:
const unsigned char LCD_MCSD = (1 << 4);
// direction of shift (right if set):
const unsigned char LCD_MCSD_RL = (1 << 2);
// turn on display shift:
const unsigned char LCD_MCSD_SC = (1 << 3);

// set interface length:
const unsigned char LCD_SETIFLEN = (1 << 5);
// set character font 5x10 (1) or 5x7 (0)
const unsigned char LCD_SETIFLEN_F = (1 << 2);
// set # of display lines 1 if 0, 2 if 1:
const unsigned char LCD_SETIFLEN_N = (1 << 3);
// set interface length 8 bits if 1, 4 bits if 0
const unsigned char LCD_SETIFLEN_DL = (1 << 4);

// move cursor into CGRAM:
const unsigned char LCD_MOVERAM = (1 << 6);

// Move cursor to display:
const unsigned char LCD_MOVEDISPLAY = (1 << 7);

#endif
```

Step-By-Step:

1. The test program for this lab was "assembled" from Lab 2 and a third party library of LCD functions found on the Internet. The library is free to use as long as credit is given to the original author. It was modified as needed to work with the LCD display and port I/O assignment. The library can be found at the following address: http://www.latke.net/lcd/.

2. This is the first lab that also uses multiple files. The best way to use a library is to include its header file in your main C file and call the available functions of the new library. Examine the header file for the LCD library. The functions listed there are available for use. Additional functions that may be found in the main C file are private to the library.

3. Besides saving time in development, studying other people's code is a great way to learn how things work and possibly improve your coding techniques.

4. Wire up the circuit as shown in the schematic.

5. Open the IDE and close any open projects.

6. Your lab instructor should provide you with the source files for this lab. Open the project file **Lab7.wsp** by selecting *Project* → *Open Project* from the menu.

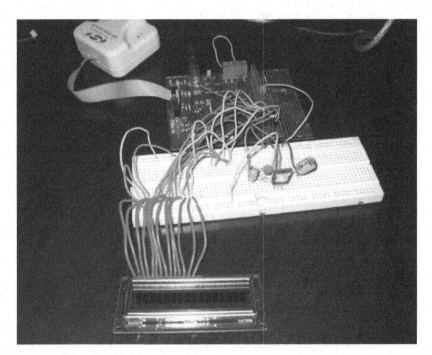

Fig. 9.17 Photo for Lab 7

7. Compile and download the program using the following steps:

 - Select **Project → Rebuild Project** from the menu or use the toolbar button.
 - Select **Debug → Connect** from the menu or use the toolbar button.
 - Click the **Download Code** button on the toolbar.
 - If your code is correct and you have a good connection to your board, the program should compile, connect and download to the 8051.

8. Press the green **RUN** button on the toolbar to run your program.
9. The LCD display should start counting up from 0. The maximum count is the storage of an integer. When the count reaches that value, it will reset back to 0 and start counting up again.
10. Reset the CPU and restart the program to watch it count again, if needed.

Lab Wrap-up:

1. Demonstrate that your program works to the lab instructor.

Questions:

1. Why did we need to include the header file *limits.h* in our program?
2. What is the maximum value for an integer?
3. The LCD display is 4 or 8 bit selectable. What does this mean? Why would you want to use only 4 bits?
4. List all of the available commands for the LCD Display. Include a brief comment and the command value. **Hint:** Use the datasheet on the CD.

Additional Exercises (Optional):

1. Modify the program to use the pushbutton on the development board (i.e. P1.7) to change the update speed of the counter. Use three speed settings. Pressing the pushbutton should cycle through the settings.
2. Modify the program to read the analog temperature sensor built into the development kit. This version of the program should just display the raw analog value coming from the ADC.
3. Modify the program from Exercise 2 to display Fahrenheit or Celsius. The temperature scale should be selectable using the pushbutton on the development board (P1.7).

9.8   Lab 8: Advanced RS232 Communications (Handshaking)

Purpose:

This lab has three main purposes:

1. Understand the fundamentals of handshaking and learn the differences between software and hardware handshaking.
2. Demonstrate software handshaking.
3. Demonstrate hardware handshaking.

Assignment:

In this lab, you will do the following:

1. Wire up a serial communications interface to communicate with a PC.
2. Use HyperTerminal to test serial communication.
3. Configure HyperTerminal for software handshaking (i.e. XON/XOFF) and run a C program on the 8051 to demonstrate that it works.
4. Configure HyperTerminal for hardware handshaking (i.e. RTS/CTS) and run a C program on the 8051 to demonstrate that it works.

Equipment:

1. Si Labs 8051 development kit
2. Line-Powered RS-232 Transceiver Chip (MAX233). This chip was chosen because it doesn't require external capacitors – an unusual feature for transceiver chips. The chip has two transceivers. The second one will be used for the RTS/CTS hardware handshaking lines.
3. Female DB9 connector with five wires for TxD, RxD, RTS, CTS and GND.
4. PC with HyperTerminal or equivalent. **NOTE:** HyperTerminal is not available in Windows Vista.

Schematic:

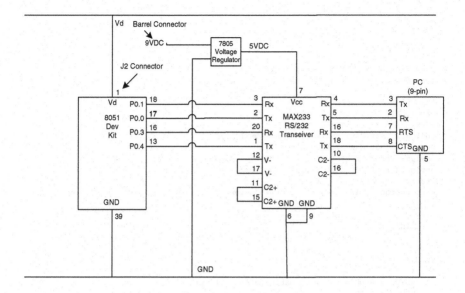

Program:

Program Listing for Lab 8 (software handshaking)

```
//-----------------------------------------------------------------------------
// Lab8soft.c (3-wire serial communication with software handshaking)
//-----------------------------------------------------------------------------
//
//
// Tool chain: KEIL Eval 'c'
//
//-----------------------------------------------------------------------------
// Includes
//-----------------------------------------------------------------------------

#include <C8051F000.h> // SFR declarations
#include <stdio.h>


//-----------------------------------------------------------------------------
// Global Constants
//-----------------------------------------------------------------------------
#define PRESSED 1
#define NOT_PRESSED 0
#define UART_BUFFERSIZE 64
#define XON 0x11
#define XOFF 0x13
#define CR 0x0D
#define LF 0x0A
```

```
//-----------------------------------------------------------------------------
// Function Prototypes
//-----------------------------------------------------------------------------

void OSCILLATOR_Init( void );
void PORT_Init( void );
void UART0_Init( void );
void Send_Str( unsigned char *s );
void Send_Char( unsigned char c );

//-----------------------------------------------------------------------------
// Global Variables
//-----------------------------------------------------------------------------
unsigned char UART_Buffer[UART_BUFFERSIZE];
unsigned char UART_Buffer_Size = 0;
unsigned char XONsent = 0;  // One shot flag
unsigned char XOFFsent = 0; // One shot flag
static unsigned char Byte;
sbit button = P1 ^ 7;       // pushbutton on development board

//-----------------------------------------------------------------------------
// main() Routine
//-----------------------------------------------------------------------------

void main( void )
    {
    WDTCN = 0xDE;       // Disable watchdog timer
    WDTCN = 0xAD;

    OSCILLATOR_Init(); // Initialize oscillator
    PORT_Init();        // Initialize crossbar and GPIO
    UART0_Init();       // Initialize UART0
    EA = 1;             // Enable interrupts

    while (1)
        {
        // Check switch status
        if (button == PRESSED && XONsent == 0) // signal to start transmission
            {
            Send_Char(XON);
            XONsent = 1;
            XOFFsent = 0;
            }

        if (button != PRESSED && XOFFsent == 0) // signal to stop transmission
            {
            Send_Char(XOFF);
            XOFFsent = 1;
            XONsent = 0;
            }

        // If the complete word has been entered via the hyperterminal followed by
        // carriage return
        if (UART_Buffer_Size != 0 && Byte == 13)
            {
            UART_Buffer[UART_Buffer_Size++] = LF; // Add LF (CR already in string)
            UART_Buffer[UART_Buffer_Size] = 0x00; // Null terminate string
            Send_Str(&UART_Buffer[0]);
            UART_Buffer_Size = 0;
            Byte = 0;
            }
        }
    }
```

```
//-------------------------------------------------------------------------------
// Initialization Subroutines
//-------------------------------------------------------------------------------

//-------------------------------------------------------------------------------
// OSCILLATOR_Init
//-------------------------------------------------------------------------------
//
// Return Value : None
// Parameters   : None
//
//
//-------------------------------------------------------------------------------
void OSCILLATOR_Init( void )
    {
    OSCICN = 0x07; // Internal oscillator -- 16Mhz
    }


//-------------------------------------------------------------------------------
// PORT_Init
//-------------------------------------------------------------------------------
//
// Return Value : None
// Parameters   : None
//
// This function configures the crossbar and GPIO ports.
//
// Pinout:
//
// P0.0   digital   push-pull    UART TX
// P0.1   digital   open-drain   UART RX
//-------------------------------------------------------------------------------
void PORT_Init( void )
    {
    XBR0 = 0x04;     // Enable UART0
    XBR1 = 0x00;
    XBR2 = 0x40;     // Enable crossbar and weak pull-up

    PRT0CF |= 0x01; // Set TX pin to push-pull
    }


//-------------------------------------------------------------------------------
// UART0_Init    Variable baud rate, Timer 2, 8-N-1
//-------------------------------------------------------------------------------
//
// Return Value : None
// Parameters   : None
//
// Configure UART0 for operation at <baudrate> 8-N-1 using Timer2 as
// baud rate source.
//
//-------------------------------------------------------------------------------
void UART0_Init( void )
    {
    CKCON = 0x20;
    T2CON = 0x34;
// The two lines below are for a clock speed of 2Mhz
//RCAP2L    = 0x2C; // 300bps (set to 294.81bps to compensate for oscillator drift)
//RCAP2H    = 0xFF; // values are from Config2 tool
// The two lines below are for a clock speed of 16Mhz
//RCAP2L    = 0x60; // 300bps (set to 294.81bps to compensate for oscillator drift)
//RCAP2H    = 0xF9; // values from Config2 tool
```

```
     // The two lines below are for a clock speed of 16Mhz
     RCAP2L = 0xCB; // 9600bps (set to 9433.96bps to compensate for oscillator drift)
     RCAP2H = 0xFF; // values from Config2 tool
     TL2 = RCAP2L;
     TH2 = RCAP2H;
     TR2 = 1;      // Start Timer2

     SCON = 0x50; // 8-bit variable baud rate;
     // 9th bit ignored; RX enabled
     // clear all flags
     ES = 1; // Enable se-rial interrupt
     }

void Send_Char( unsigned char c )
     {
     if ((c >= 0x61) && (c <= 0x7A))
        { // If lower case letter
        c -= 32;
        }

     SBUF = c;       // send character

     while (!TI) { } // wait until character has been send
     TI = 0;
     }

void Send_Str( unsigned char *s )
     {
     unsigned char ch;

     while (*s != 0x00) // keep looping until NULL termination is reached
        {
        ch = *s;

        if ((ch >= 0x61) && (ch <= 0x7A))
           { // If lower case letter
           ch -= 32;
           }

        SBUF = ch;      // send character

        while (!TI) { } // wait until character has been send
        TI = 0;
        s++;            // get next character in string
        }
     }

//-----------------------------------------------------------------------------
// UART0_Interrupt
//-----------------------------------------------------------------------------
//
// This routine is invoked whenever a character is entered on the
// Hyperterminal.
//
//-----------------------------------------------------------------------------

void UART0_Interrupt (void) interrupt 4
     {
     if (RI)         // Check if receive flag is set
        {
        Byte = SBUF; // Read a character from Hyperterminal
        RI = 0;      // Clear receive flag
```

```
            if (UART_Buffer_Size < UART_BUFFERSIZE - 2)
                {
                UART_Buffer[UART_Buffer_Size] = Byte; // Store character
                UART_Buffer_Size++;                   // Update array's size
                }
            }
        }
```

```
//-----------------------------------------------------------------------------
// End Of File
//-----------------------------------------------------------------------------
```

Program Listing for Lab 8 (hardware handshaking)

```
//-----------------------------------------------------------------------------
// Lab8hard.c (5-wire serial communication -- hardware handshaking with RTS/CTS)
//-----------------------------------------------------------------------------
//
//
// Tool chain: KEIL Eval 'c'
//
//-----------------------------------------------------------------------------
// Includes
//-----------------------------------------------------------------------------

#include <C8051F000.h> // SFR declarations
#include <stdio.h>

//-----------------------------------------------------------------------------
// Global Constants
//-----------------------------------------------------------------------------

#define UART_BUFFERSIZE 64
#define PRESSED 1
#define NOT_PRESSED 0
#define ON 0
#define OFF 1
#define CR 0x0D
#define LF 0x0A

//-----------------------------------------------------------------------------
// Function Prototypes
//-----------------------------------------------------------------------------

void OSCILLATOR_Init( void );
void PORT_Init( void );
void UART0_Init( void );
void Send_Str( unsigned char *s );

//-----------------------------------------------------------------------------
// Global Variables
//-----------------------------------------------------------------------------

unsigned char UART_Buffer[UART_BUFFERSIZE];
unsigned char UART_Buffer_Size = 0;
static char Byte;
sbit button = P1 ^ 7; // pushbutton on development board
sbit rts = P0 ^ 3;    // RTS handshaking signal from PC
sbit cts = P0 ^ 4;    // CTS handshaking signal to PC


//-----------------------------------------------------------------------------
// main() Routine
```

```
//------------------------------------------------------------------------------

void main( void )
    {
    WDTCN = 0xDE;        // Disable watchdog timer
    WDTCN = 0xAD;

    OSCILLATOR_Init(); // Initialize oscillator
    PORT_Init();        // Initialize crossbar and GPIO
    UART0_Init();       // Initialize UART0

    EA = 1;

    while (1)
        {
        // Check switch status
        // No switch debounce may mean that the CTS/RTS lines will bounce too
        // Shouldn't be a problem for the PC.
        if (button == PRESSED)
            {
            cts = ON;
            }
        else
            {
            cts = OFF;
            }

        // If the complete word has been entered via the hyperterminal followed by
        // carriage return
        if (UART_Buffer_Size != 0 && Byte == 13)
            {
            UART_Buffer[UART_Buffer_Size++] = LF; // Add LF (CR already in string)
            UART_Buffer[UART_Buffer_Size] = 0x00; // Null terminate string
            Send_Str(&UART_Buffer[0]);
            UART_Buffer_Size = 0;
            Byte = 0;
            }
        }
    }

//------------------------------------------------------------------------------
// Initialization Subroutines
//------------------------------------------------------------------------------

//------------------------------------------------------------------------------
// OSCILLATOR_Init
//------------------------------------------------------------------------------
//
// Return Value : None
// Parameters    : None
//
//
//------------------------------------------------------------------------------
void OSCILLATOR_Init( void )
    {
    OSCICN = 0x07; // Internal oscillator -- 16Mhz
    }

//------------------------------------------------------------------------------
// PORT_Init
//------------------------------------------------------------------------------
//
// Return Value : None
```

```
// Parameters    : None
//
// This function configures the crossbar and GPIO ports.
//
// Pinout:
//
// P0.0   digital    push-pull     UART TX
// P0.1   digital    open-drain    UART RX
// P0.3   digital    open-drain    RTS
// P0.4   digitial   push-pull     CTS
//-----------------------------------------------------------------------------
void PORT_Init( void )
    {
    XBR0 = 0x04;     // Enable UART0
    XBR1 = 0x00;
    XBR2 = 0x40;     // Enable crossbar and weak pull-up

    PRT0CF |= 0x11; // Set TX and CTS to push-pull
    }


//-----------------------------------------------------------------------------
// UART0_Init    Variable baud rate, Timer 2, 8-N-1
//-----------------------------------------------------------------------------
//
// Return Value : None
// Parameters   : None
//
// Configure UART0 for operation at <baudrate> 8-N-1 using Timer2 as
// baud rate source.
//
//-----------------------------------------------------------------------------
void UART0_Init( void )
    {
    CKCON = 0x20;
    T2CON = 0x34;
// The two lines below are for a clock speed of 2Mhz
//RCAP2L  = 0x2C; // 300bps (set to 294.81bps to compensate for oscillator drift)
//RCAP2H  = 0xFF; // values are from Config2 tool
// The two lines below are for a clock speed of 16Mhz
//RCAP2L  = 0x60; // 300bps (set to 294.81bps to compensate for oscillator drift)
//RCAP2H  = 0xF9; // values from Config2 tool
    // The two lines below are for a clock speed of 16Mhz
    RCAP2L = 0xCB; // 9600bps (set to 9433.96bps to compensate for oscillator drift)
    RCAP2H = 0xFF; // values from Config2 tool
    TL2 = RCAP2L;
    TH2 = RCAP2H;
    TR2 = 1;      // Start Timer2

    SCON = 0x50; // 8-bit variable baud rate;
    // 9th bit ignored; RX enabled
    // clear all flags
    ES = 1; // Enable se-rial interrupt
    }

void Send_Str( unsigned char *s )
    {
    unsigned char ch;

    while (*s != 0x00) // keep looping until NULL termination is reached
        {
        ch = *s;

        if ((ch >= 0x61) && (ch <= 0x7A))
```

```
                { // If lower case letter
                ch -= 32;
                }

        SBUF = ch;        // send character

        while (!TI) { } // wait until character has been send
        TI = 0;
        s++;              // get next character in string
        }
    }

//------------------------------------------------------------------------------
// UART0_Interrupt
//------------------------------------------------------------------------------
//
// This routine is invoked whenever a character is entered or displayed on the
// Hyperterminal.
//
//------------------------------------------------------------------------------

void
UART0_Interrupt(void)
interrupt

4
    {
    if (RI)           // Check if receive flag is set
        {
        Byte = SBUF; // Read a character from Hyperterminal
        RI = 0;       // Clear receive flag

        if (UART_Buffer_Size < UART_BUFFERSIZE - 2)
            {
            UART_Buffer[UART_Buffer_Size] = Byte; // Store character
            UART_Buffer_Size++;                    // Update array's size
            }
        }
    }

//------------------------------------------------------------------------------
// End Of File
//------------------------------------------------------------------------------
```

Step-By-Step:

1. Wire up the circuit **from Lab 6** for software handshaking.
2. Open the IDE and close any open projects.
3. Your lab instructor should provide you with the source files for this lab. Open the project file **Lab8soft.wsp** by selecting *Project* → *Open Project* from the menu. This program demonstrates software handshaking.
4. Compile and download the program using the following steps:

   – Select *Project* → *Rebuild Project* from the menu or use the toolbar button.
   – Select *Debug* → *Connect* from the menu or use the toolbar button.

- Click the ***Download Code*** button on the toolbar.
- If your code is correct and you have a good connection to your board, the program should compile, connect and download to the 8051.

5. Press the green ***RUN*** button on the toolbar to run your program.
6. Open HyperTerminal and connect to the serial port. The HyperTerminal connection should be set for 9600,8,N,1. Also set the port to software handshaking (i.e. XON/XOFF) by changing the flow control property.
7. This program is the same as in Lab 6 except that handshaking has been added.
8. The pushbutton on your SI Labs development board will be used to control the flow of data from HyperTerminal to the 8051. Pressing the button will allow characters to be received from HyperTerminal. This approach makes it easy to see handshaking in action.
9. Type a word or phrase into HyperTerminal and press the ENTER key. Nothing should happen.
10. Press and hold the pushbutton. The word or phrase should be echoed back in uppercase. The demonstration of software handshaking is complete.
11. **Tip:** If you receive some (or all) "garbage" characters back, it may be a problem with the baud rate. Check both HyperTerminal and C program settings. When designing and testing this lab, we found the internal oscillator to be inaccurate and had to experiment with the baud rate within $+/- 1\%$. This is reflected in the code comments.
12. Wire up the circuit as shown in the schematic for hardware handshaking. This circuit uses the RTS/CTS handshaking lines. These lines are typically used to keep buffers on either end from overflowing. Alternatively, the DTR/DSR handshaking lines are used to indicate that a device is powered-up and ready to communicate.
13. Now open the project file, **Lab8hard.wsp.** Compile, download and run the program.
14. Open HyperTerminal again and use the settings as before except for flow control. Set the port to use hardware handshaking (i.e. HARDWARE) by changing the flow control property.
15. The pushbutton on your SI Labs development board will be used again to control the flow of data from HyperTerminal to the 8051. Pressing the button will allow characters to be received from HyperTerminal. This makes it easy to see handshaking in action.
16. Type a word or phrase into HyperTerminal and press the ENTER key. Nothing should happen.
17. Press and hold the pushbutton. The word or phrase should be echoed back in uppercase.
18. **Tip:** If you receive some (or all) "garbage" characters back, it may be a problem with the baud rate. Check both HyperTerminal and C program settings. When designing and testing this lab, we found the internal oscillator to be inaccurate and had to experiment with the baud rate within +/- 1%. This is reflected in the code comments.

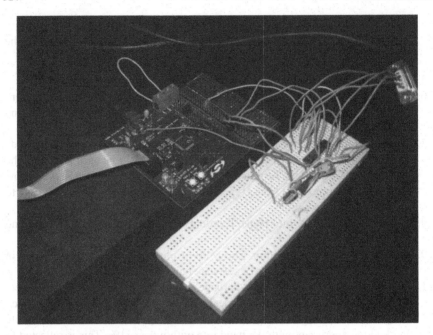

Fig. 9.18 Lab 8 Photo (5-wire, hardware handshaking)

Lab Wrap-up:

1. Demonstrate to the lab instructor that both programs are working properly.

Questions:

1. What are the pros and cons of using software versus hardware handshaking?

Additional Exercises (Optional):

1. Modify the circuit and program to verify the operation of the DTR/DSR lines.
   Hint: This mostly involves changing the wiring on the 9-pin connector.
2. This lab used the internal oscillator set at a frequency of 16MHz. This clock frequency is not optimal for generating baud rates. In fact, there are only a few baud rates that can be used at this frequency. Choose an external crystal to be installed at Q1 on the SI Labs development kit (either 11.0592MHz or 22.1184MHz). Determine the highest baud rate for the chosen crystal. Rerun the lab at this

higher baud rate without the crystal and verify that it doesn't work. Install the crystal and run the lab again. It should work correctly.

3. The software flow control is only a partial implementation – the 8051 application will send a control character to stop HyperTerminal from sending data. However, if HyperTerminal sends a control character to stop data transmission, it will be ignored by the 8051 application. Modify the code to accept XON/XOFF control characters from the PC. Since it may be difficult to overrun the buffers on a fast, modern PC, write a small program in the language of your choice on the PC side to send the XON/XOFF characters under program control. Test the programs to verify that the 8051 application stops sending data when commanded.

4. The hardware flow control is also a partial implementation. As in exercise 3, modify the program to respond to the RTS input from the PC and test with a custom PC program.

Appendix A
C programming Primer

A.1 Overview

C is a typical structured programming language. C was created by Brian Kernighan and Dennis Ritchie in the early 70s. The first well known "Hello world" C program was introduced in their "The C Programming language" book in 70's.

```c
#include <stdio.h>    /* standard library header file */
int main()
{
 printf("Hello World\n");   //display greetings on screen
 return 0;
}
```

The #include is a C preprocessor directive used to make C library functions, like printf() available to use, which is defined in the stdio.h standard library header file. There are many other standard libraries such as math.h. You can also include your own library header file you write yourself. A C program is no more than a collection of functions and data declarations.

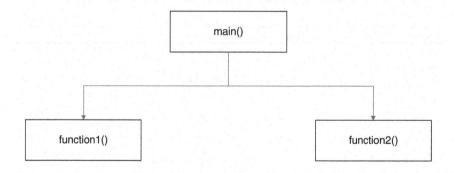

The main() function is the main entrance of the program. Here the printf() function is called by the main() function to displays formatted data on screen just like the function1() in above C program structure diagram The function1 and function2 are two task specific reusable sub-functions used(called) by the main() function The "return 0;"statement returns status zero which can be accessed at the operating system.

You might have notice that all functions are followed by (), the body of a function is embraced by curly braces {}, and all statements in C are marked with a ";". The directive doest not end with ";".

C is a case-sensitive language. There are two type of comments available: one is "//" and the other is a pair of "/*" and "*/" as shown in the example above.

A.2 Data Types in C

A.2.1 Primitive Data Types

Char types

All C integer types can be signed or unsigned and signed is default.

Specifier	Bytes	Minimum	Maximum
signed char	1	−128	+127
unsigned char	1	0	255
Char	1	−128 *or* 0	+127 *or* 255

Integer types

The integer types come with various sizes, with varying amounts of memory usage and range limit. Modifiers are used to designate the size: short, long.

Specifier	Bytes	Minimum	Maximum
signed short int	2	$-32,768(-2^{15})$	$+32,767(2^{15}-1)$
unsigned short int	2	0	65,535
signed int	2 *or* 4	$-32,768$ *or* $-2,147,483,648(-2^{31})$	$+32,767$ *or* $+2,147,483,647(2^{31}-1)$
unsigned int	2 *or* 4	0	$65,535(2^{16}-1)$ *or* $4,294,967,295(2^{32}-1)$
signed long int	4	$-2,147,483,648$	$+2,147,483,647$
unsigned long int	4	0	4,294,967,295

Floating point types

The floating-point type represents numbers with a fractional component.

Specifier	Bytes	Range	Precision
`float`	4	$(+-)3.4 \text{x} 10^{+-38}$	7 digits accuracy
`double`	8	$(+-)11.7 \text{x} 10^{+-308}$	15 digits accuracy
`long double`	8	$(+-)11.7 \text{x} 10^{+-308}$	15 digits accuracy

A floating-point constant can be either in decimal notation, e.g. 1.234 or in Scientific notation by adding e or E followed by a decimal exponent, e.g. 1.234E3 But remember this value does not match int type 1234 any more if you compare them because all float type value its precision in a approximation range.

Variables

Variables in C are used to store data. For example,

```
int a1=1,b2;
```
// define int variable a1 with initial value 1 and int type variable b2 with default 0

```
float x,y=1.2;
```
// define float type variable x with default 1 value 0.0
//and float type variable b with initial value 1.2

Variable identifier must start with an alphabet character and followed by mix of characters or digits plus underscore "_" . Any C variable must be declared before being used. Any function which returns a type of data must also be declared (prototyped) as well before being used. You will see the detailed discussion in the section of functions.

`float y = 1.2;` combines the declaration and initialization in the same line.

A C assignment statement has a form of

```
<variable> = <expression>
```

It evaluates the value of the expression on the right side and assigns the evaluated value to the target of left side variable to let it hold this value.

```
#include <math.h>
#define pi 3.14159

float x;

x=2*sin(pi/4) +sqrt(2);
```

A.2.2 Enumerated Type

The enum keyword is used to specify the enumerated type in C which represents a series of named constants. Each of the enumerated constants has type int (starting from 0) so that each enum type itself is compatible with char or a signed or unsigned integer type.

For example, consider the following declaration:

```
enum day_type { sunday, Monday, Tuesday, Wednesday,
Thursday, Friday,Saturday } day;
```

which declares the enum day_type type; the int constants Monday is zero; Saturday is 6; and the enum day_type variable day_var.

A.2.3 Pointer Type

The asterisk modifier (*) specifies a pointer type in a declaration of a variable.

```
int * ptr;
int a=1, b;
```

In this example, the specifier int would refer to the integral type, the specifier int * refers to the type "pointer to integer" so that variable a is a int type variable used to hold an integer value while the ptr variable is a pointer type variable used to refer to a int type variable. A pointer has two pieces of information: a memory address and a data type

You can use a C assignment statement to make a pointer reference a memory address as follows

```
ptr = &a;
```

Here the & is a operator named as "address of". You always associate a memory location to a pointer rather than a numeric data. You should never assign numeric value to the ptr pointer variable.

The pointed-to data can be accessed through a pointer in the way called dereferencing:

```
b = *ptr;
```

It returns the value of variable a which is pointed to by the pointer ptr.

A.2.4 Arrays

An array is used to store a set of consecutive data elements with the same data type. A fixed size array is declared as follows.

```
int a[100];
```

which defines an array named a to hold 100 values of the primitive type int. a[i] refers to i-indexed element of the array a, where i is the subscript or index operator of the array. Array subscript numbering begins at 0. The largest allowed array subscript for this array a is 99 (100 − 1).

The addresses of each of the array elements can also be expressed in its equivalent pointer notation. E.g.,

```
int x, *p = a;
```

`x=a[i];` is same as

`x=*(p+i);` or `x=*(a+i);`

Here a[i] represents the (i-1)th element in the array a.($0 <= i <= 99$)

An array name implies the location of this array, i.e. the address of the first element of the array which can be used as a pointer. To assign a value to the first element of the array a, you can do it by

`*a =3;` instead of `a[0]=3;`

Or you can do like this:

`*(a+2) =5;`

which is same as

`a[2] =3;`

You may ask whether a pointer is necessary. In many cases there are no other options to bypass it, e.g. dynamic arrays declaration for an array with variable dynamic size.

The `malloc` function in stdlib.h library can allocate memory space for an array dynamically with the pointer facility. It takes one parameter: the amount of memory to allocate in bytes. The function `malloc` returns a pointer pointing to the beginning of the allocated space.

```
int *a, n;
n=1000;
a = malloc(n * sizeof(int));
a[3] = 150;
```

Here the pointer points to an int array of 1000 elements. The pointer and array notations can be used alternatively. If the dynamically allocated memory is not needed any more, it should be released back to reused. This can be done by

```
free(a);
a = NULL;
```

which release all the space allocated to the pointer(array) a.

Multidimensional arrays

Multidimensional arrays are also supported in C as follows:

```
int a_2d[100][20];
```

Reading the subscripts from left to right, a_2d is an array of 100 elements, each element of which is an array of 20 ints. To access an integer element of 3rd row, 4th element in that row in this 2D array, you use

```
array2d[2][3]
```

A.2.5 Char and Strings

In C, a character literal is represented by single-quotes, e.g. **'B'**, and have type **int** (not **char**). A string literal is represented by double quotes ("), e.g. **"B"**, in a null-terminated format. The difference is that **"B"** represents a pointer to the first element of a null-terminated array, whereas **'B'** directly represents the ASCII value (66). "" is a empty string with a null(\0) but empty char '' is invalid.

If you wish to include a double quote inside the string, you must escape it with a backslash (\), e.g. \''A pair of double quotes\''. To include a literal backslash, use \\. The other escape usages are \'(single quote), \n(new line), \r(carriage return), \b(back space), \t(tab), \f(line feed), and more.

A string is an array of char type elements. You can initialize a string like this

```
char str[] = ''Hello world!'';
```

or

```
char str[13];
str[0]='H';
str[1]='e';
. . .
str[11]='!';
str[12]='\0';      // the null char which means the
                   // end of string EOS
```

You can also use char point to handle a string.

```
char *strp = ''How are you?'';
```

You can print a string by printf function using either the name of the string or the name of the pointer.

```
print(''%s'', str);    // print Hello world!
print(''%s'', strp);   // print How are you?
```

You can get input for a string variable str from keyboard as

```
scanf(''%s'', str);
```

String Library functions

The string.h library provides many most commonly used string functions:

- strcat(dest, source) appends the string source to the end of string dest
- strchr(s, c) finds the first instance of character c in string s and returns a pointer to it or a null pointer if c is not found
- strcmp(a, b) compares strings a and b returns negative if a is less than b, 0 if equal, positive if greater in dictionary order.
- strcpy(dest, source) copies the string source onto the string dest
- strlen(st) return the length of string st

A.2.6   Structures and Unions

The structure type in C is similar to record type in other language. A struct type has
a set of named members with various types.

```
struct point
{
    int x;
    int y;
}
```

```
point p1, p2;    //two pint type variables p1, p2
```

You can initialize a point struct variable p1 simply by

```
point p3 = {2,3};
```

Now p3.x is 2 and p1.y is 3, where p3.x and p3.y refer to the coordinate x, y of
the point p3.

```
struct circlr
{
    point center;
    Float area;
}c1,c2;   // You can also declare variables when you
          // define the structure.
          // two circle type variables c1, c2
```

Here c1.area refers the area of c1 and c1.ceter.x and c1.center.y are the coordi-
nates of the center of the circle c1.

Union is similar to variant record type in other language that may hold different
types and sizes at different time without the need to allocate additional memory
space for each new type. The size of a union is equal to the size of its largest member.
In most cases you see the member of a union is a large array because it can save
space in this way.

```
union share
{
    int    x[1000];
    float y[500];
} n;
```

In this example, the members x and member y overlap because they share same
memory space. Once a new value is assigned to a member such as y[0], the existing
data in x[0] and x[1] are wiped over with the new data. In other word, member x
and member y should be used in sequence instead of interleave.

A.2.7 User Defined Type with typedef

typedef is often used to define a new data type by giving a new name to an already defined type, struct, or union types.

```
typedef float real; //rename float to real
real r, s;
typedef struct {
    float x;
    float y;
} point;
point first, second;  // two variables of type point
```

With the new defined data type point, it's easier to create more complex types such as triangle.

```
typedef struct {
    point v1;
    point v2;
    point v3;
} triangle;
```

In addition, you can define a constant variable PI by a C preprocessor define directive as

```
#define const PI 3.14159
```

which can be referenced in many places in a program and one only need to change its definition in order to adjust its value.

This directive is also often used to define a macro such as

```
#define ABS(x)  ((x) < 0) ? -(x) : (x)
```

which can be used ABS(2-4) where the expression 2-3 substitute for x and return a $+1$ value.

There are many other preprocessor directive in C such as

```
#ifndef
// followed by a name. If that name is not defined then
// it is true.

#else //This is part of #ifndef preprocessor statement.

#endif
```

Because you might define your own macro or const variable but it might conflict with the existing definitions in the header files you include in your program. By this directive, you can avoid such conflicts.

A.2.8   Variable Scope Specifiers

Every variable has its visibility scope. Variables declared within a block or a function by default has automatic storage scope which may only be used within functions or blocks where they are defined. They are also called local variables because their scope is local to the function or block where they are defined. Here a block is specified by curly braces {}.

The `extern` specifier indicates that the data variable has been defined elsewhere either outside block or outside of the file. Sometimes a C program consists of multiple files. If a function may need to access a variable defined in another file then it must use an extern specifier to reference that variable across files.

file_1.c

```
main ()

{
    extern int i;
}
```

file-2.c

```
int i

function()
{
}
```

In this example, the function `main()` in file_1 can use the variable x defined in file_2.

Another scope specifier is called `static`. The name `static` is given to variables which can hold their values between calls of a function: they are allocated only once and their values are preserved between function calls. Every global variable, defined outside all functions and blocks, has the type static storage duration automatically while local variable defined within functions has automatic storage duration. A local variable does not preserve its value across function calls.

A.3   Operators

There are many C operators. You can classify them into number of categories: arithmetic operators, logical operators, relational operators, and other operators.

A.3.1   Arithmetic and Shift Operators

$+ - * / \%$

You should note the /(division) and %(module) operations values.

E.g. $5/9 -> 0$(quotient of integer ion) and $9/5 -> 4$(remainder of integer division)

All these operator can work with assignment operator $=$, such as $a+ = 2$ is short of $a = a+2$.

Parentheses ( ) are used for forcing a priority over operators such as $a^*(b+c)$.

C also supports unary operators

$++ -- + -$

$++ (--)$ is an unary increment (decrement) operator(add one to/ subtract one from).

$a++;$ //is same as $a = a+1;$

$a--;$ // is same as $a = a-1;$

decrement: subtract one from

A.3.2 Bitwise Operators

C supports 6 bitwise operators listed in the table below. They are widely used in embedded software due to memory space saving and time reduction.

Operator	Function	Operand1	Opramd2	result
&	AND	00000101(5)	00000110(6)	00000100(4)
|	OR	00000101(5)	00000110(6)	00000111(7)
^	XOR	00000101(5)	00000110(6)	00000011(3)
~	One's complement	00000101(5)		11111010(250)
>>	Shift right	2		00000001(1)
<<	Shift left	2		00010100(20)

```
x = 5;
x <<= 2; // same as x = x << 2;
```

A.3.3 Relational Operators

operator¿		function	Oprand1	Operand2	result
==	¿	is equal to	5	5	true
!-	¿	is not equal to	3	5	false
>	¿	Is greater	5	3	true
	¿	than			
<	¿	Is less	5	3	false
	¿	than			
>=	¿	Is greater	5	5	true
	¿	than or			
	¿	equal to			
<=	¿	Is less	55		false
	¿	than or			
	¿	equal to			

The values which they produce are called true and false. As words, "true" and "false" are not defined normally in C, but you can define them as constant macros

```
#define TRUE 1
#define FALSE 0
```

C assumes zero value as False and any non-zero values as True. E.g.

```
(1 != 0)
```

has the value "true" (which could be any non- zero). The statement:

```
(1 == 0)
```

would be false, so the expression has a zero value.

A.3.4 Logical Operators

operator	function	Operand1	Operand2	result
%%	AND	$1 > 2$	$3! = 4$	false
||	OR	$1 > 2$	$3! = 4$	true
!	NOT	$!(1 > 2)$		True

A.4 Functions

A.4.1 Function Definition

A C function performs a specified task. You have seen the main() function and printf() function in the hello world program. A function definition consists of a return type (void if no value is returned), a function name, a list of parameters in parentheses (void if there are none), and various statements in the body of the function. A function with return type should include at least one return statement:

```
<return-type> functionName( <parameter-list> )
{
    <statements>
    return <expression of type return-type>;
}
```

where <parameter-list> of n parameter variables is declared as data type and parameter variable name separated by a comma:

<data-type> p-var1, <data-type> p-var2, ... <data-type> p-varN

A function without return value is a action which itself is a C statement. A function with return value can not be used as a statement, Such function has a value which can be part of other expression.. Here is an example of add function which is called by the main() function. The add function is defined before it is used by main() function.

```c
#include <stdio.h>

int add(int x, int y)
{
    return x + y;
}

int main(int argc, char* args[])
{
    int a,b, sum ;
    scanf(<< %d %d >>, &a, &b) ;
    sum = add(x,y) ;
    printf("%d", sum);
    return 0;
}
```

You can also give a prototype of the function add() prior the main() function, and give the definition of the add function later.

```c
#include <stdio.h>

int add(int x, int y); //prototype of the add function

int main(int argc, char* args[])
{
    int a,b, sum ;
    scanf(<< %d %d >>, &a, &b) ;
    sum = add(a,b) ;
    printf("%d", sum);
    return 0;
}

int add(int x, int y); //function add definition
{
    return x + y;
}
```

A.4.2 Function Parameters

There are two type parameters:: *value* parameters and *variable* parameters. Value parameters are one-way communication carrying information into a function from the function caller. Variable parameters are two-way communication which can alter the values of the parameters the caller passed in.

A.4.2.1 Value Parameters

The add() function above carries two value parameters x and y. Once a value of actual parameter a (argument) is passes into a function its value is copied to the formal parameter x. same as b and y. After that the connection between actual argument a(b) and formal parameter x(y) are disconnected.

In the add() example, if you provide 3 for a and 4 for b from keyboard, then the formal parameter x will get value 3 from the actual argument a and the formal parameter y will get value 4 from the actual argument b, and the add(3,4) function call will return a 7 to variable sum.

A.4.2.2 Variable Parameters

One way to return data back is to use the return statement but at most one data can be returned by the return statement. A variable parameter can be used to alter a actual argument or return a value. You can see that a variable parameter is a pointer type parameter from the following example. This is also why pointer is so important in C.

```
#include <stdio.h>

modify ( int *x, int *y);

main ()
{
int a=2, b=3;
modify (&a,&b);
printf (" %d  %d", a, b)
}

modify ( int *x, int *y)
{
*x = *x + 1;
*y = *y - 1;
}
```

The ampersand & operator can be read as "the address of " and * operators can be read as "the contents at the address pointed to by ". So, the statement $^*x =^* x + 1$ can be interpreted as

Add 1 to the contents at the address pointed to by pointer x and assign it to the contents of the address pointed to by pointed to by x. Because the pointer x is associated with the address of actual argument a so that the effect of this statement is $a = a + 1$ which increments a by 1.

Finally, $a = 3$ and $b = 2$.

Try the function with value parameters in next program, see what happens.

```
#include <stdio.h>

modify ( int x, int y);

main ()
{
int a=2, b=3;
modify ( a, b);
printf (" %d  %d", a, b)
}

modify ( int x, int y)
{
x = x + 1;
y = y - 1;
}
```

A.5   Control Structures

Any structured program can be constructed by three constructs: sequence construct, selection construct, and loop construct.

Sequence construct organize statements in a sequence and they are executed sequentially.

A compound statement or a block

```
{
statement-1;
statement-1;
...
statement-1;
}
```

is a typical sequence construct where each individual statement-i can be a assignment statement, if selection statement, while loop statement, or another compound statement.

A selection construct provides conditional branch and decision making logic. The typical C statements are if-else statement and switch statement.

A loop construct provides the repetition logic and its C statements are while-do, for, and do-while statements.

Any C program can be programmed with assignment statement, if statement, and while statement only. The other statements just provide alternate convenience in programming.

A.5.1 Selection Statements

C has two types of selection statements: if statement and switch statement.
The syntax of if statement is

```
if (<condition>)
    <statement1>
[else
    <statement2>]
```

The <condition> is a logical expression. If the <condition> is nonzero (true), control forwards to <statement1>. If the else clause is present and the <logical expression> is zero (false), control will switch to <statement2>. An else always matches the nearest previous unmatched if clause in a nested if – else statement. Here the <statement1> and <statement2> can be another if statement nested there.

Here is an example of if statement which assign a bigger value to variable big out of variables x and y.

```
int x, y big;
scanf("%d %d", &x, &y);
if (x>y) big =x ; else big = y ;
```

A nested if statement is given as follows

```
if (temp < 70)
    {
    printf ("failed");
    }

else

    {
    if (result < 80)
        {
        printf ("passed");
        }
```

```
    else

        {
        if (result < 90)
            {
            printf ("good!");
            }
        Else
            printf("excellent!");
        }


    }


}
```

The switch statement forwards control to one of several statements depending on the value of an expression, which must have integral type. The most often seen types for the expression in the switch statement are char, int, enum types. Here <statement 1> and <statement 2> are often compound statements. Actually, any switch statement can be implemented by an if statement. The syntax is as follows:

```
switch (<expression>)
{
    case <label1> :
        <statements 1>
        break;
    case <label2> :
        <statements 2>
        break;
    default :
        <statements 3>
}
```

if none of the case labels match to the expression in the parentheses following switch, control goes to the default label, or if there is no default label, control moves to next statement. A simple switch example is given as follows.

```
int digit;
scanf("%d", &digit);
switch (digit)
    {
    case 0 : printf ("failure");
            break;
    case 1 : printf ("failure");
            break;
    case 2 : printf ("pass");
            break;
```

```
case 3 : printf ("good");
         break;
case 4: printf ("excellent");
        break;
default: printf ("error");
        break;
};
```

A.5.2 Loop Statements

C provides three types of loop, while, do while and for.

The while loop repeats an action until the loop termination condition is false-(zero). This is useful where the programmer does not know in advance how many iterations the loop needs.

The do while loop is similar to while loop, but the loop termination test occurs after the loop body is executed. This ensures that the loop body is run at least once.

The for loop is frequently used, usually where the loop will repeat a fixed number of iterations.

A.5.2.1 while Loop

The while-loop has a condition:

```
while (<condition>)
   {
   <statements>;
   }
```

and the statements in the curly braces are executed repeatedly as long as the condition remains nonzero (true). The <statements> can be a compound statement which consists of a block of statements, another nested while loop statement, or any other statements.

A simplest while loop can be written as

```
while(1);
```

This is an infinitive loop which runs forever and never stop. You may ask what application it has. You know any operation system itself is an infinitive loop and any embedded software is designed as a infinitive loop as well in the following pattern.

```
init();
while(1)
{
Process-1();
.  .  .
process-n();
}
```

The following C program counts the number of spaces in a input line.

```
#include <stdio.h>

main ()
{
   char ch;
   int count = 0;

   printf ("Input a text line\n");

   while ((ch = getchar()) != '\n')
   {
   if (ch == ' ')
     {
        count++;
     }
   }
   printf("# of space = %d\n", count);
}
```

You can also have loop statement in a function. Here is a function to count the number of characters in a string which is similar to strlen() function in string.h.

```
int count(char s[])   //same int as count(char *s)
{
    int i = 0;

    while (s[i] != '\0')    //'\0' is the EOL mark
                            //of null char
       i++;

    return i;

}
```

This function has a char pointer type parameter which takes an. array location. i.e. a char string. It is a variable parameter rather than value parameter. The environment passes the location of a string (not copy the string or array to the parameter). After the function is called, the parameter s points to the beginning of the array passed in.

In the loop, while the current character read isn't null, the index is incremented and the test is repeated.

```
char str[] = "Hello world!";

int i= count(str);
```

A string is represented as an array of characters terminated by a null character '\0'. The size of the array is unknown so this function can work for a string of any size.

When a string str is passed to the function as an argument the function call count(str) returns the length of a string 12.

A.5.2.2 for Loop

If the number of iterations of the loop is known in advance, the for loop is a good choice.

The syntax of the for loop is:

```
for (<statements1>; <condition>; <statements2>)
{
    <statements>
}
```

A for loop normally has a control variable associated with the loop. In next example, variable is such a control variable which is used to refer the subscript of each element in an array.

```
int i, data[]={1,2,3,4,5};

for(i=0; i<4; i++)
    data[i]++;
```

The control heading of the for loop statement has three sections separated by semicolons.

Initialization section: <statements1>:

It initializes the control variable. This statement is only run once before the loop is entered.

This section can include multiple statements separated by commas e.g. i = 0, j=0.

Loop termination condition section: <condition>:

It specifies the condition for the loop termination. The condition is evaluated at the beginning of each iteration and the loop is terminated (exited) if the condition is not met,

```
e.g. i < 20 && j<10.
```

Step forward section <statement2>

It updates the value of the control variable otherwise the loop may go forever and never stop. The third section is run every time the loop body is completed. This is usually an increment of the loop control variables, e.g. i++, j++ are common statements in this section.

Any of the three sections in a for loop may be omitted. A missing second section represents a nonzero value indicating always true, and creating a potentially infinite loop.

A simplest for loop statement may look like

```
for( ; ; );
```

It is an unconditional infinitive loop without initialization, without termination condition, without control variable updating, and without the loop body.

Here is an example of function which calculates the summation of the integers stored in an array. The function takes two parameters: the array and the number of elements.

```
int sum(int array[], int count)
{
        int total = 0.0;
        int i;

        for(i = 0; i < count; i++)
                sum += array[i];

        return sum;
}
```

The following function returns the largest element of first n elements of an integer array.

```
int max(int array[], int n)
{
        int max = array[0];
        int i;

        for(i = 1; i < n; i++)
        if(array[i]>max)max = array[i];

        return max;
}
```

Any for loop can also be implemented by a while loop. For example,

```
for (i=0; i<10; i++)
    { s += a[i] }
```

is equivalent to

```
i=0;
while (i<10)
{
    s += a[i];
    i++;
}
```

You may often see the nested for loop in C programming. Assume you have a
2-D int array (2 x 3) and you want to get the total value of the elements in the array.
You can simply use a nested for loop to do this job.

```
int a[][] = {{1, 2, 3},{4, 5, 6}};
int s=0;

for(int i=0; i<2; i++)
   for(int j=0; j<3; j++)
      s+=a[i][j];
```

A.5.2.3   do while Loop

The do while loop is similar to while do loop except it will run the statements in
the body of loop at least once because it test the loop condition at the end of each
iteration.

```
do
    <statements>
while ( <condition> ) ;
```

A.5.3   break and continue Statement in a Loop

The break statement is used to exit from a loop, and move the control to the next
statement following the loop. It forces an early exit from the loop when a certain
exit condition is met. The break statement always associates with an if statement
within loop. In a nested loop the break statement exits the current(inner most loop)
to resumes the enclosing loop where it left.

The continue statement within a loop will skip the rest statements in the current
iteration and moves the control to the loop termination condition test section to
determine whether to continue a new iteration within the same loop. Like a break,
continue statement always works with an if statement. Here is a loop that prints out
first n even numbers and skips all odd numbers.

```
for(i = 0; i < n; i++)
{
    if(i % 2 != 0) continue;          //if i is odd,
                                      //skip printing
    printf("%d\n", i);
}
```

A.5.4 goto Statements

C has a goto statement which permits unstructured jumps to be made. Its use is not recommended, so we'll not discuss it in detail here. The goto statements transfer control unconditionally.

The goto statement looks like this:

```
goto <label> ;
```

In case you like to break out of more than one nested loop you can use goto statement.

```
for(i = 0; i < m; i++)
{
    for(j = 0; j < n ; j++)
    {
        . . .
        if(condition) goto label_1;
        . . .
    }

}
Label_1:puts("done");
```

A.6 Reserved Keywords

The following words are reserved, and may not be used as identifiers:

auto	extern	short
break	float	signed
case	for	sizeof
char	goto	static
const	if	struct
continue	inline	switch
default	int	typedef
do	long	union
double	register	unsigned
else	restrict	void
enum	return	volatile
		while

A.7 Command-line Arguments

You can pass command line arguments to a C program. The main() function has two predefined parameter variables: int argc holds the count of the command-line arguments in and the char *argv[] (array of char pointers) holds character string arguments. If the C executable program name is myprg created by C compiler then

```
myprg abc 123
```

results in

```
argv[0] = "myprg"
argv[1] = "abc"
arv[2] = "123"
arvc = 2.
```

```
#include <stdio.h>

int main(int argc, char *argv[])
{
    int i;
    for (i = 0; i < argc; i++)
        printf ("%s ", argv[i]);
    printf ("%c\n", '!');
    return 0;
}
```

The exeution of the following command line

```
$ myprg Hello world
```

will display "hello world!" on the screen.

A.7 Command-line Arguments

Appendix B
Getting Started with The Keil μVision IDE

B.1 Introduction to the Keil μVision IDE

The Keil μVision IDE is an integrated embedded software development environment for project management, program editing, debugging, and simulation. It is an
excellent development tools for beginner students and professionals for the 8051
microcontroller embedded software development.

This appendix provides a getting started guide for the embedded C51 beginners. The standalone Keil Software development tool is widely used in embedded
C software development for 8051, 151, 251, and 166 microcontroller families. This
tool suite includes C compilers, cross-compilers, assemblers, real-time executives,
debuggers, simulators, and integrated environments. The Keil Software delivers its
software in two types of kits: evaluation kits and production kits.

The free evaluation kit let you generate applications up to 2 Kbytes in size and
only includes a limited version of RTOS - RTXTiny. This kit can be used to generate
small target applications. The Keil evaluation μVision3 development tools for 8051
Microcontrollers are available to download at

https://www.keil.com/c51/demo/eval/c51.htm and the getting started tutorials of
Keil μVision3 development are available at http://www.keil.com/uvision/ide_ov_
starting.asp

B.2 Run a Keil μVision IDE Project

Many built-in example programs in the Keil μVision IDE help you get started with
the kit and devices. The Keil μVision Debugger can simulate on-chip peripherals
such as Interrupts, I/O Ports, A/D and D/A converter, and UART serial ports. Simulation helps you understand system configurations, and write and test applications
program prior loading the executables into target devices. You will practice a Keil
μVision IDE built-in Hello project first which just simply displays a "Hello, world"
greeting message on the serial port. You can start our own projects with Keil μVision
IDE after you complete this Tutorial.

First, start up the Keil μVision IDE: `Programs -> Keil μVision3`

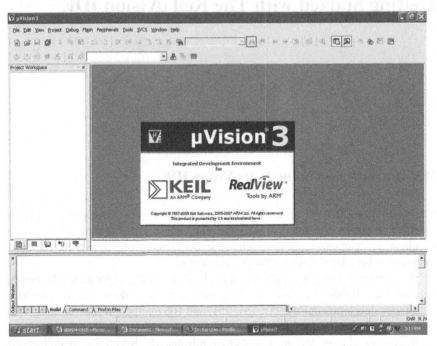

All the C51 example projects are available in <Keil installation directory> \c51\examples.

Go to Keil IDE menu: `project -> open` and browse to the Hello folder under the examples folder. Click the Hello project to open it as follows.

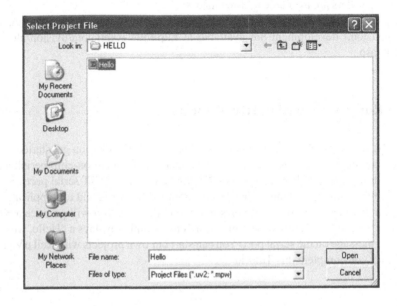

Double click on HELLO.C and you see the HELLO.C source code in the editor window, you need to compile and link this project before execution. Go to `Project -> Build Target` to build the project. If you don't see any error in the output window below the editor window, then

Go to `Debug -> Start/Stop Debug Session` to initialize debugger and starts program execution till the main function.

Go to `View -> Serial Window-> UART #1` to activate the window so that you will be able to see the greeting message in this serial port.

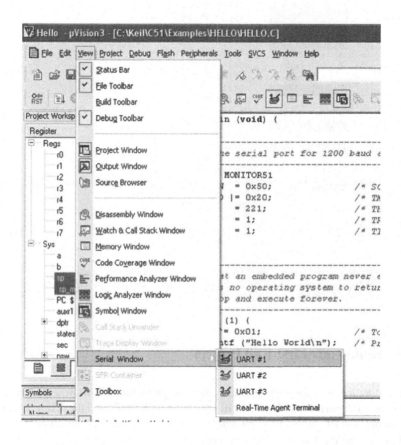

You can run the program either go to `Debug -> Run`, or click the Run button on the toolbar to begin executing your target program in the μVision debugger. The greeting messages are displayed in the serial windows continuously (due to the loop) until you stop it with the "Stop" button on the toolbar.

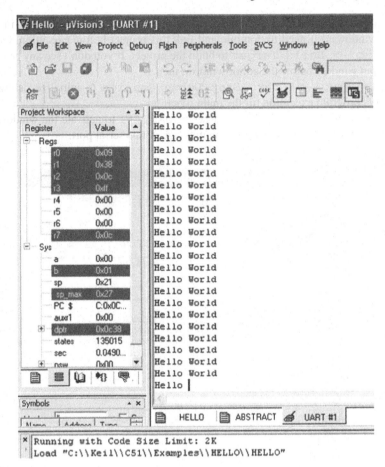

B.3   Build your First Keil Project

In this practice, you are going to build a new project which allows you to input data to the port P2, perform a bitwise XOR operation with 0x0F, and the result is sent to the output port P1. In this lab, you will learn how to interact with the simulated pins of I/O ports in the Keil μVision simulator. When starting a new project, simply go to the menu bar and select Project -> New μVision Project.

Specify the name of the new project as *first*.

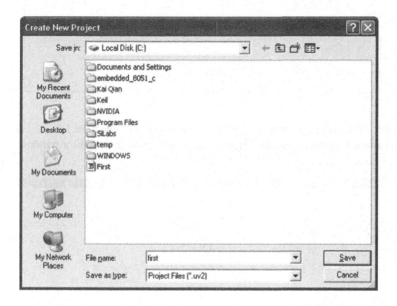

You must select the microcontroller you use from the Device Database and the µVision IDE sets all compiler, assembler, linker, and memory options for you.

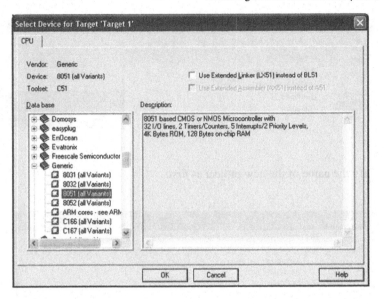

After click the OK button, you go to the menu bar and select File -> New to create a new C source code file. Type in the source code in the editor window.

```
#include <reg51.h>
void main (void)
{
P2 = 0xFF;                        // Setup P2 for Input
while (1){
    P2 ^= 0X0F;
    P1 = P2;                      // Write XOR of P2 to P1
  }
}
```

Save it as *p2_p1.c* in a folder as follows.

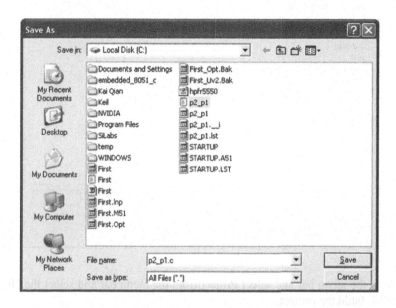

Right click on the "Source Group 1" and select "Add Files to Group" to add the C source file into the group of the project.

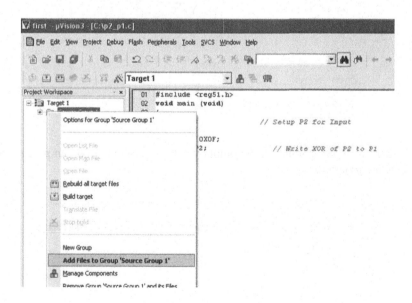

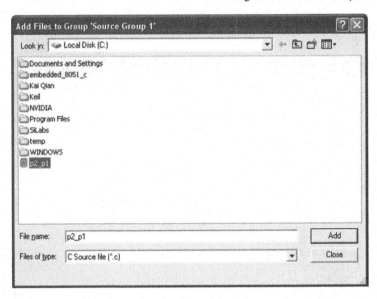

Go to the menu bar and select Project from the menu bar and select the "Build target" to build the project.

If there is no error found in the output window as follows you can proceed to execute the program.

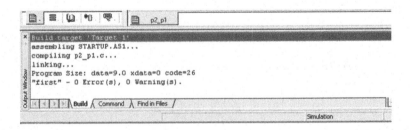

Click the "Debug" button on the toolbar as shown below.

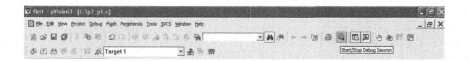

In order to check the status of the I/O, select the Peripherals from the menu bar, then select I/O-Ports, Port 1 and Port 2 as follows.

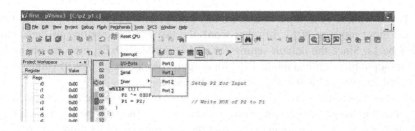

The yellow cursor moves to the first line in the main function after you start the Debug and the IDE then waits for you to instruct it further. The breakpoints are trigger points that halt program execution for debug purpose. You can set break-points while writing your source code or while debugging your program. Here are few often used buttons for breakpoint setting:

The "Insert/Remove Breakpoint" button sets or unsets an execution break-point on the current cursor line.

The "Enable/Disable Breakpoint" button enables or disables an existing breakpoint on the current cursor line.

Move the editor focus to the last line of the loop and click   button, you will see a Red stop mark set to this line. The other debug options are explained below:

The "Step Over" button on the toolbar executes one line of C code (single-step) at a time. The µVision supports various methods of single-stepping through your application.

The "Step Into" button executes one line of C code (single-step) and it will step into function is a function call is encountered.

The initial debug setting is shown below.

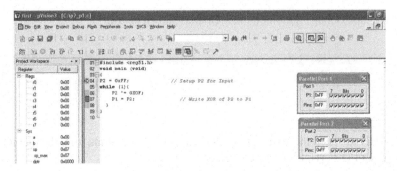

If you want to read input data from any port pins, the pins of the port must be in the input mode in 8051. In other word, the last previous writing to these pins must be 1s. Since the default setting for all I/O ports are 0xFF, they are set in the input/output bidirectional mode. E.g., for output, you can set bit 0 of P1 (upper row) to 0 and the pins of bit 0(lower row) also changes to 0.

If you change the pins(lower row) of the bit 2 of P1 to 0, the bit 2(upper row) of P1 is unchanged as shown in the following P1 window. The pin is assumed connected to outside for input and output but the upper low bits represent the data in the port register. The port data will not change until you read the data on the pins to the port register by C assignment statement. That is why the bit 2 of the port 1 has different data in the upper or lower rows.

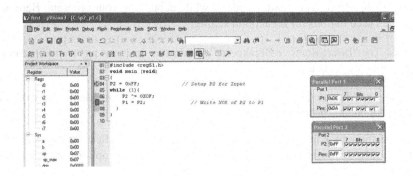

After you click the "Step Over" button again, P2 is updated to 0xF0. Since the last writing to bit 0 of P2 was 0, you can not interact with the pin of bit 0 of P2 because it is not in the read input mode.

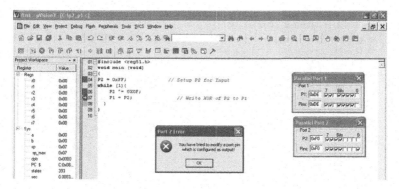

But you can still interact with the P1 to simulate inputs as follows because the last writing to P1 was all 1s.

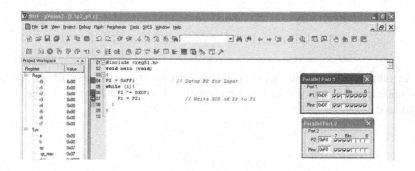

Run one more line of C code with the "Step Over" button and you will see P1 is replaced by P2.

Click the Run button, the program stops at the breakpoint. P2 is updated to 0xFF by the XOR operation. Notice that the data read from P2 comes from the port register not from the input pins of P2 at this time. You will fail in attempting to interact with the lower 4 bits of P2 because the last writing to these 4 bits was 0.

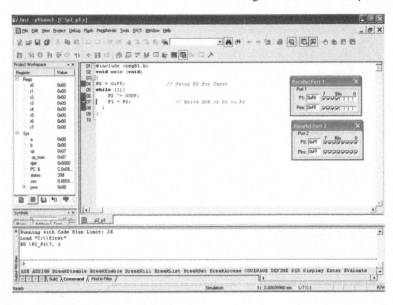

In other word, in order to simulate the real inputs to the pins of any ports, the corresponding bits the last writing must be 1 so that the port is in the input read mode.

Appendix C
Getting Started with Silicon Laboratories C8051F005DK Development

In this section you will have a hands-on lab exercise with an 8051 based microcontroller board. All the embedded system labs in this book are designed with the Keil 8051 software and the C8051F005DK development kit by the Silicon Laboratories, Inc. If you don't have this kit with you at this time you can use Keil software to simulate and practice this lab. The C8051F005DK kit is a 25 MIPS 8051 microcontroller with 32K in-system programmable FLASH, 256 bytes RAM, 2K-bytes XRAM, SPI, UART; 12-bit 8-channel A/D and 12-bit 2-channel D/A. Its Integrated Development Environment (IDE) is a complete, standalone software program that provides designers with the Keil software 8051 development tools (assembler-A51, C compiler-C51, linker-BL5, debugger, project interface, configuration wizard) that make the embedded software design and testing much easier. The picture below shows the target board and USB debug adapter which connects a JTAG connector on the board to PC USB port for embedded software debug and test in emulation, and deployment. The Joint Test Action Group (JTAG) is the usual name for the IEEE 1149.1 Standard Test Access Port and Boundary-Scan Architecture for test access ports used for testing printed circuit boards. The C8051F005DK development kit is available at https://www.silabs.com/products/mcu/Pages/C8051F005DK.aspx you can purchase.

The target board has a C8051F005 microcontroller chip and 64 pins I/O connector for all I/O signals. In addition, it provides a power connector(AD adapter is included in the kit) and power indicator, a system reset button, a user switch, a user LED, ADC/DAC connector, a JTAG interface connector, and a proto board.

The 64-pin I/O connector provides access to most of the necessary signal pins on the C8051F005 MCU. Each pin is also replicated in the through-hole prototyping area near the I/O connector. A list of pin descriptions is provided in Table 1.

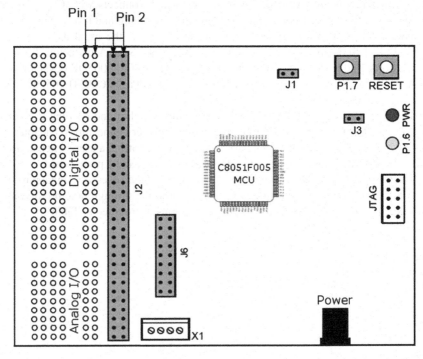

Table C.1 Pin descriptions for the I/O connector on C8051F005 evaluation board.

Pin	Description	Pin	Description
1	+VD (digital)	28	P3.7
2	XTAL1	29	P3.4
3	P1.6	30	P3.5
4	P1.7	31	P3.2
5	P1.4	32	P3.3
6	P1.5	33	P3.0
7	P1.2	34	P3.1
8	P1.3	36	/RST
9	P1.0	39,41,42	GND (digital)
10	P1.1	45,47,63	GNDA (analog)
11	P0.6	46,64	+VA (analog)
12	P0.7	48	DAC0
13	P0.4	49	CP1−
14	P0.5	50	DAC1
15	P0.2	51	CP1+
16	P0.3	52	CP0−
17	P0.0	53	VREF
18	P0.1	54	CP0+
19	P2.6	55	AIN0
20	P2.7	56	AIN1
21	P2.4	57	AIN2
22	P2.5	58	AIN3
23	P2.2	59	AIN4
24	P2.3	60	AIN5
25	P2.0	61	AIN6
26	P2.1	62	AIN7
27	P3.6		

The C8051F005DK kit comes with a CD of development Kit Tools which includes all required software you need to install and a document CD. In case the CD does not work for your platform for any reason you can download the software online. The current IDE kit software and the required Keil software for the kit are available online to download at https://www.silabs.com/products/mcu/Pages/SoftwareDownloads.aspx

You need install following three software components.

1. Development Kit IDE

https://www.silabs.com/Support%20Documents/Software/mcu_ide.zip

2. **Configuration Wizard**

   https://www.silabs.com/Support%20Documents/Software/ConfigAndConfig
   2-Install.zip

3. **The Keil Compiler Tools Evaluation**

   https://www.silabs.com/Support%20Documents/Software/KeilV8Tools_
   Installer.zip

   The supporting materials for Silicon Labs development kit can be found at:
   https://www.silabs.com/support/pages/support.aspx?ProductFamily=Precision+
   Mixed-Signal+MCUs

After you download above software you can set up the target board and debug
adapter following the instructions on the quick-start chart which comes with the kit.
The following steps show the software installation.

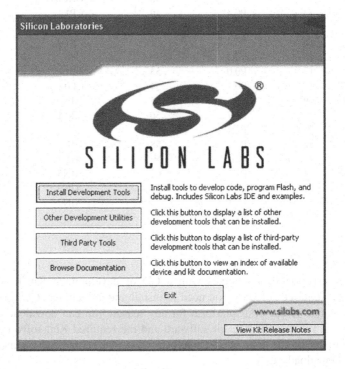

Select the kit you have as follow.

Select the components you want to install.

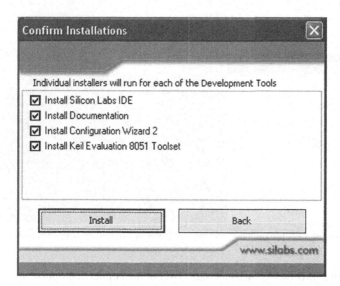

Start the installation now.

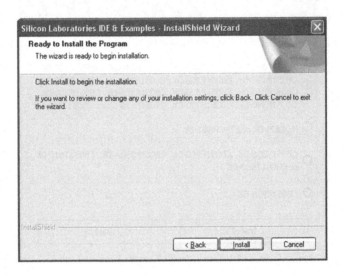

After you installed the downloaded Keil software kit you can kick off the IDE: go to Programs -> Silicon Laboratories -> Silicon Laboratories IDE to start up the IDE.

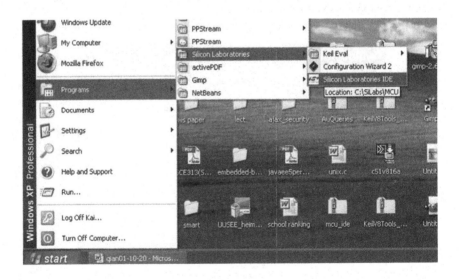

First, set the USB Debug Adapter and JTAG in the connection option.

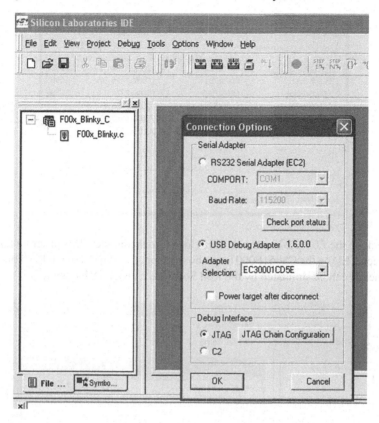

Let's practice a built-in project called blinky which is available in the silabs\ mcu\examples\blinky directory.

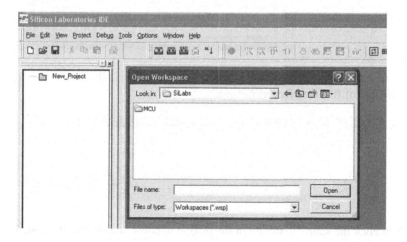

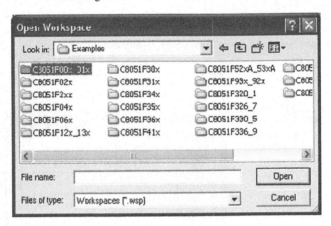

Click on the f00x_blinky.C file to load it to the project. This program flashes the green LED on the C8051F000 target board about five times a second. All on-chip peripherals can be simulated by the Keil Software μVision Debugger.

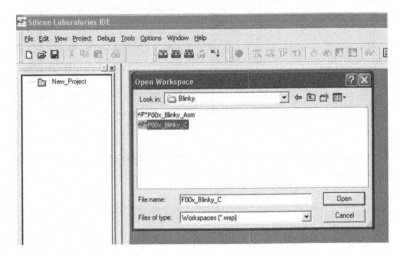

Now you see this source C file is added into the project in the project window on the left side of IDE interface as follows.

You click the source code file in the project window and display the code in the edit window. You can skip the code details for the time being.

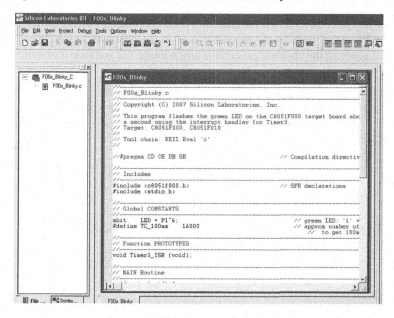

Go to `Project` on the menu bar and select the `build target` option or simply click the "`Build`" icon on the menu bar to build the relocatable object file. Check the compilation result in the output window below the edit window.

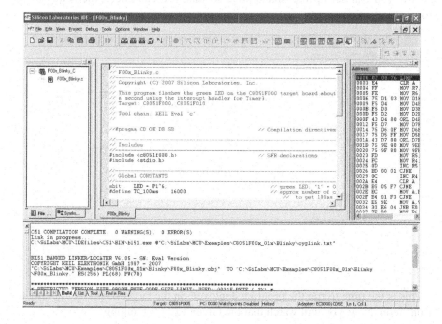

Now you can download the program into the target board by clicking the "Download the Program" icon on the menu bar next to the green circle run "icon". This step will generate the absolute executable target image file and lode it into the target board.

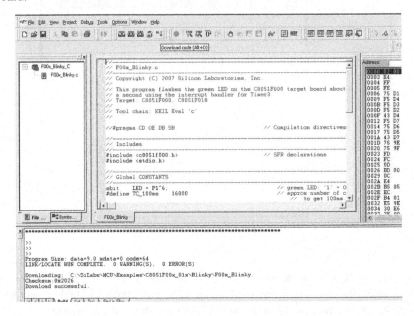

Now you can set up the breakpoints so that you can check the status of the program execution.

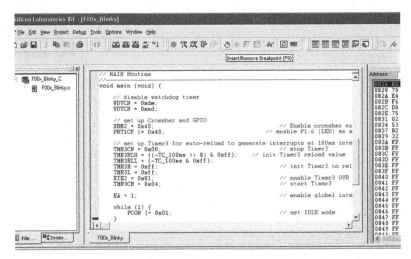

This is the time to run the program deployed on the target board by clicking the "Run" icon. Now, you will watch that the Green LED is blinking.

Appendix D
Counter with 7-Segment Numeric Display

D.1 Overview

In this lab, we will build a counter circuit using a 7-segment display with a push button to increment the numeric value shown. The circuit is built entirely on the SiLabs C8051F005 evaluation board's prototyping area. Each of the segments is controlled by a port on the 8051 and is connected via the 64-pin I/O connector, which provides easy access to the pins on the microcontroller.

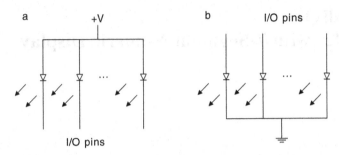

Fig. D.1 7-segment display (a) common anode and (b) common cathode setups

The 7-segment display contains seven LEDs that light up one segment each. The LEDs are setup in either a common anode or common cathode configuration. Figure D.1a shows a common anode device, where all the anodes, the plus ends, are tied together; the LED cathodes are pinned out. Common cathode devices, Figure D.1b, have all the negative ends tied together.

The 7-segment display that we use is the NTE3061. In addition to the seven segments, it also has a decimal point LED, and everything is connected in the common anode configuration. We will keep it simple and connect the common anode to the supply voltage of the 8051. The LEDs are rated to drop 1.7V and 20mA current in standard forward operation. By placing a resistor in series with each LED, we can limit the current the LED can draw. Without this resistor, the excess current can overheat and destroy your LEDs!

A quick calculation tells us what value resistor we need. The supply voltage from the evaluation board is 3.0V. This means that 1.7V drops over the LED and the remaining 1.3V must drop over the resistor. Applying $V = IR$, we see that the optimal resistance is $(1.3V)/(20mA) = 65\Omega$. Of course, it is not necessary to exactly hit this value. A slightly smaller or larger resistance simply means your LED will shine a bit brighter or dimmer, respectively.

The program is a continuous loop that changes the 7-segment display to reflect the value of the 'counter' variable. This variable is incremented each time the user presses the on-board push button 'SW2' that is internally tied to port 1.7. Timer 3 is used to run a debounce function that makes sure the counter increments only once per button press.

D.2 Equipment

Here are the components used to build this lab:

- (1) Silicon Labs C8051F005SDK Evaluation Board with USB Debug Adapter
- (1) NTE3061 7-Segment Display
- (8) 100Ω Resistors

D.3 Schematic

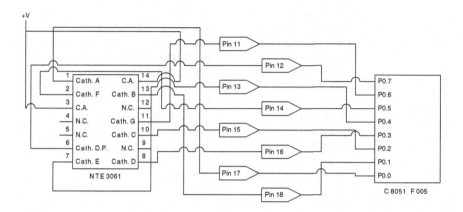

D.4 Building the Circuit

1. Layout the NTE3061 and eight resistors on the prototyping area as shown in the picture below.

2. Connect each resistor lead closest to the NTE3061 to the adjacent pin on the device. Use the schematic as a guide.
3. Connect either common anode pin on the NTE3061 to the digital supply voltage at the top of the prototyping area, as shown below.
4. Connect the other end of each resistor to its own I/O port pin. See Appendix C for a description of each pin on the 64-pin I/O connector. Follow the table below, or you will have to change the source file in order for the numeric display to show correctly.

NTE3061	64-pin I/O connector
Pin 1 (LED A)	Pin 17 (P0.0)
Pin 2 (LED F)	Pin 14 (P0.5)
Pin 3 (common anode)	Pin 1 (VD+)
Pin 4 (not connected)	N/A
Pin 5 (not connected)	N/A
Pin 6 (LED D.P.)	Pin 12 (P0.7)
Pin 7 (LED E)	Pin 13 (P0.4)
Pin 8 (LED D)	Pin 16 (P0.3)
Pin 9 (not connected)	N/A
Pin 10 (LED C)	Pin 15 (P0.2)
Pin 11 (LED G)	Pin 11 (P0.6)
Pin 12 (not connected)	N/A
Pin 13 (LED B)	Pin 18 (P0.1)
Pin 14 (common anode)	Pin 1 (VD+)

D.5 Code

```
//-----------------------------------------------------------//
//   COUNTER.C: This program controls a counter on a         //
//      7-segment display. The user can push a button        //
//      on the test board to increment the counter.          //
//-----------------------------------------------------------//
#include <c8051f000.h>            // SFR declarations
#include "stdio.h"
//-----------------------------------------------------------//
//      16-bit SFR definitions                               //
//-----------------------------------------------------------//
sfr16 TMR3RL = 0x92;             // Timer3 reload
sfr16 TMR3 = 0x94;               // Timer3

sbit segmentA = P0^0;
sbit segmentB = P0^1;
sbit segmentC = P0^2;
sbit segmentD = P0^3;
sbit segmentE = P0^4;
sbit segmentF = P0^5;
sbit segmentG = P0^6;
sbit segmentDP = P0^7;
sbit button = P1^7;


//-----------------------------------------------------------//
//   Global Variables                                        //
//-----------------------------------------------------------//
int counter = 0;
int iStatus = 0;
```

```
      int iDebounce = 0;

      //---------------------------------------------------//
      // Function Prototypes                              //
      //---------------------------------------------------//
      void Timer3ISR();
      bit Debounce();

      void main (void) {
            EA = 0;              // disable all interrupts

            WDTCN = 0xDE;        // disable watchdog timer
            WDTCN = 0xAD;

            OSCXCN = 0x00;       // external oscillator off
            OSCICN = 0x07;       // internal oscillator set to
                                 // 16MHz

            XBR2 = 0x40;         // enable xbar weak pull-up
            PRT0CF = 0x00;       // configure all to open-drain
            PRT1CF = 0x00;       // configure all to open-drain

            TMR3CN = 0x02;          // initialize Timer3 to
            TMR3RL = (-16000/12);   // overflow approximately
            EIE2 | = 0x01;          // every 1ms. Enable Timer3
            TMR3CN | = 0x04;        // interrupt

            EA = 1;              // enable all interrupts

            while (1) {

            switch (counter) {
                  case 0:
                        segmentA = 0;
                        segmentB = 0;
                        segmentC = 0;
                        segmentD = 0;
                        segmentE = 0;
                        segmentF = 0;
                        segmentG = 1;
                        segmentDP = 1;
                        break;
                  case 1:
                        segmentA = 1;
                        segmentB = 0;
                        segmentC = 0;
                        segmentD = 1;
                        segmentE = 1;
                        segmentF = 1;
```

```
        segmentG = 1;
        segmentDP = 1;
        break;
case 2:
        segmentA = 0;
        segmentB = 0;
        segmentC = 1;
        segmentD = 0;
        segmentE = 0;
        segmentF = 1;
        segmentG = 0;
        segmentDP = 1;
        break;
case 3:
        segmentA = 0;
        segmentB = 0;
        segmentC = 0;
        segmentD = 0;
        segmentE = 1;
        segmentF = 1;
        segmentG = 0;
        segmentDP = 1;
        break;
case 4:
        segmentA = 1;
        segmentB = 0;
        segmentC = 0;
        segmentD = 1;
        segmentE = 1;
        segmentF = 0;
        segmentG = 0;
        segmentDP = 1;
        break;
case 5:
        segmentA = 0;
        segmentB = 1;
        segmentC = 0;
        segmentD = 0;
        segmentE = 1;
        segmentF = 0;
        segmentG = 0;
        segmentDP = 1;
        break;
case 6:
        segmentA = 0;
        segmentB = 1;
        segmentC = 0;
        segmentD = 0;
        segmentE = 0;
```

```
                        segmentF = 0;
                        segmentG = 0;
                        segmentDP = 1;
                        break;
                case 7:
                        segmentA = 0;
                        segmentB = 0;
                        segmentC = 0;
                        segmentD = 1;
                        segmentE = 1;
                        segmentF = 1;
                        segmentG = 1;
                        segmentDP = 1;
                        break;
                case 8:
                        segmentA = 0;
                        segmentB = 0;
                        segmentC = 0;
                        segmentD = 0;
                        segmentE = 0;
                        segmentF = 0;
                        segmentG = 0;
                        segmentDP = 1;
                        break;
                case 9:
                        segmentA = 0;
                        segmentB = 0;
                        segmentC = 0;
                        segmentD = 1;
                        segmentE = 1;
                        segmentF = 0;
                        segmentG = 0;
                        segmentDP = 1;
                        break;
                default:
                        segmentA = 1;
                        segmentB = 1;
                        segmentC = 1;
                        segmentD = 1;
                        segmentE = 1;
                        segmentF = 1;
                        segmentG = 1;
                        segmentDP = 1;
            }
        }
    }
    void Timer3ISR () interrupt 14 {
        TMR3CN &= ~ (0x80);
        if(Debounce())
```

```
            if(++counter > 9)
                counter = 0;
}
bit Debounce() {
    // if iStatus = 0 then looking for valid key press
    // if 1, then looking for valid key release
    if (!iStatus) {
        if (iDebounce <= 5) {
        if (button == 1)
            iDebounce++;
        else
            // input still bouncing, reset
            iDebounce = 0;
    }
    else {
            // key held for 6ms, change iStatus and
            // signal valid keypress detected
            iStatus = 1;
            iDebounce = 0;
            return 1;
    }
    }
    else if (iStatus == 1) {
        if (button == 0)                // no key pressed
            iDebounce++;
        else
            // still bouncing, reset
            iDebounce = 0;
        if (iDebounce > 5) {
            // no key held for 6ms
            iStatus = 0;
            iDebounce = 0;
        }
    }
    return 0;
}
```

References

1. Hello: Your first Embedded Program.
   http://www.keil.com/support/man/docs/uv3/uv3_ex_hello.htm
2. Evaluation Software Overview, http://www.keil.com/demo/
3. μVision® User's Guide, http://www.keil.com/support/man/docs/uv3/
4. μVision IDE Overview, http://www.keil.com/uvision/
   http://www.keil.com/uvision/ide_ov_examples.asp
5. RTX RTOS Tiny, http://www.keil.com/rtx51/,
   http://www.keil.com/support/man/docs/tr51/
6. Quick Start of μVision3 Keil software, http://www.keil.com/product/brochures/uv3.pdf

Embedded Software Development with C

Dr. Kai Qian: Dr. Kai Qian is a Professor of Computer Science and Software Engineering at the School of Computing and Software Engineering, Southern Polytechnic State University. He has published over 50 research papers in various professional journals and proceedings of international conferences. He got his Ph.D. of Computer Science and Engineering from University of Nebraska in 1990. Dr. Qian has taught embedded systems courses for many years. Dr. Kai Qian has authored books in Component-Oriented Programming with Wiley in 2005; Java Web Development (2007), Web Development with JavaScript & Ajax Illuminated (2009), and Software Architecture & Design Illuminated (2009), with Jones & Bartlet.

David den Haring: David den Haring is a Project Manager at Atronix Engineering, Inc. located in Norcross, Georgia. Atronix is a system integrator specializing in automated control systems and middleware that integrates the factory floor with enterprise-level systems.

David received his Bachelor Degree in Computer Science from Southern Polytechnic State University in 1998 and has 20 years of industry experience.

Li Cao: Li Cao received his Bachelors Degree in Electrical and Computer Engineering from the University of Illinois at Urbana Champaign.

He has previously worked at NTT/Verio Inc. and NYSE and is currently a Masters student in Electrical and Computer Engineering at the University of Texas at Austin.

Index